The History of Roche Abbey

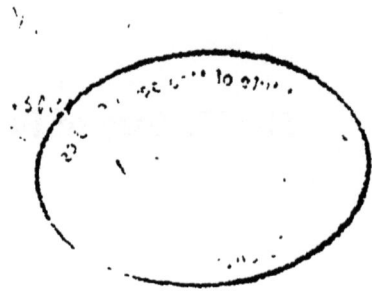

Roche Abbey.

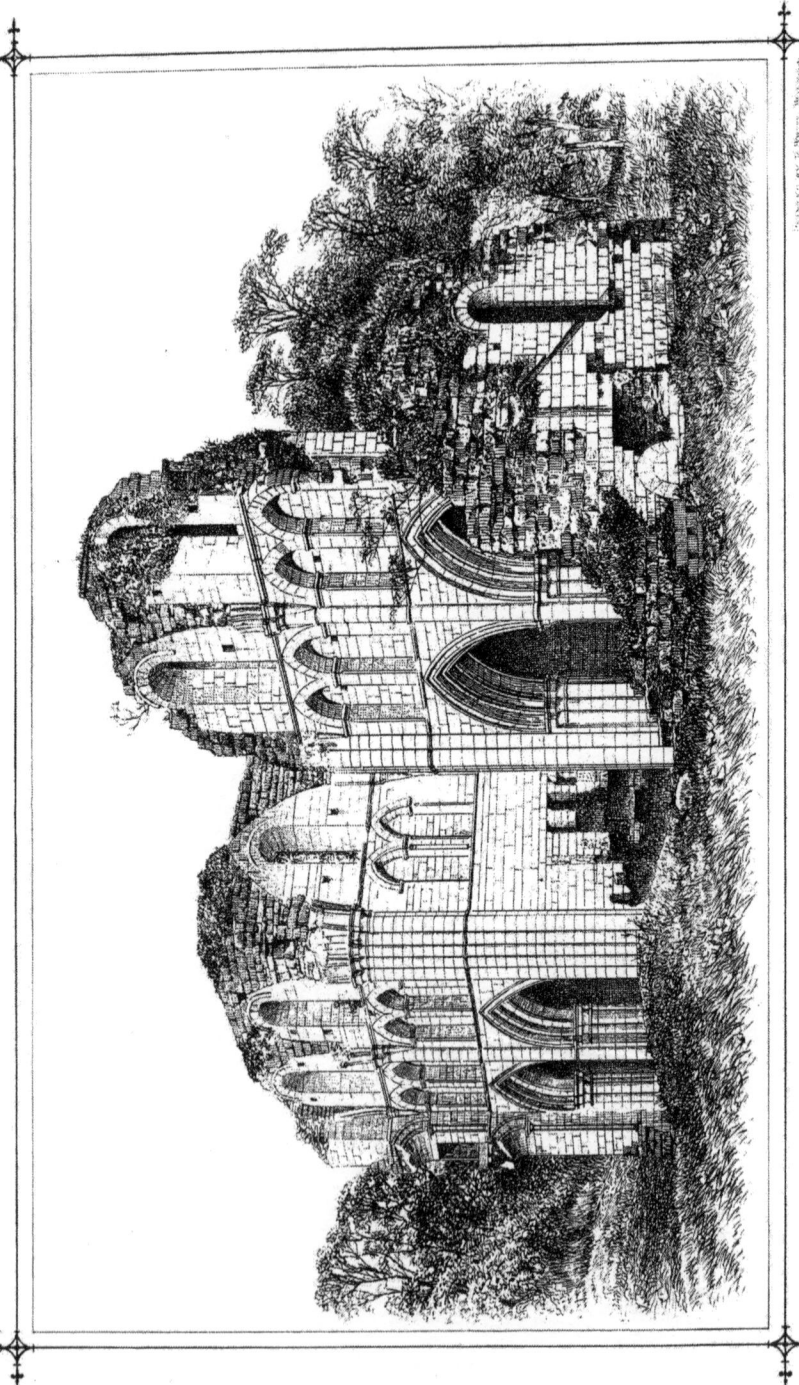

ROCHE ABBEY

Yorkshire.

THE
History of Roche Abbey,

FROM ITS

FOUNDATION TO ITS DISSOLUTION,

BY

James H. Abeling, M. D.

"When the substance of these fabricks shall have passed away, their very shadows will be acceptable to posterity."—*Fuller.*

Worksop:
ROBERT WHITE, PARK STREET.
MDCCCLXX.

To

The Right Honourable The Earl of Scarborough,

This Volume

Is,

By his Lordship's permission,

Dedicated

By one of the many thousands who would

Gratefully acknowledge the kindness which permits them

to visit and enjoy

The Picturesque Beauties of the Valley

and

Ruins of Roche.

THE PREFACE

"THE art of phyfic, which I have profeffed (with competent fuccefs) in this county, not being able for any long time to continue the people living in it, I have charitably attempted, notwithftanding the difficulty and almoft the contrariety of the ftudy, to practice upon the dead, intending thereby to keep all which is, or can be, left of them, to wit, the fhadow of their names, (better than precious ointment for the body,) to preferve their memory, as long as may be, in the world, though for this latter undertaking I expect no more glory than I have gotten riches by the former," thus wrote *Dr. Thoroton*, in the preface to his "Hiftory of Nottinghamfhire." Almoft the fame words are repeated by *Dr. Burton*, in the preface to his "Monafticon Eboracenfe," And now for the third time they appear in this preface, becaufe they exactly exprefs the feelings of the Author.

As far as he is concerned, the prefent "undertaking" is purely a work of love, at the fame time he has fpared no expenfe in collecting materials and no time in endeavouring to place them before the public in an acceptable form. His aim has been to make the volume intelligible to the general reader, and with that view all charters have been tranflated and foot-notes have been appended where obfcurity feemed to exift. The Author, however, cannot think his work anything like perfect; ftill he has the fatisfaction of knowing that feveral documents have been refcued from oblivion which were faft becoming unreadable from extreme age, and that fome points of doubt with regard to the hiftory of the Monks and their Abbey which have hitherto exifted, have been finally fettled.

In thanking his numerous friends for their kind affiftance the Author is met at once by the melancholy fact that during the time this Volume has been going through the prefs, two from whom he received a large fhare of help, are no more. To that good and learned man, the Rev. J. Eaftwood, M.A., he was efpecially indebted for many ufeful fuggeftions and for carefully correcting all the tranflations; and to Mr. W. M. Campfall he muft always feel thankful for the fervice he rendered in preparing many architectural drawings. To the Earl of Scarborough, the Author is greatly obliged for his kindnefs in allowing excavations to be made, to determine the ground plan of the Abbey, and to Mr. G. Naylor Vickers he is indebted for affiftance in carrying them out. He would alfo wifh to exprefs his deep fenfe of obligation to the Rev. John Stacye for his invaluable aid, and to Mr. Theophilus Smith, to Mr. W. Swift, Mr. J. Bohler, The Rev. J. T. Jeffcock, F.S.A., Dr. Sykes, and Mr. C. Jackfon for the kind affiftance they have each rendered.

Contents.

List of Subscribers	viii
Reference to Plates	xii
Introduction	xv
The Abbots	1
The Possessions	97
The Architecture, Monastic Buildings, and their Remains	161
Addenda	179
The Flora of Roche	181
Index	189

List of Subscribers.

His Grace The Duke of Norfolk, E.M.
His Grace The Duke of Devonshire, K.G., L.L.D.
His Grace The Duke of Newcastle.
The Right Honourable The Earl of Scarborough.
The Right Honourable The Earl de Grey and Ripon, K.G.
The Right Honourable The Earl of Effingham.
The Right Honourable Lord Wharncliffe.
The Right Honourable Lord Foley.
The Right Honourable Lord Halifax.

Abbot, G. L.	Sheffield.
Aldam, W.	Frickley Hall, Doncaster.
Anderson, Sir C. H. I, Bart.	Lea, Gainsborough.
Appleton, Rev. J., M.A.	Worksop.
Aveling, Stephen T.	Lessnes Heath, S.E.
Aveling, Thomas	Rochester.
Aveling, Miss	Needham Hall, Wisbeach.
Baines, William L.	Bawtry.
Barber, Fairless	Castle Hill, Rastrick.
Baxter, Dudley R.	Doncaster.
Bent, Rev. G.	Worksop.
Bentley, Robert J.	Finningley Park, Bawtry.
Binney, J.	Sheffield.
Bower, E. C.	Wadworth Hall, Doncasrer.
Bragg, William, F.R.G.S.	Shirle Hill, Sheffield.
Brereton, Charles	Beverley.
Brodhurst, G.	London.
Broomhead, Barnard P.	Sheffield.
Broomhead, John	Blyth.
Broughton, John	Peterborough.
Brown, Sir John	Endcliffe Hall, Sheffield.
Brown, John	Misson.
Catling, Mrs. Robert	Needham Hall, Wisbeach.
Chaloner, Edward	Hermeston Grange, Worksop.
Chrimes, Richard	Moorgate Grove, Rotherham.
Close, Thomas	Nottingham.
Cocking, Charles C.	Wath-upon-Dearne.
Coney, John	Awkley, Doncaster.
Corbitt, William	Rotherham.
Coulson, Mrs.	Bellaport Hall, Market Drayton
Coupland, J. M.	Tinsley.

LIST OF SUBSCRIBERS.

Dawson, George - - - Thorncliffe.
Depledge, John - - - - Thorncliffe.
Drabble, James - - - - Carlton.
Drury, Robert - - - - Sheffield.
Dunn, Miss - - - - Bideford.
Dunhill, John - - - - Cliftonville, Brighton.

Ellenberger, Dr. - - - - Worksop.
Emsley, Samuel - - - - Sheffield.

Frith, John - - - - Sheffield.
Flockton, Thos. J. - - - Sheffield.
Foljambe, F. J. Savile - - - Osberton.
Forrest, Charles - - - Lofthouse, Wakefield.
Fowler, William - - - Whittington Hall, Derbyshire.
Free Library - - - - Sheffield.

Gardner, Samuel - - - Archer House, Abbeydale, Sheffield.
Gatty, Rev. Alfred, D.D. - - Ecclesfield.
Guest, John - - - - Moorgate Grange, Rotherham.

Habershon, Matthew Henry - - London.
Hadfield, M. E., F.I.B.A. - - Sheffield.
Hailstone, Edward, F.S.A. - - Horton Hall, Bradford.
Hatfield, George - - - The Hermitage, Doncaster.
Haywood, George - - - Moorgate, Rotherham.
Hogg, John - - - - Doncaster.
Holmes, H. T. - - - - The Laurels, Shortlands.
Holmes, George - - - Harthill.
Horncastle, John - - - Edwinstowe.
Hotten, John Camden - - - London.
Hoyle, F. W., F.G.H.S. - - Eastwood Lodge, Rotherham.
Hoyle, W. Dickon - - - London.
Hoyle, W. P. - - - - Ferham House, Rotherham.
Hubbard, Edward Isle - - - Rotherham.
Hugo, Rev. Thomas, M.A., F.R.S.L., F.S.A. - West Hackney, Stoke Newington.
Huntsman, Benjamin - - - West Retford Hall.

Ingleby, William - - - Sheffield.

Jackson, Charles - - - Doncaster.
Jackson, Rowland - - - Leeds.
Jackson, Samuel - - - Attercliffe.
Jeffcock, John - - - Cowley Manor, Sheffield.
Jeffcock, John T. - - - Cowley Manor, Sheffield.
Jenkinson, William - - - Sheffield.
Jewitt, Lewellyn L., F.S.A. - - Winster Hall, Matlock.
Jubb, James Shemeld - - - Morthen Hall.

Latimer, William - - - Anston.
Lawton, Miss M. - - - Sheffield.
Laycock, R. - - - - Wiseton, Bawtry.
Leader, J. D. - - - - Sheffield.

Lincoln Diocesan Architectural Society - Lincoln
Linley, Robert - - - - Netherholme, Worksop.
Livesey, Rev. J - - - - Sheffield
Longden, Henry - - - - Sheffield
Lowther, Sir Charles, Bart - Swillington House, Leeds.

Makin, W. - - - - Attercliffe.
Marrian, Thomas - - - Sharrow Grange, Sheffield
Massey, Henry - - - - Worksop.
Metcalf, A. - - - - Retford
Miles, Mrs - - - - Firbeck Hall.
Milner, Henry B W. - - West Retford House.
Moore, Rev Edward, F S A - Spalding
Moore, Thomas - - - Sheffield.
Morris, Richard M. - - - Worksop.
Munk, W, M D. - - - London.

Natorp, Gustavus - - - New York
Newton, Thomas - - - Chapeltown
Newton, W - - - - East Retford
Nicholson, G. P - - - Wath-upon-Dearne

Padley, James Sandby - - Lincoln.
Parker, Thomas W - - - Rotherham.
Peacock, Edward, F S A - Bottesford Manor, Brigg.
Pearson, Thomas J - - - Worksop
Peech, John - - - - Wentworth
Peel Park Library - - - Manchester.
Perrot, Eugene H - - - Rotherham
Plant, Edwin - - - - West Retford

Ramsden, Robert J. - - - Carlton Hall
Rawlinson, Robert, C B, C E, F G S - London
Reed, Mrs - - - - Elm
Roberts, Samuel - - - Queen's Tower, Sheffield
Robinson, Mrs - - - - Rotherham.
Rodgers, Jeremiah - - - Doncaster
Rodgers, Thomas - - - Sheffield
Rolleston, George, M D F R S - Oxford
Rotherham Library - - - Rotherham
Rotherham, Mrs. A. - - Throapham.
Rotherham, Mr. Alexander, Jun - Throapham.

Sales, J. - - - - Rotherham
Sanderson, George - - - Manchester.
Science and Art Department - South Kensington.
Sheffield Library - - - Sheffield
Sheardown, J B - - - Doncaster
Shillitto, F W - - - Rotherham
Shortridge, William - - Chipping House, Heeley
Shuttleworth, J J - - - Bath
Sisk, Rev. T. Ignatius - - St. Bernard's Abbey, Leicestershire

Siddall, Joseph - - - Wath-upon-Dearne
Smith, R. Moffatt, - - - Manchester.
Smith, Theophilus - - - Sheffield

LIST OF SUBSCRIBERS.

Smith, John Russell	London.
Spurr, H. A.	Blackburn.
Stacye, Rev. John	Sheffield.
Stevenson, W. H.	London.
Swift, William	Sheffield.
Sykes, Dr.	Doncaster.
Tasker, Rev. C. W.	Glossop.
Teulon, W. M.	London.
Tipping, Rev. Vernon	Lawton.
Thompson, Lady Mary	Sheriff Hutton Park, York.
Trollope, The Rev. Archdeacon, F.S.A.	Leasingham.
Tylden-Wright, F.G.S.	Woodlands, Worksop.
Vickers, Edward	Brighton.
Vickers, G. Naylor	St. Petersburgh.
Vickers, Henry	Holmwood, Ecclesall.
Vickers, T. Edward	Bolsover Hill, Sheffield.
Wake, Bernard	Sheffield.
Wake, William	Sheffield.
Walker, Thomas	Woodlands, Doncaster.
Ward, A. J.	Sheffield.
Wardell, James	Leeds.
Watson, Henry E.	Park Cottage, Worksop.
Webster, Henry	Sheffield.
Weightman, J. G.	Collingham.
Weldon, John	London.
Weldon, Walter	London.
Wentworth, Godfrey	Woolley Park, Wakefield.
Whall, John	Worksop.
Wilcockson, W. H.	Nottingham.
Willoughby, The Hon. and Rev. C. J.	Wollaton.
Winn, C.	Nostel Priory, Wakefield.
Wise, John R.	Edwinstowe.
Wood, John	Sheffield.
Yates, James	Oakwood Hall, Rotherham.

Reference to the Plates.

FRONTISPIECE.—General View of Ruins from south-west.

PLATE   I.—Plan of Abbey Grounds, shewing old boundary wall.

    II.—Ground Plan of Abbey Church (restored), the dark portions indicate the present remains.

    III.—Elevation of interior of North Transept (east wall), with plan of Piers.

    IV.—Perspective details of Capitals, &c.,

      Fig. 1. Centre Pier in east wall of north transept, from north-east.
      „ 2. Side of south-east Tower Pier from south transept chapel.
      „ 3 and 4. Cap and Base from north window in chancel.
      „ 5. Cap from south window in chancel.
      „ 6. Corbel Pillar supporting the groined roof of chancel (north side).
      „ 7. Ditto   ditto   (south side).

    V.—Fig. 1. Enlarged Plan of Tower and Nave Piers.
      „ 2. Enlarged Plan of Piers to north transept chapels.
      „ 3. Section of Capital of transept Pier.
      „ 4. Section of Base to   ditto.
      „ 5. Section of Arch Moulding to same.
      „ 6. Section of Groined Moulding in aisles (transverse).

    VI.—Fig. 1. Plan of Pier (displaced).
      „ 2. Section of Tower Arch Moulding.
      „ 3. Ditto of String inside chapter house.
      „ 4. Plan of West Door Jamb (clear opening of door, 5ft.5in.).
      „ 5. Section of Moulding, now in possession of Mr. Crossley, of Maltby.
      „ 6. Section of Mouldings to Jamb of Doorway into chapter house.
      „ 7. Section of String of chapter house (exterior).
      „ 8. Section of Base Mould of chapter house (exterior).

REFERENCE TO THE PLATES.

PLATE VI.—Fig. 9. Section of String (triforium).
," 10. Section of Parapet (chancel).
," 11. Section of Label.
," 12. Section of String (clerestory).
," 13. Section of Groin Moulding (transept, &c.).
," 14. Section of Groin Moulding (diagonal).
," 15. Section of Groin Moulding (early decorated), found in Chapter House.
," 16. Section of String (interior).
," 17. Section of Base Moulding.
," 18—22, Sections of Bases to Window Shafts, &c.
," 23. Section of Base to west Door Jamb.
," 24. Section of Capital.
," 25 and 26. Sections of Window Shafts.

VII.—Fig. 1. Section of Arch Mould (transitional), found near chapter house.
," 2. Section of Cap and Base to Shafts (decorated).
," 3. Elevation Section of Corbel, next entrance from Abbey Buildings to south transept.
," 4. Section of Piscina Mould.
," 5. Section of Window Jamb Moulding (transitional).
," 6. Section of Angle Shaft.
," 7—9. Sections of Window Jamb Mouldings in south chapel (decorated).
," 10. Section of Arch Moulding (decorated).
," 11. Plan of Window in south Transept chapel (decorated).
," 12. Elevation of Window in ditto (restored).

VIII.—Fig. 1, Present condition of Easter Sepulchre (?) in north wall of chancel.
," 2. Piscina in south wall of north transept chapel.

IX.—Various ancient incised Masons' Marks found on Roche Abbey.

X.—Fig. 1. Secretum of Roche Abbey.
," 2. Matrix of the same.
," 3. First common Seal of Roche Abbey.
," 4. Last ditto, attached to the Surrender Deed.

XI.—Fig. 1. Fragment of Capitals of West Door Jamb, found near the quarries, together with portion of String.
," 2. Cap and Base (perpendicular).
," 3—6. Various Fragments (transitional).

XII.—Fig. 1—5. Fragmentary portions of the Easter Sepulchre, (?) &c., (decorated), discovered in excavating below it.
" 6. Ancient Copper Key found in ruins (Weight, 2¾oz).

XIII.—View of Abbey Gatehouse, from south-east.

XIV.—Plan of Abbey Gatehouse.

XV.—Fig. 1. Plan of Jamb Mouldings of Gatehouse.
" 2. Section of Arch Moulding of Gatehouse.
" 3 and 4. Sections of Base Mouldings of Gatehouse.
" 5. Section of Groin Moulding (transverse).
" 6. Section of Groin Moulding (diagonal).
" 7—9. Capitals.
" 10 and 11. Corbels.

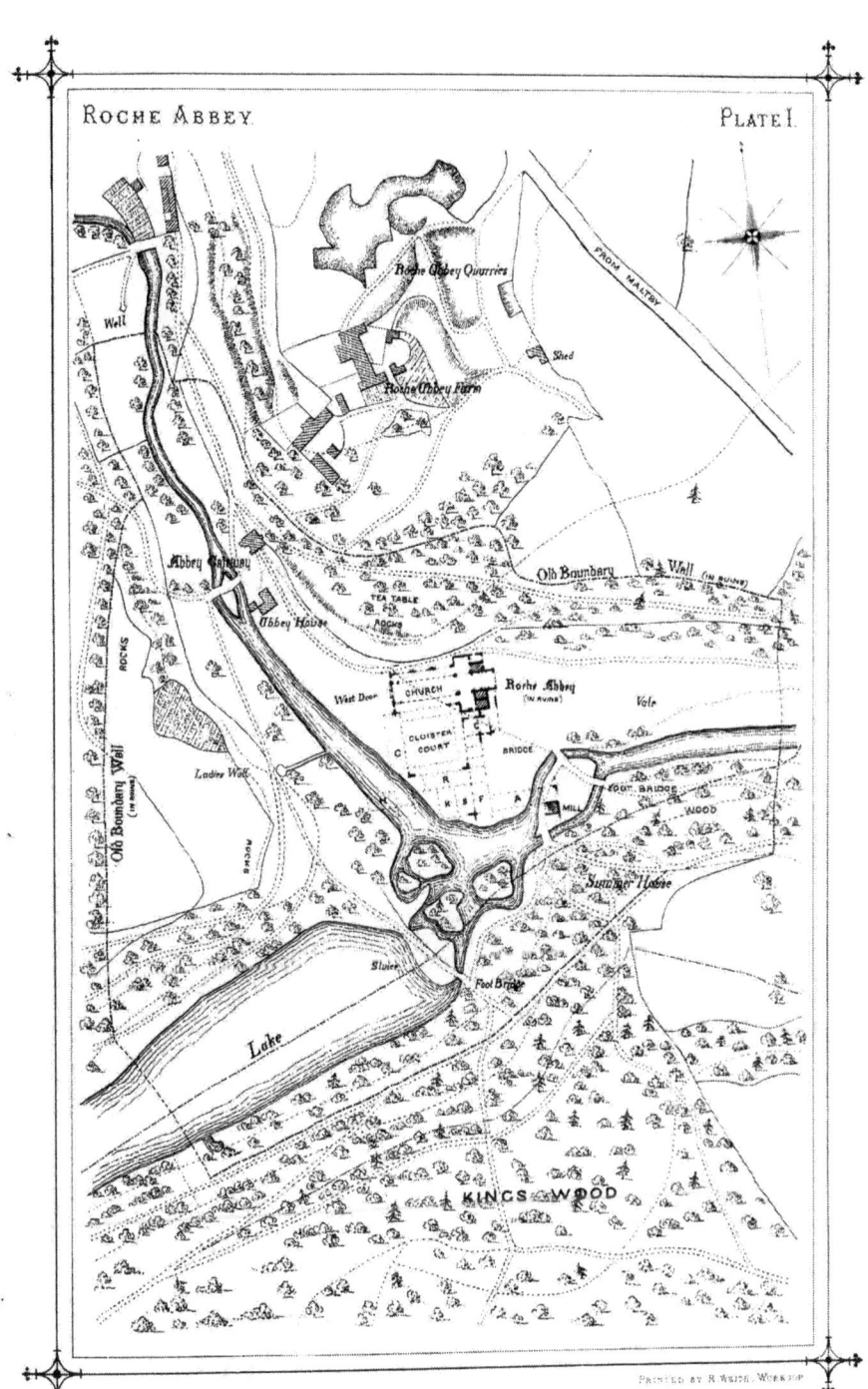

Roche Abbey. Plate II.

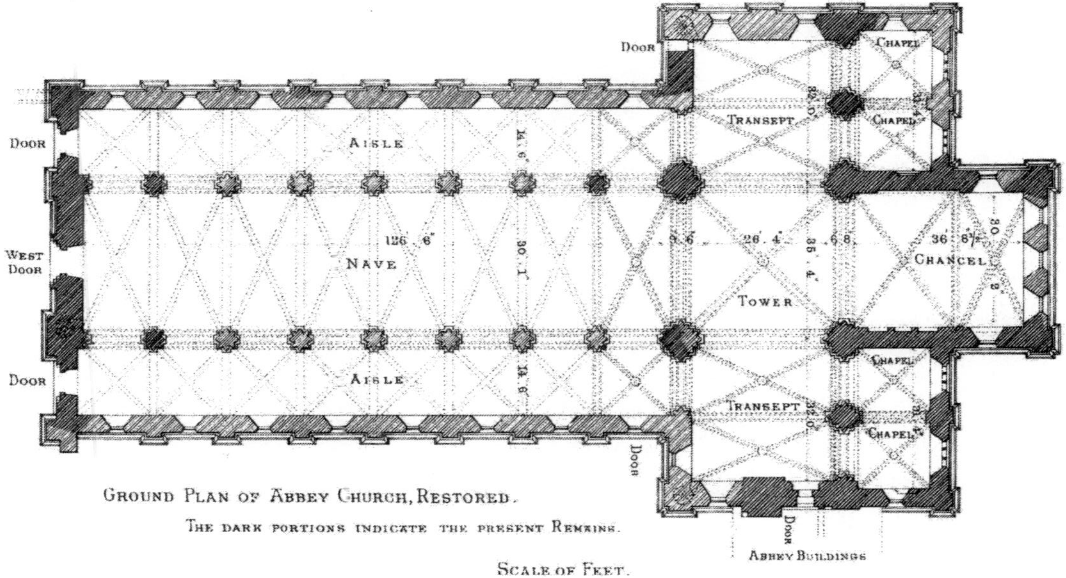

Ground Plan of Abbey Church, Restored.

The dark portions indicate the present Remains.

Scale of Feet.

10 5 0 10 20 30 40 50 60 70 80 90 100 110 120 130 140 150

Printed by R. White, Worksop

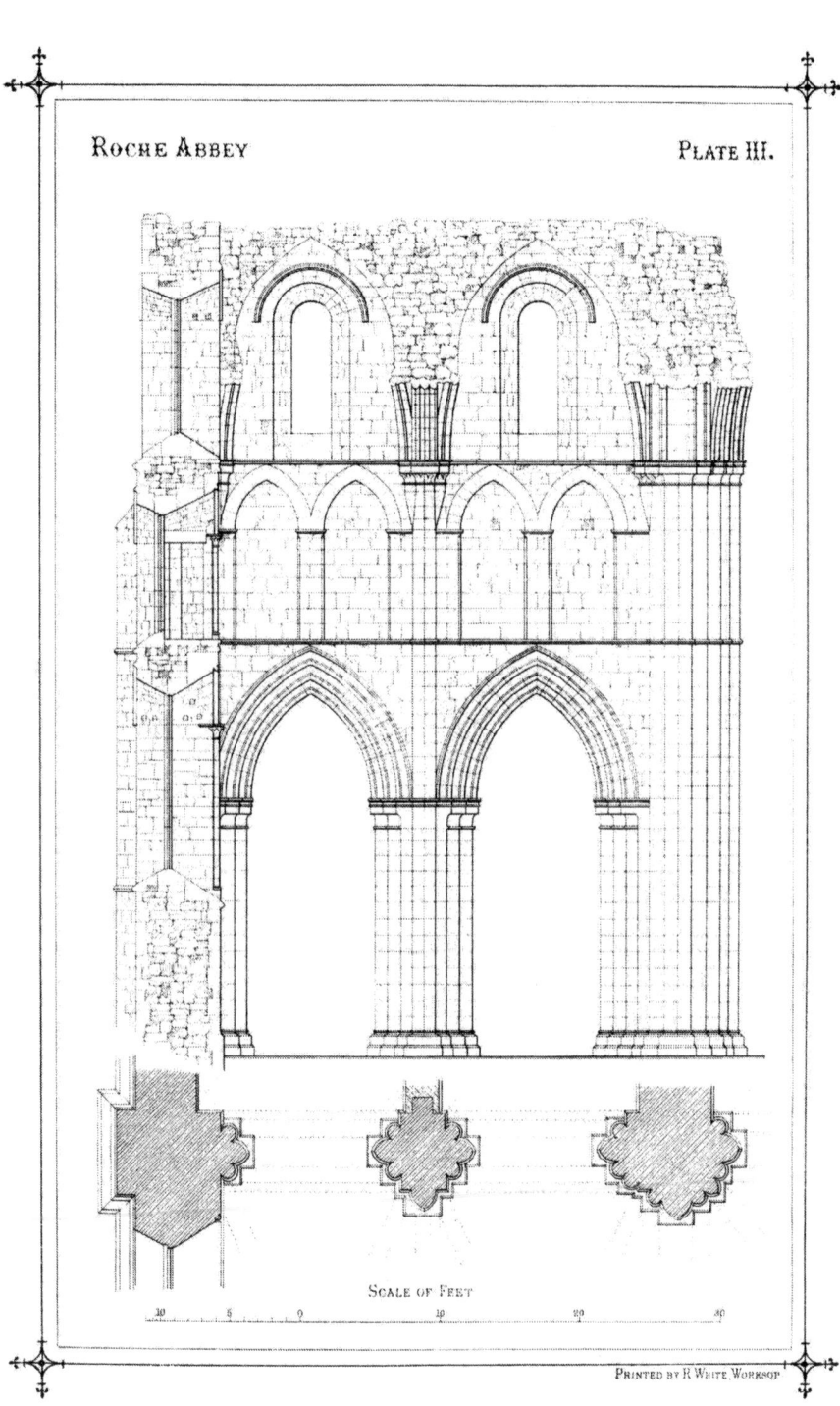

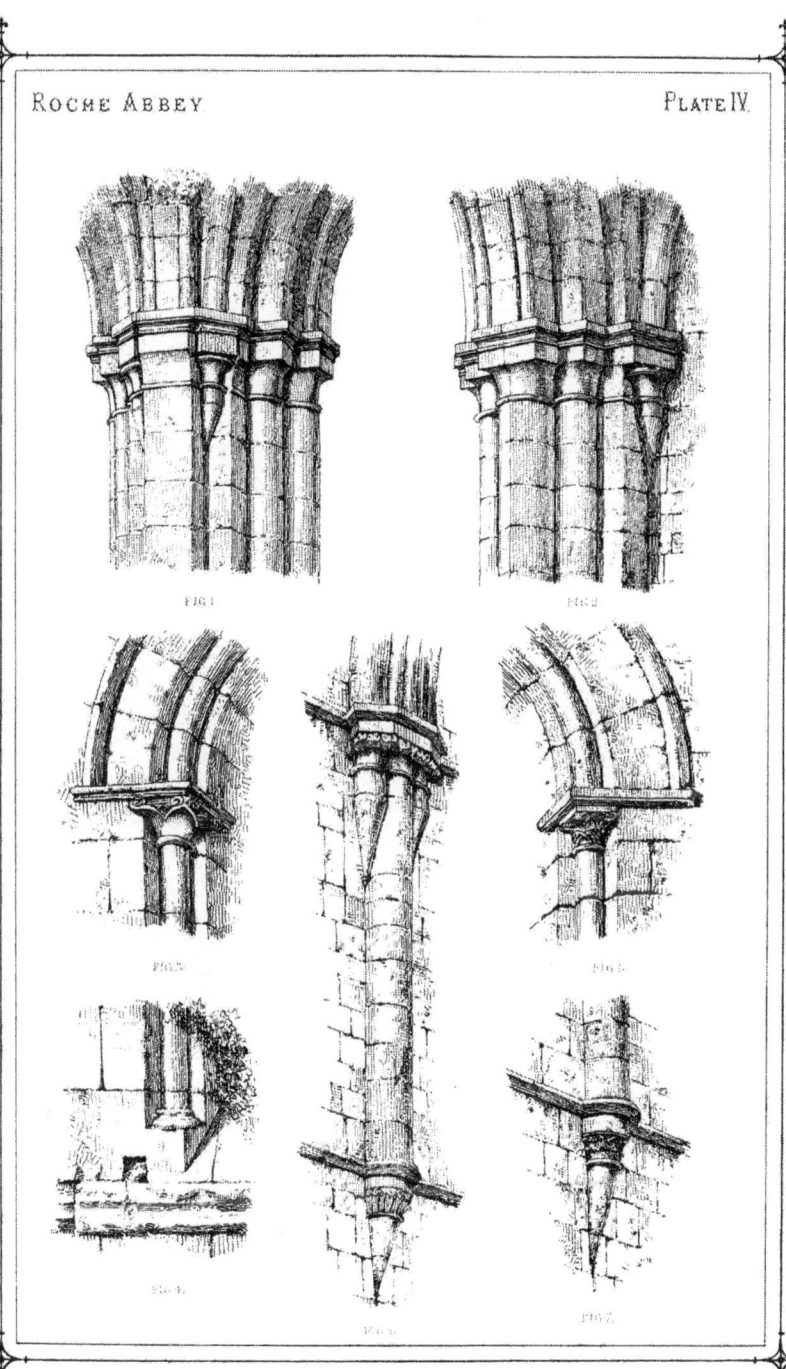

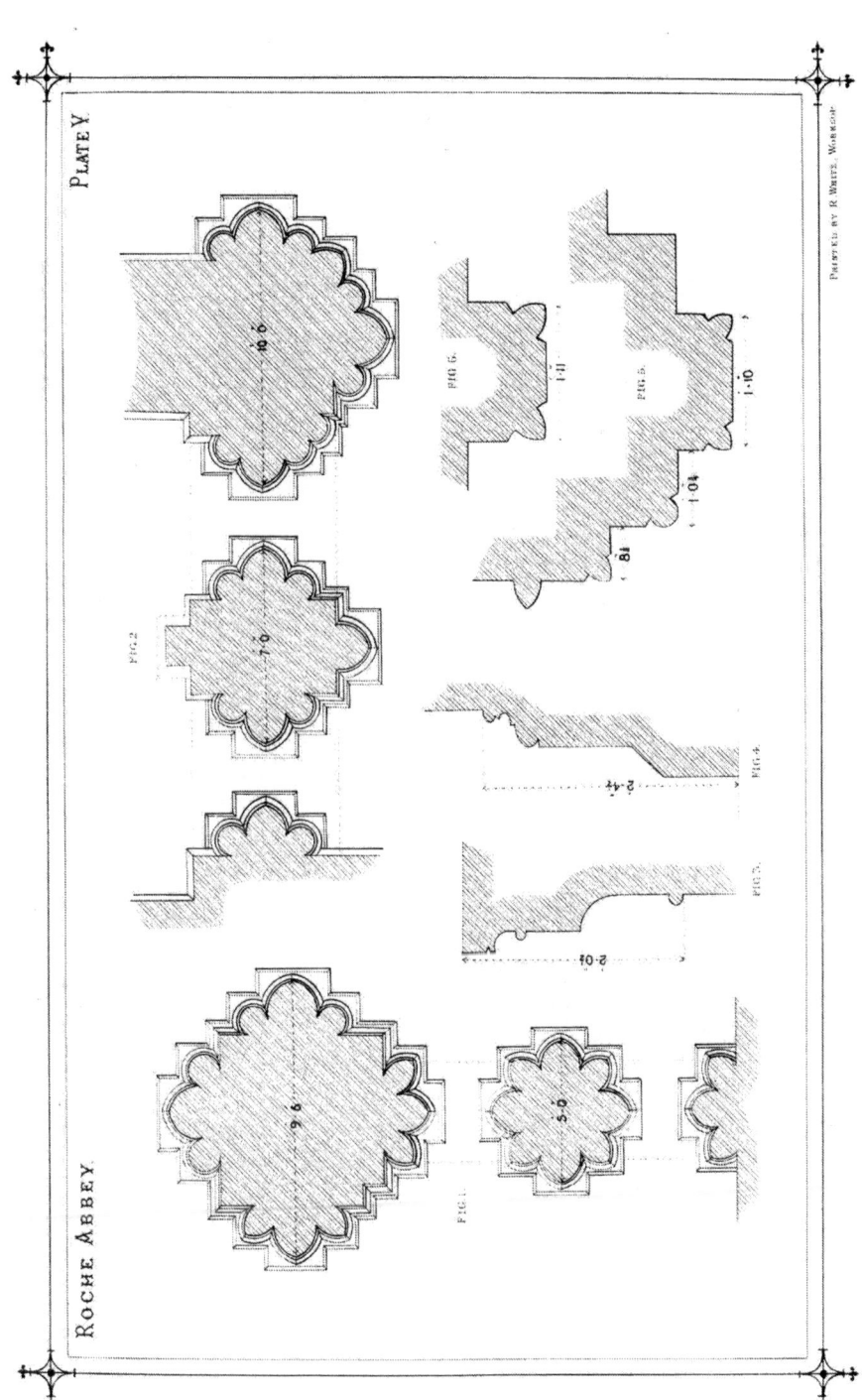

PLATE VI.

ROCHE ABBEY

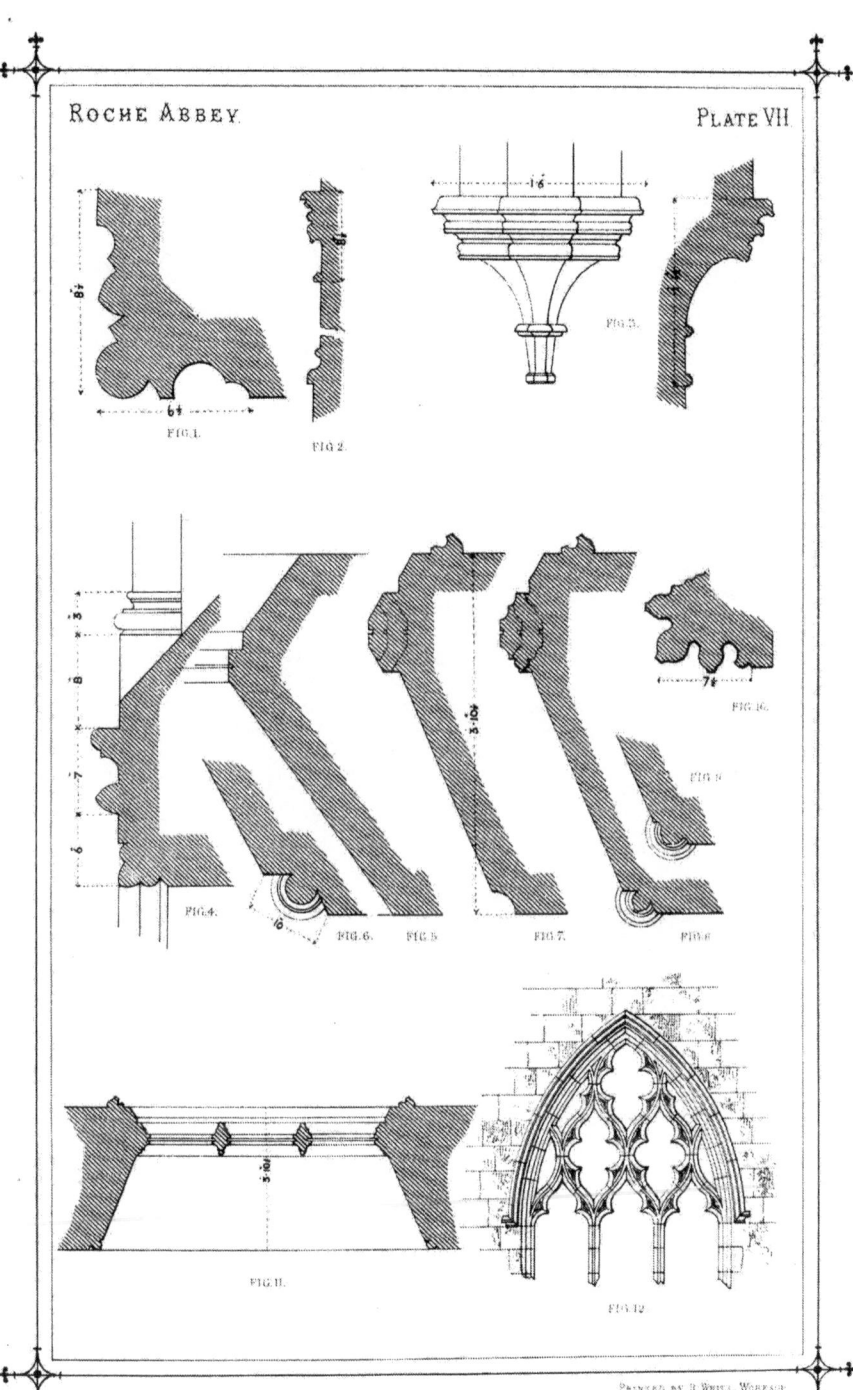

ROCHE ABBEY   PLATE VIII

Roche Abbey   Plate IX

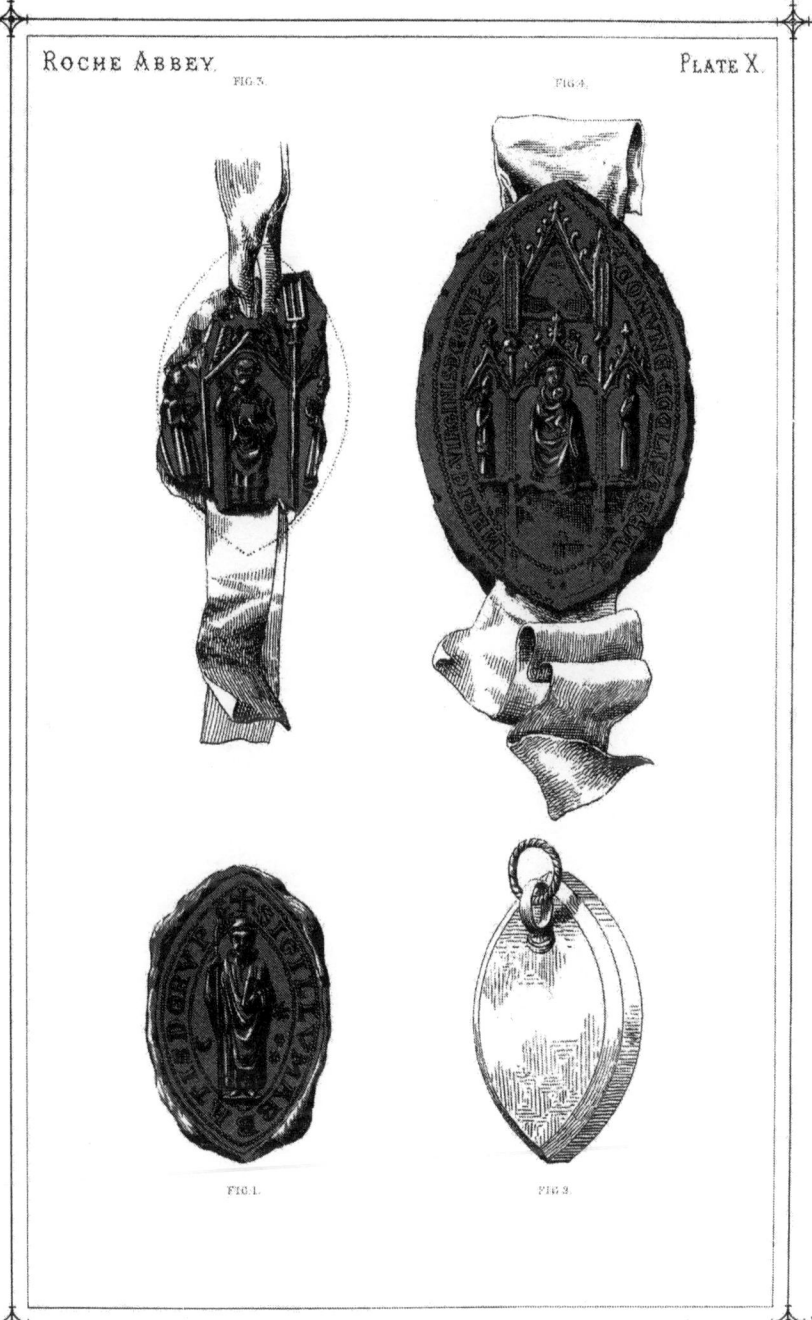

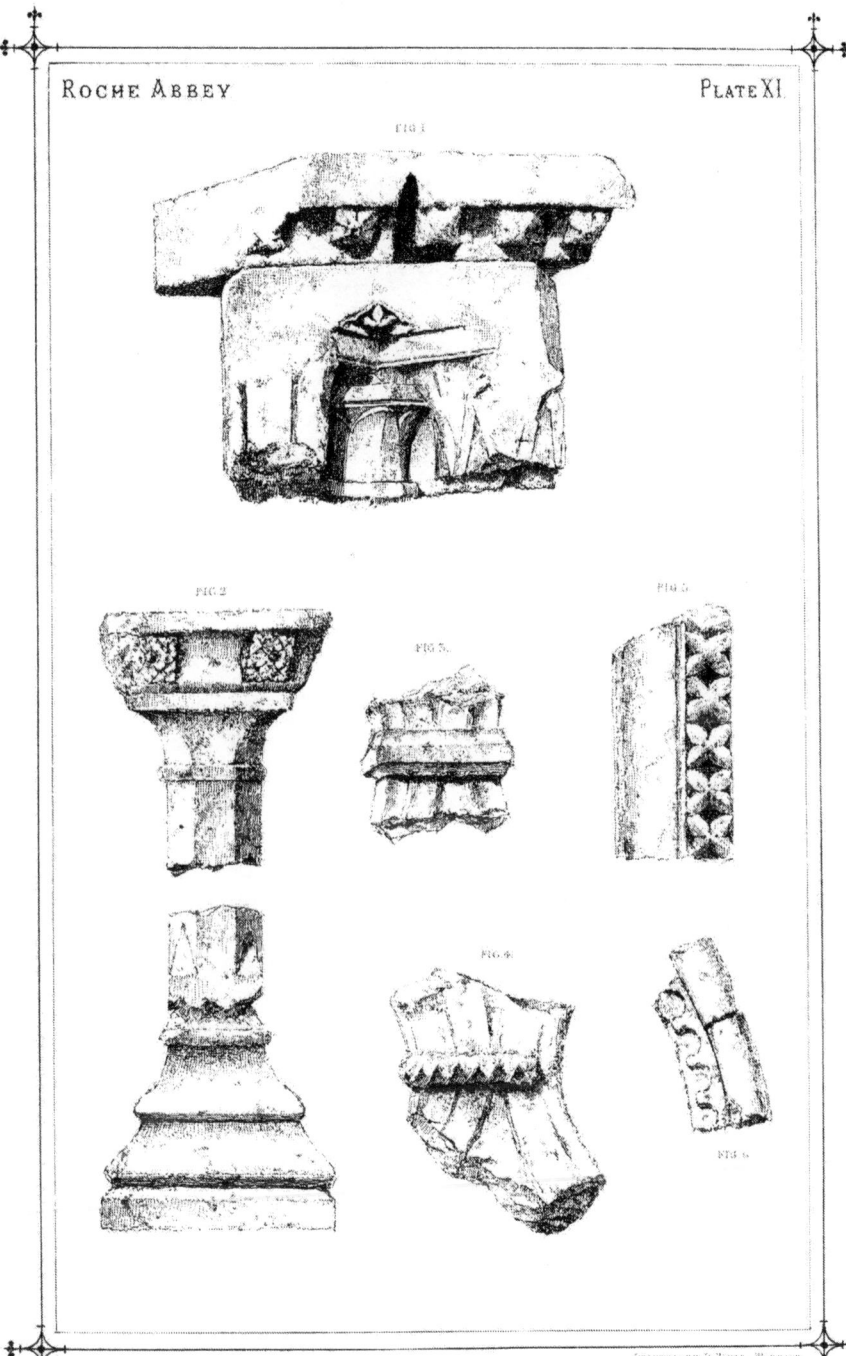

Roche Abbey. Plate XII

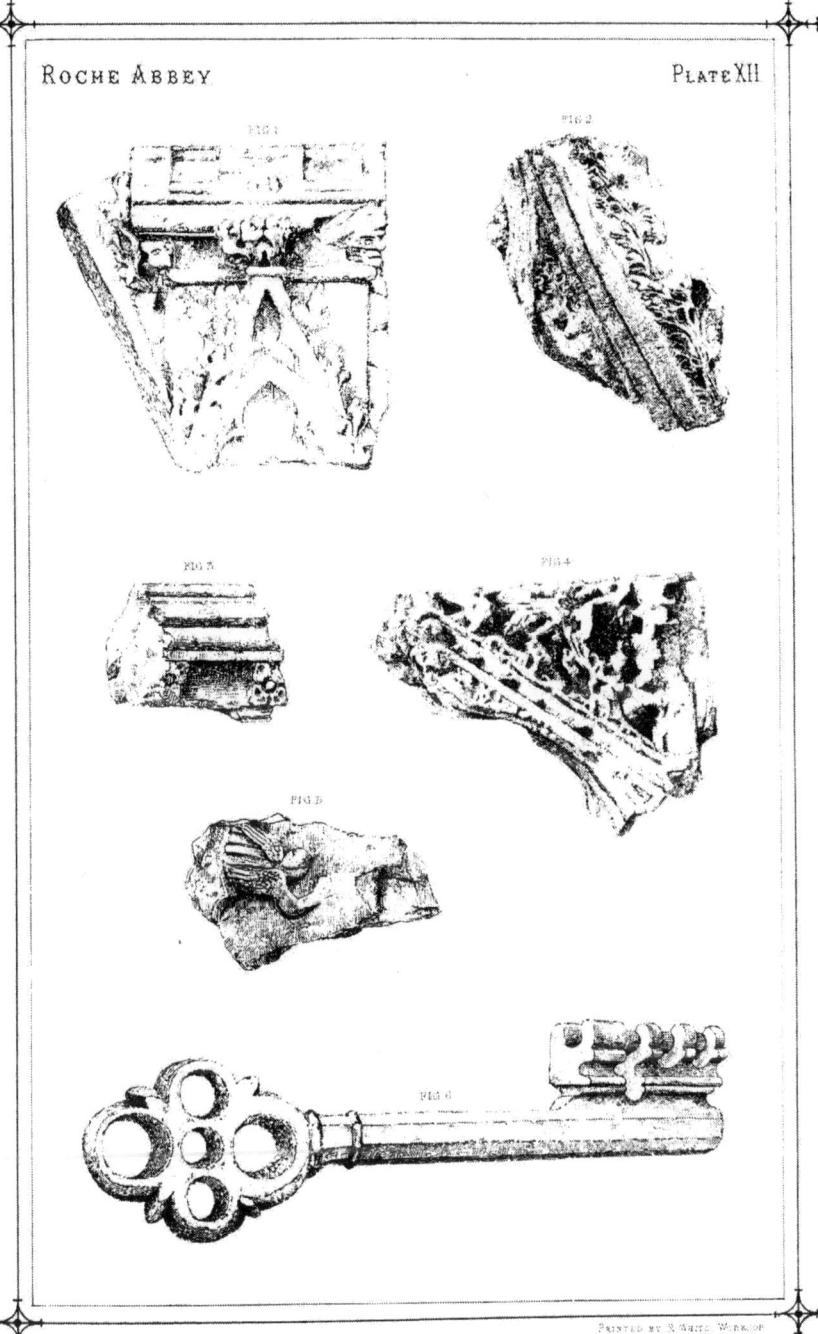

ROCHE ABBEY.

PLATE XIII.

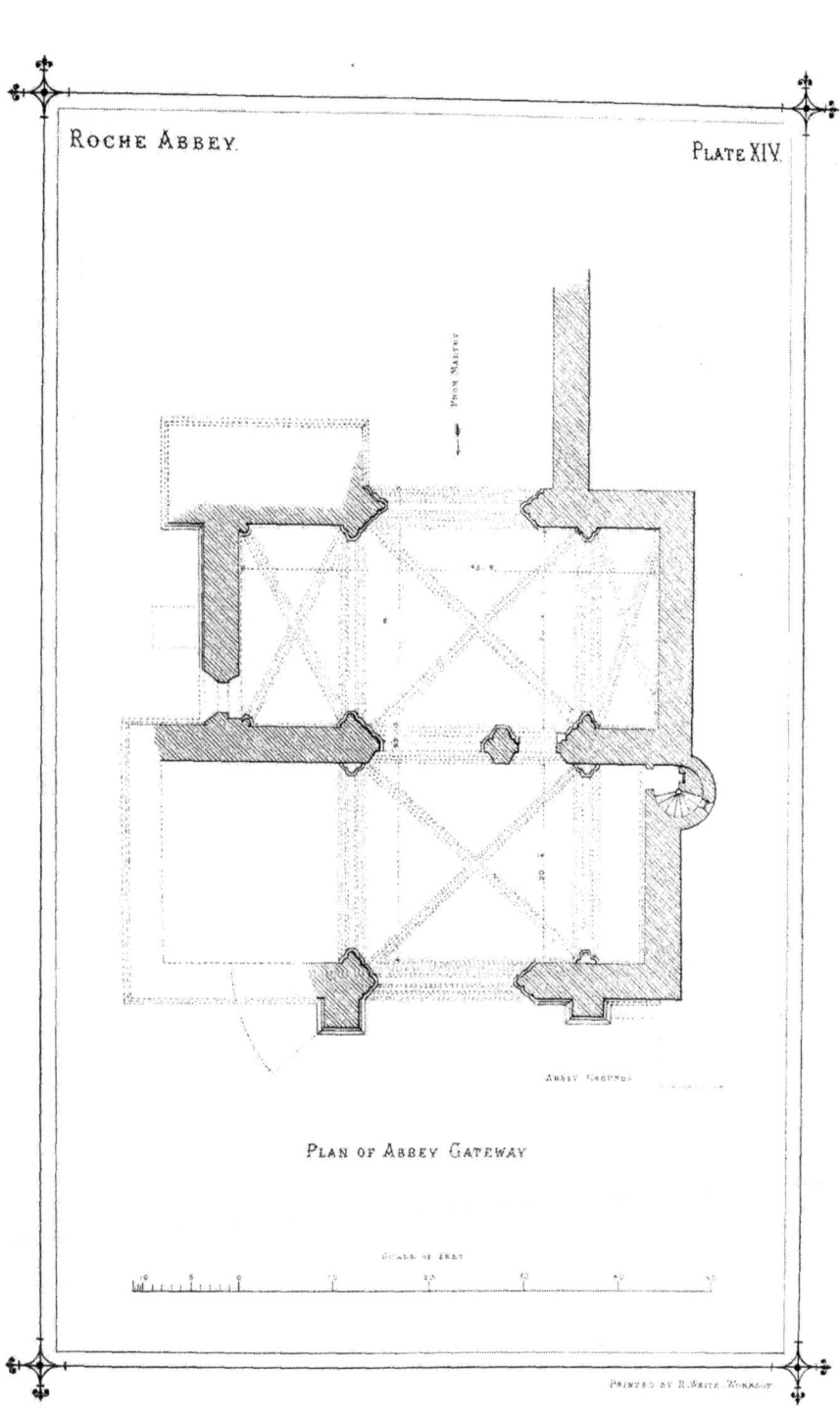

PLAN OF ABBEY GATEWAY

ROCHE ABBEY. PLATE XV.

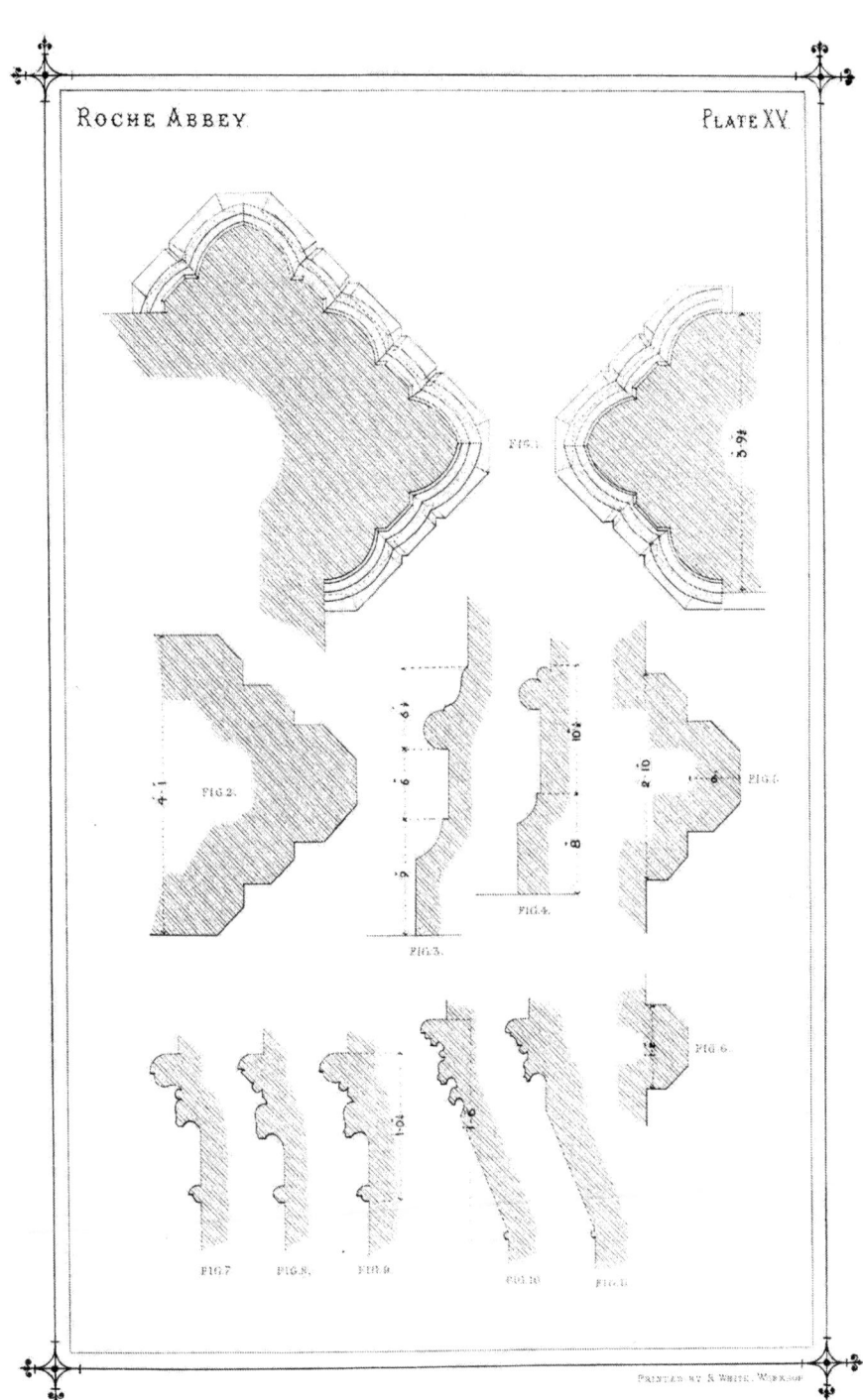

The Introduction.

THE INTRODUCTION

IN the beginning of the twelfth century, after the Crusaders had taken Jerusalem and had completed the massacre of its inhabitants, after they had fallen down, their swords still streaming with the blood of women and children, before the holy sepulchre, weeping in the ecstasy of their devotion; and after Robert, Duke of Normandy had lost his crown by loitering upon the road, to espouse Sibylla, the daughter of an Italian Count: Henry I. foreseeing that his usurped crown would sit uneasily, endeavoured, by a charter which he then passed, to gain the confidence and love of his subjects.

He, in this charter first makes great concessions to the church, promising "that at the death of any Bishop or Abbot he never would seize the revenues of the See or Abbey during the vacancy, but would leave the whole to be reaped by the successor; and that he would never let to farm any ecclesiastical benefice, nor dispose of it for money." The King had also another object in conciliating the favours of the clergy and especially of Anslem who, from his zeal and piety of character, had obtained great authority in the kingdom. Henry proposed to marry Matilda, daughter of Malcolm III. King of Scotland, and niece to Edgar Atheling, but as that princess had been brought up in the nunnery of Rumsey, the legitimacy of the act became a matter of doubt and the religious prejudices of his subjects had to be overcome; which difficult task the church alone could perform.

The concessions contained in this charter, and other things tending to give confidence to the clergy, caused religious houses to spring up so fast, that during the thirty-five years in which Henry reigned no less than one hundred and fifty were established. Five new orders also came into England during this reign, and one of these was the Cistercian, to which order the monks of Roche Abbey belonged.

Of all the orders which sprung from the Benedictines, the Cistercian was the most popular. Their first monastery was at Cisteaux—now Gilley-les-Citeaux—about twelve leagues to the north of Chalons-sur-Saone. To this place Robert, Abbot of Molesme, having obtained the Pope's sanction, retired together with twenty-one of his brethren. Cisteaux at that time, 1098, was a dense and tangled wilderness, inhabited only by wild beasts, but Robert de Molesme disgusted with the laxity of those he had left, was determined, most effectually, to separate himself from the world. The more wild and uninviting the place, therefore the more tempting was it to this ascetic Abbot He immediately commenced cutting away the thorns and crowded trees, and under the protection of Otho, Duke of Burgundy, and the Bishop of Chalons, soon laid the foundation stone of the first Cistercian Abbey

The first Abbey of this order in England seems to have been at Waverley, in Surrey, founded about the year 1128, thirty years after Robert de Molesme's entrance into the wilderness of Cisteaux *Mr. Rastal*, however, in his Chronicles says that "the order of Cysteaux was first brought into England by Walter Espeke, who founded the first Abbey of that religion at Ryvall" Although this abbey may not have been the first in England, it was, doubtless, the first in Yorkshire.

The rules of the Cistercian order were very strict, but did not last so long. Their houses were to be built in solitary places, and to be dedicated to the Holy Virgin All secular affairs were to be placed in the hands of lay-brothers Their revenues were to be divided into four parts—to the bishop a fourth; to the priests a fourth, to the exercise of hospitality a fourth, and a fourth for widows and orphans, the sick, and repairs of the church and cloisters. They were not to possess any churches, altars, ovens, mills, towns, or serfs. They were not to permit any women to enter their Abbeys or any dead to be buried there They were to wear no leather, linen, nor fine woollen cloth, neither were they, except on a journey, to put on any breeches, taking heed to deliver them up, fair washed, upon their return They were to have two coats with cowls, which they might lessen but not augment, and in which habit they were to sleep They were to observe strict silence, save to their Abbot or Prior, to "devise extraordinary afflictions for their own bodies, to the intent their souls may be advantaged," to fast, to prostrate themselves before visitors, and to wash their feet*

The Cistercians were sometimes called "White Monks" owing to the colour of their habit, which consisted of a white cassock with a narrow scapulary. According to a legend of this order this colour was assumed at the wish of the Virgin Mary, intimated in a vision to St. Bernard When they were at work or abroad a black gown fastened about the waist with a black girdle of wool was worn over the white to protect it from dirt They also wore a cowl and a hood of black. The lay-brothers and novices were always clad in a dark colour.

---

* Peter, of the Grandimont order, wore upon his naked body a coat of mail; his bed was made of a hard board, having neither straw nor coverlet, "with often kneeling, kissing of the ground, and beating it with his forehead and nose, he rendered his knees and hands hard like a *callus*, or horn, and his nose crooked"

INTRODUCTION.

The Cistercians performed their devotions seven times in the twenty-four hours, as follows:

Nocturnal	at 2 a.m.
Prime	at 6 a.m.
Tierce	at 9 a.m.
Sexte	at noon.
None	at 3 p.m.
Vespers	at 6 p.m.
Compline	at 7 p.m.

The vestments, utensils, and ornaments of the church were ordered to be very plain. The crosses were to be of painted wood uncarved, and the candlesticks of iron. Pictures and painted glass were not to be allowed.

From the following history the reader will learn that this humility and self-denial did not last long. Wealth, even when it entered the walls of a monastery could not leave luxury without; nor could the monk exercise the power which the ignorance and superstition of the people allowed him without pride. Not many years had elapsed from the institution of the order, before the Cistercian Abbot might have said with the Benedictine, "my vow of poverty has given me 100,000 crowns a year, my vow of obedience has raised me to the rank of a sovereign prince."

When the bold usurper, Stephen, obtained his throne the power of the church had become so great that the mitre might be said to rule the crown, and it is doubtful whether that monarch would have so easily received from the prelate the rite of royal unction and consecration, had it not been for the interest and assistance which he obtained through his brother Henry, who was at that time Bishop of Winchester.

Stephen, like his predecessor, well knowing the importance of securing the good-will of the clergy, lost no time in passing a charter in which he made most liberal promises to the church; and hoping still further to steady his tottering crown, pleased the Pope by desiring him to ratify, by a bull, his groundless title.

Religious houses, during the reign of Stephen, continued to be established, notwithstanding the misery and confusion in which the kingdom was involved, even with greater rapidity than in the time of Henry. "Emperors and Empresses, Kings and Queens, Dukes and Duchesses, exchanged the sceptre and the ducal coronet for the crosier, deserted their thrones and honours in order to assume the titles of ecclesiastics and to wear their habits, and instead of labouring to conquer the world, forsook it, and thereby gained a greater victory—a victory over themselves."

During the short space of eighteen years and nine months which Stephen reigned, no less than one hundred religious houses were founded. At this period the Cistercians gained the summit of their popularity, no fewer than thirty-two abbeys of that order having been added to the thirteen already existing. Among the thirty-two Cistercian Abbeys founded in the reign of Stephen, was one vieing with others in magnificence and interest, the Abbey of Sancta Maria de Rupe, or Roche Abbey.

The Abbey of Roche was situated near the south-eastern extremity of the county of York, within a short distance from the boundary of Nottinghamshire; its site being about nine miles from the towns of Doncaster and Worksop, somewhat less from that of Rotherham, and still nearer to the once celebrated castles of Tickhill and Conisbrough.

It seems desirable for a more distinct understanding of the following history of the place, that a slight sketch should be premised of the general history of the adjoining district and its early lords, some of whom were among the founders and principal benefactors of Roche Abbey.

Previously to the Norman Conquest the lands in this neighbourhood were held by a variety of proprietors, of whom the chief were Earls Harold and Edwin, respectively Lords of Conisborough and Laughton. Shortly, however, after that great event, almost the whole of the manors about here became the prey of three great companions in arms and also family allies of the Conqueror, these were Roger de Bush, Robert, Earl of Morton, and William de Warren—of these Roger de Bush held the largest share, if we include his manors in the county of Nottingham, where he was lord of not less than 170 estates, and also many in the county of York. The head of his fee was, at first, placed at Blyth, in Nottinghamshire, but afterwards removed to Tickhill where he commenced the erection of a castle, on a site which had formerly been occupied as a Brigantian stronghold. The castle of De Bush soon rose to such importance as to give a new name, that of Tickhill, *i e* The Wick Hill or Castle Hill, to the vill, to which it was adjacent, which had previously been called Dadesley, under which designation it appears in the Domesday survey. It is a remarkable fact, however, and one worthy of observation, that this castle, which conferred a name on the town with which it was connected, and on the Honour of which it formed the head in the earliest documents in which it is mentioned, is called the castle of *Blythe*, that is, no doubt, the castle of the *honour*, not of the vill of Blythe. This latter place, Roger de Bush had given as endowment for a Priory of Benedictine Monks, which he founded there in A D 1088. He died in A D 1099 leaving a son of the same name, who did not long survive him, and died without offspring. After the death of the latter, the extensive fee which they had enjoyed was, for some time, either in the hands of the crown, or of persons to whom it was temporarily assigned by the sovereign, till it was restored to a descendant of the house of De Bush in the person of Alicia, Countess of Augi or Eu, who held it in the reign of Henry III, and whom we shall hereafter meet with in our history. This great lady derived her pedigree from Beatrix, the sister of Roger de Busli, and although she did not appear to have had so good a title to the honour as the representatives of the male branch of the family, who derived their origin from Ernaldus a brother of Roger, who disputed it with her, yet she contrived to maintain her position, chiefly it would seem by royal favour, until, according to *Dugdale*, she forfeited it about 37th Henry III.[a]

Among the numerous manors which Roger de Busli held hereabouts, Maltby, in which the Abbey of Roche was mainly seated, formed a not unimportant one. Previously to the Norman Conquest, it had been the property of one Elsi, but at the time of the great survey it was held, in part, in demesne by Roger himself, and the rest was cultivated by his villeins and borderers. Shortly, however, after that date, it appears that Roger subinfeuded his brother Ernaldus here, as also at Kimberworth and other places, where his family held, on the whole, as much as six knight's fees. At Kimberworth the descendants of Ernaldus had long a mansion and a park; they possessed also Sandbeck, immediately adjoining our Abbey, with which valuable estate we shall find one of his race, the great heiress of the house, Idonea, the widow of Robert de Vipont endowing the brotherhood of Roche. Richard de Busli, the co-founder of the Abbey, was the grandson of Ernaldus. He was not only liberal to this house, but also a benefactor to a kindred establishment, that of Kirkstead, in Lincolnshire, the monks of which had already gained a footing on the confines of his estate at Kimberworth, where they had a small establishment and some property, at the place afterwards called Thundercliffe Grange. To these brethren, about the year 1160, he granted sufficient land for the erection of four ironworks, two for smelting the ore and two for forming it into bars, together with liberty to dig for ore in any part of his Kimberworth manor: they were also to have liberty to pasture their horses and cattle there, and to collect dry wood. There is little doubt, that the building erected by the monks at that time, as a stable for their beasts, and residence for their forgemen exists, little altered, at the present day. It stands, in a very elevated situation, adjoining the road from Rotherham to Wortley, within a short distance of the "Keppel Column," and is well worthy of observation, as a very ancient and curious structure. Maltby, and the other estates of this branch of the De Busli family, continued in the hands of persons of that name till the reign of King John, when they passed by the marriage of Idonea, the heiress of the house, with Robert de Viteri Ponte or Vipont, into this latter name. Here they continued for three generations, till they again passed by the marriage of two co-heiresses, Isabel and Idonea, into other families; the former, being the elder sister, having in 52nd Henry III married Roger son and heir of Roger Lord Clifford; the younger, 1st Roger de Leyburn, and 2ndly John de Crumbewell, who had in her right the manor of Kimberworth. She died without issue, and it would

---

[a] Rot. Fin. 37th Henry III., Baronage, vol. i., p. 137.

appear before her death had conveyed the manor of Maltby to her nephew, Robert de Clifford, and in this great family the manor was vested, with slight intermissions, till the reign of Queen Elizabeth, when it was sold in 1587 by George the 3rd, Earl of Cumberland, of that race, to Sir Edward Stanhope, whose son again sold it to Sir Nicholas Saunderson, from whom it has descended to its present noble owner, the Earl of Scarborough. The family connexions of the De Busli race will perhaps be more clearly understood from the following pedigree derived from *Thoroton's* "History of Nottinghamshire."

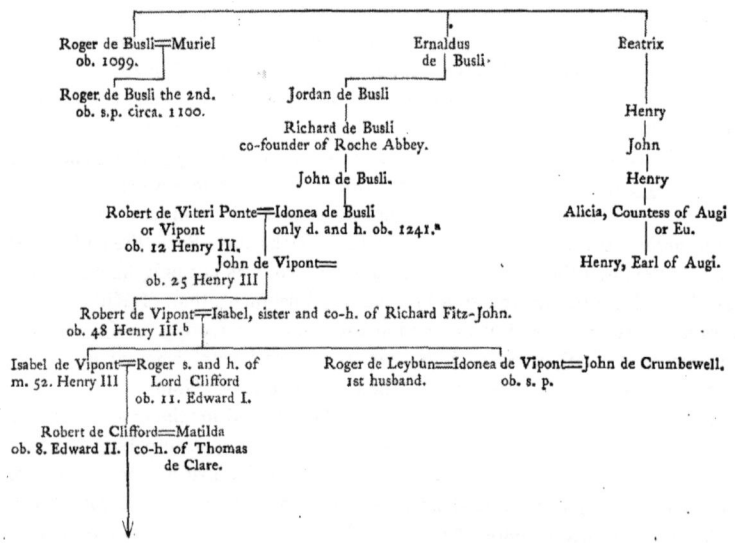

Another great lord of the soil in this neighbourhood at the time of the Domesday survey, as we have already intimated, was Robert, Earl of Morton, the half-brother of William the Conqueror. He held a vast number of manors in Yorkshire, the greater part of which were apportioned to two subinfeudatories, Richard de Surdeval and Nigel de Fossard. Some few, however, he retained in his own hands, and of these was the one with which we are now principally concerned, that of Hooton, afterwards distinguished from several others of the name, within a short distance, by the addition of Levet, from the name of the family which subsequently possessed it. This small manor detached from his other estates, and surrounded by those of Roger de Busli, had strangely escaped the rapacious maw of that great leviathan of manors hereabouts. It was held in demesne by Earl Robert, and cultivated by his villeins and

---

[a] Excerpta é Rot. Fin. Henry III. vol. i. p p. 357, 371.
[b] ,,   ,,   vol. ii. p. 410.

INTRODUCTION.

borderers, but it did not long continue in his possessions, for it was soon forfeited together with all his other English estates, and appears then to have become vested in the family of Fossard, who thus were elevated to the position of chief tenants. They did not, however, occupy the land themselves, but subinfeuded the house of Vesci, Lords of Rotherham, and these again invested with the actual possession of the soil, a family named Fitz-Turgis. The first person of this race of whom we find mention is Richard Fitz-Turgis, also named De Wickersley, from his having become possessed of the manor of that place, which he held of the Lords of Bentley, the Newmarches, and they again of the castle of Tickhill. It was this Richard, who was so happily joined in the bonds of christian brotherhood, but too rare in such cases, with his neighbour De Busli, Lord of Maltby, whose estate there was separated from his own, only by a small brook, as heartily to co-operate with him, in the foundation of the Abbey of Roche. He was succeeded in the estate by a son, who was also a benefactor to the house, and the latter by a daughter named Constantia his sole heiress, who carried the property into the family of De Levet by her marriage with William de Levet. With the Levets the manor continued till the time of Henry V. about which period they disappear. It then seems to have become the property of the Cliffords, and is mentioned among the places of which Thomas, Lord Clifford died seised in 1454. From that time its descent, it is believed, has been the same with Maltby, to the Earl of Scarborough.[a]

The other principal fee in this neighbourhood whose lords were special benefactors of Roche, was that of Conisborough. This manor with its numerous dependencies, as already intimated, had before the Conquest been the property of Earl Harold, afterwards King of England, but after that event became the portion of William de Warren, who married Gunnora, the daughter or rather daughter-in-law of the Conqueror. The lands of his Yorkshire fee lay not only at Conisborough and in various townships extending to the extreme confines of the county southward, but also beyond Doncaster, where Hatfield and a large surrounding district was dependent upon it: there being, however, an extensive tract of country intervening which was not in Warren's possession. And it was, as we shall see, at Hatfield and its neighbourhood that the Abbey of Roche was specially benefited by that great family. The manor of Conisborough remained in the family of Warren till the time of Edward III, when their possessions came into the hands of the crown. It was settled on the Princes of the house of York, and became the property of Edmund of Langley a younger son of the King. At the castle here it would appear that he sometimes resided, and here his second son Richard, who enjoyed the title of Earl of Cambridge, was born. This Prince married, as his second wife, Maud a daughter of Thomas, Lord Clifford, who as we shall find in our subsequent history, made

---

[a] Hunter's "South Yorkshire," vol. i. p. 265.

her will at Roche Abbey, in which she directed that her body should be buried there.

It appears unnecessary to pursue this general history any further, so much, however, it seemed desirable to premise, in order to enable the reader more intelligently to peruse the following history.

This history will be found digested under the three following principal heads.

    I.—THE ABBOTS.
    II.—THE POSSESSIONS.
    III.—THE ARCHITECTURE, MONASTIC BUILDINGS, AND THEIR REMAINS.

And under these heads, it is trusted, that a full and accurate account will be furnished respecting the venerable and interesting Abbey of Roche.

The Abbots.

List of the Abbots of Roche Abbey.

1.	Durandus	1147
2.	Dionysius	1159
3.	Roger de Tickhill	1171
4.	Hugh de Wadworth	1179
5.	Osmund	1184
6.	Reginald	1223
7.	Richard	1238
8.	Walter	1254
9.	Alan	1268
10.	Jordan	***
11.	Philip	***
12.	Thomas	1286
13.	Stephen	1287
14.	John	1300
15.	Robert	1300
16.	William	1324
17.	Adam de Gykellswyk	1330
18.	Simon de Baukewell	1349
19.	John de Aston	1358
20.	Robert	1396
21.	John Wakefield	1438
22.	John Gray	1465
23.	William Tikil	1479
24.	Thomas Thurne	1486
25.	William Burton	1488
26.	John Morpeth	1491
27.	John Heslington	1503
28.	Henry Cundal, surrendered in	1538

THE ABBOTS.

Durandus.

1147—1159.

URANDUS, bearing in his hand a crofs of wood, and followed by twelve monks,[a] in imitation of Chrift and his twelve Apoftles, might have been feen, in the middle of the twelfth century, wandering about a defolate and trackless foreft—which, at that time, covered the South of Yorkfhire—in fearch of unappropriated land in a retired fituation, where he might lead a holy life, and by labour win from the earth the little fuftenance which his abftemious habits demanded. With much "Travail and hungre, thurfte, and colde," he might have been feen to enter a namelefs valley, whofe tangled flopes were fheltered from the inclemency of the North by a range of lofty gray and venerable looking rocks. And as the good Durandus entered, we ftill may picture the flafh of joy which croffed his weary countenance when he became convinced, from its wildnefs and extreme folitude, that the long-fought refting place had been found. And as he ftood elated at the fitnefs and beauty of the fpot, imagination ftill may fhow us the monks approaching, one, with tidings of a fpring, furpaffing in purity any he had before met with; and another, with awed and eager ftep, relating that, wandering near, he has found hewn out upon a rock, by God's own hand, an image of our Saviour on a Crofs! And may we not ftill in our

[a] "For thretteene is a convent as I geffe."—Chaucer.

minds fee Durandus and his twelve bowed down before that myftic rock in filent thankfulnefs and deep devotion?

This valley, fo peaceful and retired, and contrafting fo ftrongly with the turmoil and buftle of the world, and the horrors of civil war (at that time being carried on between Stephen and Matilda,) is fituated in the parifh of Maltby, and the ftream which paffes through it formed the boundary line between the lands of Richard de Bufli, and Richard Fitz Turgis, lords of Maltby and Hooton. In this valley—this lonely and beautiful wildernefs—Durandus and his followers fettled down under the title of "Monachi de Rupe," or 'Monks of the Rock,' living for a time in rude huts under trees, and depending partly upon their own exertions and partly on the charity of others for their fupport. How long the community remained in this condition is not known, but it is not probable that their privations lafted long, for in thofe days the endowment of a religious houfe was looked upon as a high privilege, and lords of the foil loft no time, when an opportunity prefented itfelf of doing that which they believed would both immortalize their names and fave their fouls!

Upon the 30th day of July,[a] in the year of grace 1147, the Houfe of Roche was founded by Richard de Bufli and Richard Fitz Turgis. The following are tranflations of the foundation charters:—

Charter of Richard de Busli,[b] concerning the Foundation of the Abbey of Roche.

"BE it known to all who fee or hear thefe letters that I, Richard de Bufli, with confent of my wife and heirs, have given to God and St. Mary, and to the Monks of the Rock, for the falvation of my foul, and the fouls of all my anceftors, the whole wood from the middle of the road from Eilrichethorpe to Lowthwaite, and fo far as the water which is the boundary between Maltby and Hooton, and the two farts[c] which belong to Gamul, with a great culture which is there adjacent and common of pafture for a hundred fheep, in number fix fcore, in the foke[d] of Maltby, by this tenure, that they build their Abbey on whichfoever

---

[a] Mr. Hunter makes this date "June," but he is evidently in error, for the paffage in the "Succeffio Abbatum," "tertio kalendas Augufti," can mean nothing elfe than the third day from the kalends of Auguft.—"South Yorkfhire, vol. i. p. 269."

[b] Richard de Bufli was grandfon of Arnaldus, who was brother to Roger de Bufli, an eminent Aorman, who followed the Conqueror, and obtained great poffeffions.

[c] A piece of wood land turned into arable.   [d] Territory.

DURANDUS.   5

side of the water they pleafe, according as the fituation of the place fhall be more fuitable, Richard de Bufli and Richard Fitz Turgis agreeing between themfelves that both fhould be the founders of the Abbey, on whichfoever's property the Abbey may be built, as a perpetual charity, free and quiet from all fecular fervice or gift. Before thefe witneffes, Adam de Newmarch, Hugh de Stainton, Odo Filius Johannis, Willielmus Filius Raveni, Jordan Painel, Gamel Filius Befingi, Hugh de Langthwaite, Robert de Scalzebi, William le Buteiler, William de Mileri, Robertus, Filius, junior, Richard Barbot, Gervafe de Barneby, Swein, fon of Tor and Jordan, his fon."

The Charter of Richard Fitz Turgis, respecting the Foundation of the Abbey of Roche.

"BE it known to all who fee and hear this Charter, that I, Richard Fitz Turgis, with the confent of my wife and heirs, have given to God, St. Mary, and the Monks of the Rock, for the falvation of my foul, and the fouls of my anceftors, the whole land from the borders of Eilrichethorpe, as far as the brow of the hill beyond the ftream which runs from Fogfwell, and fo to a heap of ftones which lies in the fart of Elfi, and fo beyond the road as far as the Wolfpit, and fo by the head of the culture of Hartfhow to the borders of Slade Hooton; all that land, and all that wood below thefe bounds and common of pafture of all my land, and fifty cart loads every year in my wood of Wickerfley, where I fhall provide, or fome one on my behoof, for a perpetual charity, free and quiet from all fecular fervice, on this condition— that they build an Abbey on whichever fide of the water they pleafe, according as the fituation of the place fhall appear beft, Richard Fitz Turgis and Richard de Bufli agreeing between themfelves, and conceding that both be founders of the Abbey, on whofefoever fide of the water it may happen to be. Before thefe witneffes, Adam de Newmarch, Hugh de Stainton, Odo Filius Johannis, Willielmus Filius Raveni, Jordan Painel."

In thefe fancy-bazaar and begging-letter days it is difficult to enter into the feelings of two men, who, in the twelfth century, were fo much in earneft, and fo full of faith, that they could without hefitation give up fo large a portion of their poffeffions for the purpofe of building and endowing a monaftery, wherein a few ſtrolling monks, who had choſen to ſettle upon the borders of their eſtate, might live and worſhip God after their own faſhion. Two great inducements for ſuch a ſacrifice are, however, prominently mentioned in both charters. The firſt is—"the ſalvation of their ſouls and thoſe of all their anceſtors" (no ſmall boon!); and the ſecond is, the honour of being founders. The whole of their lands and woods were given to God, St. Mary, and the Monks of the Rock, "on this *condition*, that both be founders."

The building of the Abbey, doubtleſs, commenced at once, as both wood and good building ſtone were to be procured on the ſpot in abundance, no delay would be occaſioned in collecting materials. Durandus would, therefore, have the pleaſure of ſeeing the firſt ſtone of his Abbey laid, and of dedicating it, as was the Ciſtercian cuſtom, to the Bleſſed Virgin Mary. At the laying of the foundation of Croyland Abbey, which took place a few years earlier, the pious Abbot Toffred began by ſaying prayers, and ſhedding a flood of tears. Then thoſe who had come to aſſiſt in the ceremony each laid a ſtone, and upon it depoſited a ſum of money, a grant of lands, tithes, or patronages, or a promiſe of ſtone, lime, wood, labour, or carriage, to aſſiſt in building. Richard de Buſli and Richard Fitz Turgis moſt likely followed the liberal cuſtom of the ſtone-layers at Croyland, and Robert de Scalzebi and Adam de Newmarch probably followed their good example, they having been two of the earlieſt benefactors of the houſe, and, as the reader may have noticed, two of the witneſſes to the foundation charters.

It has been a ſubject of doubt from which abbey Durandus and his monks came, and ſome, not content with the ſufficiently difficult taſk of deciding from which of the Britiſh abbeys they were derived, have gone ſo far as to ſuggeſt the poſſibility of their foreign origin.

Theſe doubts, however, need no longer exiſt, as there is ſufficient evidence to prove beyond a doubt from whence they came. From the narration of Hugh, a monk of Kirkſtall, which is printed in the *Monaſticon Anglicanum*, vol. v., p. 299, we learn the following:—

In the fifth year of the foundation of Fountains Abbey, a noble man, Ranulph de Merlay, came to viſit that abbey, and ſeeing the converſation of the brethren was ſtruck with compunction, and under the Lord's inſpiration, for the redemption of his ſoul, aſſigned a certain place in his patrimony for building a monaſtery. The Abbot of Fountains accepted the offering, and the building having been arranged in due form, he conſtructed an abbey which he called Newminſter. And this was the firſt daughter of the Church of Fountains, as yet the only one of her mother. In the fifth year of its foundation a convent was sent out from Fountains to Newminſter, with Abbot Robert, a holy and religious man, formerly monk of Whitby, who joined himſelf with thoſe who left St. Mary's Abbey, York, to found Fountains. Thus Newminſter had its beginning. And this was the firſt plant which proceeded from our vineyard. The holy ſeed flouriſhed in the ſoil, and as if received into the boſom of a fertile ground, forthwith increaſed into a ſtalk, and from a few grains aroſe a copious crop. For emulating the fecundity of her mother, ſhe brought forth three daughters—Pipewell, Salley, and Roche.

The truth of this narration is corroborated in many ways. Dr. Whitaker, in his *Hiſtory of Craven*, p. 36, gives a charter,[a] ſhewing that Swain Fitz Swain ſold to Robert, the Abbot of Newminſter, ſome land to build an abbey upon of the Ciſtercian order (Salley Abbey.) In the *Monaſticon Anglicanum*, vol. v. p. 34, there is alſo a charter proving that the original monks of Pipewell came from Newminſter: and the evidence is completed by the letters[b] of the Abbot of Newminſter to the Archbiſhop of York, requeſting him to confirm the election of the Abbots of Roche. The Abbot of Newminſter, in one of theſe, ſtyles himſelf "*Father Abbot and immediate Viſitor of the Monaſtery of Roche.*" Henry, prior of Roche was elected abbot of Newminſter in 1216.

The Abbey of Newminſter is ſituated at a ſhort diſtance from Morpeth, in Northumberland. One doorway alone of the original building remains. From this monaſtery then, the "Monks of the Rock" came, ſent forth by St. Robert,[c] the firſt abbot of Newminſter, a Yorkſhireman by birth: and it is not unlikely that he aſſiſted them as he did the monks of Salley in their early poverty.

After having lodged for ſome time in huts, living on "boiled leaves and herbs," as the monks of Fountains had firſt done, and with the proſpect of winter before him, how gladly muſt they have received the meſſage of the lords of Maltby and Hooton, offering to build and endow them an abbey! How ſpeedily, too, muſt the ſcene have changed! Where a few ſilent monks had been dwelling in

---

[a] Dr. Whitaker has miſtaken the meaning of the words "novi monaſterii" in this charter, and places Robert, the Abbot of Newminſter, at the head of the abbots of Salley.

[b] See page 62.

[c] The life of St. Robert is given in Alban Butler's "Lives of the Saints," under June 8th. Should it not be June 7th?

folitude, a throng of noify workmen now appear. And inftead of the peace which had hitherto reigned, the rattle of carts, the tramp of horfes, and the founds of pickaxe and fpade are heard. It muft have been an anxious and a happy time for the good Durandus, as he walked among the labourers, watching their daily progrefs, and pondering upon the glory of the future. In the crafh of falling timber, and in the founds of mafon's tools chipping and fhaping the fair white ftone, he, perhaps, forefaw his beautiful abbey already ftanding, capped with pinnacles and towers, furrounded with fruitful gardens, orchards, and barns well ftored! Death, however, prevented the good old abbot from feeing all his wifhes fulfilled. In 1159, after he had held his abbacy twelve years, Durandus died.

Reft, Durandus! The materials of the crumbling abbey will foon fall over thy mouldering bones. The trees thou felledft have been replaced, and now, with outftretched arms, thefe younger fons of the foreft reclaim the ancient foil. Yea, in the very fane where noble arches fprung, rough branches wave; now flowers only cenfe the air; and for the folemn mafs, now noify jackdaws fit and mock with fcornful laughs!

> "The owl of evening and the woodland fox
> For their abode the fhrines of Waltham choose.
> Proud Glaftonbury can no more refuse
> To ftoop her head."

Dionysius.

1159—1171.

DIONYSIUS was elected second Abbot of Roche in the year 1159. Who he was, or from whence he came, are matters of doubt; but there is reason to believe that he was one of the original followers of Durandus, and perhaps, sub-prior to the community previous to his election to the abbacy.

The twelve years during which Dionysius governed the abbey of Roche, exactly coincide with the period during which Henry II. and Thomas à Becket were struggling for the ascendancy. And strange to say, this Royal quarrel threatened at one time to seriously affect the happiness of the poor "monks of the Rock;" for Henry, hearing that Thomas à Becket (who had fled the country) had assumed the habit of the Cistercian order, and was living with Gwarine, Abbot of Pontiniac, wrote to that abbot and threatened to drive out from his realm all the monks of his order if he continued to harbour him in his abbey. Happily for Dionysius and his monks however, Thomas à Becket left Pontiniac, and so the king had not the chance of putting his threat into execution.

The life of Dionysius as abbot must have been very quiet and prosperous. Property came flowing in, and the possessions of the abbey were becoming rapidly more extended. In the time of Alexander, Abbot of Kirkstal, who lived contemporaneously with Dionysius, Henry de Laci, lord of Pontefract, granted and confirmed the donation which Richard de Wickersley, and Roger and Jordan Hoten, made to the Monks of the Rock, of common pasture of all the territory of Hotun. The following charter of Richard de Busli, son of the founder, was probably also granted at this time:—

Charter of Richard de Busli, of Elrichthorpe.

"TO all the sons of Holy Mother Church, as well present as future, Richard de Busli, greeting! Be it known to all that see and hear thefe letters, that I, Richard de Bufli, with the advice and confent of my wife and heirs, have given to God, St. Mary, and the Monks of the Rock, for the falvation of my foul and thofe of all my friends, Elrichthorpe, and whatever belongs to it in all things. And I have granted to them the land of William de Alz which my father gave them, and the land which the aforefaid monks have of my Knight of Scalzebi.—Witneffes, William, his fon and heir; R., his fon; Ralph, the prieft; Hugh, the clerk of Rotherham; Robert de Bufli; William de Sandebi; Mr. William de Duningeton; Richard Baret; William Barbot; and Ralph de Turlavefton."

Dionyfius, fave attending a general chapter now and then, and looking after his revenues, could have had little elfe to do than to fuperintend the building of his abbey, the walls of which by that time muft have reached a goodly height. A few pointed arches, were perhaps, already completed, and had received their fhare of admiration and aftonifhment, for in thofe days the pointed arch was a great novelty, the round or Norman arch being the form, which had up to that time been ufually employed.

Dionyfius ceafed to be abbot in 1171.

Roger de Tickhill.

1171—1179.

THANKS to the cuftom which the monks had when they left the world of leaving their furnames behind them, and of affuming by way of diftinction the names of the places from whence they came, we are able to learn that by this time, the Monks of the Rock had begun to receive brothers from the towns and villages near them; and that Roger, the third abbot of Roche, came from the neighbouring parifh of Tickhill.

The building of the Abbey muft have been carried on very actively during the time of abbot Roger; and we find from the following charter of John, fon of the founder, that the Houfe of De Bufli ftill remained firm friends to the monks:—

The Charter of John de Busli, the son of Richard de Busli.

"TO all the fons of Holy Mother Church, prefent and future, John de Bufli, greeting! Know that I have granted and confirmed by this my charter, to God, St. Mary, and the Monks of the Rock, for the falvation of my foul, and the fouls of my father and mother, and all my anceftors and heirs, all the donations and liberties, without refervation, which Richard de Bufli, my father, gave them, and confirmed by his charters; fo that the ditch of the aforefaid monks as it has been made around the wood fhall remain for good and peace, without any clamour, common from me and my heirs, except the aerie of fparrow-hawks, which the aforefaid monks have granted me. I have granted alfo, to the aforefaid monks, to make ditches and enclofe their fields between the wood of Maltby and the fields of Sandbec, below their boundaries at their pleafure, keeping the two roads untouched, to wit, Bolgate and the road which comes from Blythe. All thefe I have granted and confirmed to the aforefaid monks, for a pure and perpetual charity, free and quiet from all secular service, and from everything which belongs to the estate; so that I and my heirs shall warrant and defend that charity against all. Before these witnesses, Nicholas, the parson of Tickhill; Humphrey, the clerk; William, chaplain of the castle; Robert Fitz Payne; Ralph, his son; Hugh Scausby; Hugh, the son of Robert; Robert of Bereus; Hugh le Engleis; and Thomas, the servant. In the court of Tickhill."

Works on falconry name the kind of hawk assigned to different ranks. The sparrow-hawk is that assigned to the priest.[*] A hawks aerie was returned in Domesday-Book, among the most valuable articles of property which a person could possess; and doubtless this one was much prized by John de Busli. From it probably he obtained the sparrow-hawk, which had to be rendered yearly by the De Busli's to the Fossard's for the tenure of Bawtry. And this may have been one cause for retaining it.

Blythe mentioned in the above charter was one of the five places licensed by King Richard I. for tournaments, and Roger de Busli placed a colony of monks there; "founding the priory not improbably" says Mr. Hunter, "that there might be those at hand who could minister religious consolation to the knight who might chance to be mortally wounded in those dangerous encounters, or medical assistance, for the monks were often skilled in the healing art, to those more slightly injured." Matthew Paris tells us of a tournament which was held here in 1256; "about Whitsuntide," says he, "a general tournament was held at Blythe, according to the laws and discipline of chivalry, at which the King's eldest son Edward attended in linen clothing and light armour to be instructed in the laws of chivalry. Many nobles who endeavoured to gain knightly renown there, were unhorsed, beaten, crushed and trampled under foot; of whom one was William Longsword, who never afterwards recovered from the effects of his injuries."

Roger de Tickhill was abbot of Roche for eight years. He ceased to be abbot in 1179.

[*] "There is a Spare-hawke; and she is an hawke for a preeft." Dame Julyan Bernes on Hawkynge, WYNKYN DE WORDE, 1496.

Hugh de Wadworth.

1179—1184

HUGH DE WADWORTH, Mr. Hunter says—"appears to have been an active superior, as in his time the Confirmation from the Pope was obtained, and Roxby grange bought." But that indefatigable historian is in error when he states that this abbot obtained the Confirmation charter. This writing is addressed to Osmund, the next abbot, and bears a date two years later than that of Hugh de Wadworth's death.

There can be little doubt but that Abbot Hugh came originally from the neighbouring parish of Wadworth, and not improbably he was a member of the family of that name, which at that time resided at Wadworth. He certainly had one great family likeness to them, namely, that of borrowing money from the Jews at York. Peter de Wadworth fell into sad trouble with these Hebrew gentlemen, and was helped out of his difficulties and assisted in his "great necessity" by the monks of Roche, who had previously received great favours from the family.

The only act which can positively be ascribed to Hugh de Wadworth, is the rather discreditable one of having involved the Abbey in great debt to the Jews of York, for the purpose of purchasing Roxby grange, in Lincolnshire.

He held his abbacy five years, and ceased to be abbot in 1184.

Osmund.

1184—1223.

SMUND had the moſt proſperous and the longeſt reign, ſave one, of all the Abbots. He came from Fountains Abbey, where he had held the office of "Cellarer," in the year 1184. Ambitious and active, all things proſpered in his hands, and under his rule the Abbey became ſpeedily rich and powerful.

His firſt great act was that of obtaining from Pope Urban III. a Confirmation of all the gifts which the monaſtery had up to that time received. The following is a tranſlation of it :—

Confirmation of Pope Urban iii.

"URBAN biſhop, ſervant of the ſervants of God, to his beloved ſons, Oſmund, abbot, of Roche, and his brethren as well preſent as future, profeſſing a regular* life—ſalvation in Chriſt. To all thoſe who chooſe a religious life it is fitting that apoſtolical guardianſhip be at hand, leſt, haply the attacks of any one's temerity ſhould either call them off from their purpoſe, or (which God forbid!) break in upon the ſtrength of their ſacred bond. Therefore, beloved ſons in the Lord, we favourably aſſent to your juſt requeſts, and after the example of our predeceſſor, of happy memory (Pope Lucius ;) take under the bleſſed Peter's and our own protection, and fortify by the privilege of this writing the aforeſaid monaſtery of Roche, in which ye are bound under a divine ſervitude; in the firſt place decreeing that the monaſtic order which is acknowledged to have been inſtituted in the ſaid monaſtery according to the rule of the Lord and the bleſſed Benedict, and the inſtitution of the Ciſtercian brothers, be inviolably obſerved in the ſaid place for all time. Next, that whatever poſſeſſions and whatever goods the ſaid monaſtery poſſeſſes at preſent,

* I.e. Monaſtic.

or in future, by the grant of Pontiffs, largefs of Kings or Princes, offering of the faithful or in any other juft modes by the help of the Lord it may obtain, remain firm and entire to you and your fucceffors, according to the very words in which we have thought right that thefe things fhould be expreffed.

Of the gift of Richard de Builli, (called alfo Bufli,) and Richard de Wikerflai, the place itfelf in which your Abbey ftands.

Of the gift of Lord King Henry II., one hundred acres in Lindric, near the faid Abbey.

Of the gift of the fame perfons, the grange of Aggecroft with its appurtenances.

Of the gift of the fame Richard de Bufli and Hugh de Drigwrt, Lambecroft (Lambcote) with its appurtenances.

Of the gift of Leo de Manners, Brancliffe with its appurtenances.

Of the gift of William Avenell, Anes (Oneafh) with its appurtenances.

Of the gift of Walter de Scoteni, Rokefby (Roxby,) with its appurtenances.

Of the gift of Ralph Tortemayns, Todwick with its appurtenances.

Of the gift of Symon, fon of Symon, land in Infleby with its appurtenances.

Of the gift of Hamelin Bardolf and Robert Fitz Eudo, land in Winterington with its appurtenances.

Of the gift of Robert de Scalcebye and Adam de Newmarch and Roger de Mar, Newfome with its appurtenances.

Of the gift of William Vavafour, Thurnfcoe with its appurtenances.

Of the gift of Gervas de Barnby, a grange in Barnby and Bramwith.

Of the gift of Thomas de Armthorpe, a grange in the faid town.

Of the gift of Robert Fitz Payne, Wellingley with its appurtenances, and all the lands which ye have in the territory of Wadworth.*

Of the gift of William de Moles and William Fitz Gerard, Sezacres with its appurtenances.

Of the gift of Simon de Plefley, Afhover (Derbyfhire,) with its appurtenances.

Of the gift of Robert, fon of Glai, land and wood of Cumrefbruig (Coningfborough,) as far as to Witewell between the road and the brook.

* The gift of Eudo son of Godfery de Wadworth, says Dr Burton

Of the gift of William the Fleming, all the land which Ligulf held and a certain essart between Hestwell and the essart of Orm, the man of Adam Fitz Swayn, with all appurtenances.

Of the gift of Gerard de Stirap, turbary in the territory of the same town.

Verily, let no man presume to extort from you tithes of your labours, which with your own hands or at your own expense you cultivate, as well from lands cultivated as uncultivated, or of the nourishment of your animals, under pain of &c. Given at Verona, by the hand of Albert, priest of the Holy Roman Church, cardinal and chancellor, the seventh day of April, in the fourth indiction, in the year of the incarnation of our Lord MCLXXXVI, but in the first year of the pontificate of the most Holy Pope Urban III."

Having obtained this important charter which not only confirmed the possessions of the monks, but exempted them from paying tithes, Osmund next applied to King Richard, and obtained from that monarch a remission of the 1300 marks borrowed from the Jews of York by his predecessor Hugh de Wadworth. The Jews were so hated at this time that this dishonest interference of the King would be looked upon rather as a virtuous action than otherwise. The sums which the Jews lost in this way must have been enormous.

Osmund also obtained from King Richard a charter which confirmed to the monks the Abbey and all that belonged to it, and granted to them many rights and privileges, not the least important of which was that of allowing them to hold a court of their own, in which they might judge thieves, trespassers, &c. The following is a translation of it:—

Confirmation of King Richard i.

"RICHARD, by the grace of God, King of England, &c., all, &c., know that I have granted, and by the present charter confirmed to God, and the Church of Saint Mary of Roche, and the monks serving God in the same, the Abbey itself, with all its appurtenances, to wit, whatever they have in the territory of Maltby and Hooton, and in the grange of Brancliffe, and whatever they have in the territory of Takewith, Bramley, and the grange of Lambcotes, and whatever they have in the territory of Stainton and Wadworth, and the grange of Wellingley, and the grange of Newhum, and whatever they have in the territories of Scoreby of Marr, Thurnscoe, Armthorpe, Barnby, Bramwith, and the grange of * * * with all their appurtenances; and whatever they have in the territories of Ashover, Torworth, Fairwath, Oldcotes, Stirap,

Winterington, Rifby, and the grange of * * * with all their appurtenances; and all the poffeffions which the faid monks have, or which they may hereafter reafonably acquire, in granges, houfes, buildings, men, fervices, rents, lands, meadows, paftures, commons, woods, ponds, waters, ftews, mills, fifheries, turbaries, in-ways and paths, free introits and exits, and all other poffeffions and liberties, within the towns and without, and in all other places, as the reafonable charters and handwritings of the donors and vendors teftify. Wherefore, I will, and firmly enjoin, that the aforefaid Abbey and monks, have and hold all the aforefaid, well and peaceably, fully, entirely and honourably, in free and perpetual almoigne, free and quiet from all gilds, fcutages, pleas, quarrels, fummonfes, county meetings, wapentakes, trithings, aids to fheriff, and all other aids and all other charities, and from frankpledge and murder, and all other cuftoms and occafions which appertain to me. I grant alfo, that the faid monks fhall have the rights of a Court of their own, over all their tenements, and men with foke, and fac, and toll, and theam, and infangthef. And I enjoin alfo, that the faid monks and brethren be free and quiet from all toll and cuftom which belongs to me throughout my realm, of all things which they fhall buy or fell for their own ufe, or caufe to be carried out or brought in by land or water. And I forbid there being put in any plea concerning any tenement of theirs except before me or my Chief Juftice. Witnefs, the King."

Ofmund alfo obtained a further confirmation from the Countefs of Eu, of which the following is a tranflation :—

Confirmation of the Countess of Eu.

"TO all the fons of Holy Mother Church, prefent and future, Alice, Countefs of Eu, formerly wife of Ralph de Ifondun, Earl of Eu, greeting! Know all of you that I in my widowhood, and being in full power over my own body, for the welfare of the foul of the faid Ralph my lord, and for the welfare of my own foul, and that of Ralph my fon, and all my anceftors, and heirs have granted, and by this my charter have confirmed to the Monks of the Abbey of St. Mary of Roche, the fite of the faid Abbey, and the grange of Aggecroft, with the appurtenances, and the wood of Lindric as it is bounded by a ditch, in pure and perpetual alms, and moreover, all the lands and poffeffions which they hold in the Barony of Tickhill, with the appurtenances, liberties, commons and eafements in woods and plains, and in all places as the reafonable charters of the donors and vendors thereof contain and testify. Witness, Lord William Earl Warren, my uncle; Philip de Ulecotes; William de Cressi; Mavesin de Hersy; Baldwin his brother; Mathew de Shepeley; knights. Given at Tickhill in the year of grace 1219."

In the seventh or eighth year of Osmund's presidency he was made proctor for Cardinal Stephen of all his rents in England, in such sort, says a valuable old deed giving the list of the early abbots, "that he received of the goods of the said Cardinal at different times of the year by annual payments to the amount of 400 marks, out of which money they provided handsomely for themselves, and were enriched to such an extent that they were reckoned wise men, and lacking no temporal good." The monks had also from this same Cardinal the prebend of Laughton.

Roche Abbey seems not only to have been fortunate at this time in having an illustrious abbot, but also in possessing monks of more than ordinary ability. The names of the four following have been preserved:—

HELIAS, who was elected abbot of Kirkstal in the year 1209. The following account of him is copied from a deed quoted by Stephens from *Thoresby's MSS.* "Helias of worthy memory, formerly monk of Rupe, an industrious man, and well versed in temporal affairs, having taken upon him the government, had enough to do according to time and place to gather what had been scattered and to preserve what had been gathered, and the Lord was with him. Nor did he want tribulation at his first promotion; for the noble Roger Lacy, patron of the monastery, being ill advised by some persons, conceived so much anger against the said abbot, that he would not vouchsafe to see nor admit him into his presence; but the Lord in whose hand are the hearts of princes and their councils, assuaged his passion and rancor, and converted it into perfect favour and affection, for he afterwards was very familiar and intimate with the abbot, and not a little promoted the affairs of the house." Helias held the abbacy of Kirkstal twelve years.

HENRY, who was elected abbot of the monastery of Newminster, near Morpeth in Northumberland.* This Abbey was founded for Cistercian Monks from Fountains, and the connection which existed between it and Roche points still to the suggestion already made, that the original monks of Roche came from Fountains. Henry, who had been prior of Roche was elected abbot of Newminster in 1216.

* Chronicle of Melrose, p 194

THEODORE, another monk who lived during the reign of Osmund, and was probably of high standing; he took precedence in signing before Henry, prior of Worksop, a deed in which a son of Girard de Furnival gave to the monks of Kirkstal the moiety of a mill at Hansworth Woodhouse.

REGINALD, whose name appears coupled with that of Osmund in 1202,[a] was probably the monk who was elected abbot of Roche after Osmund.

In 1223 Osmund died after a reign of thirty-nine years.

[a] Fines Ebor in the Augmentation Office, IV John.

Reginald.

1223—1238.

DURING Ofmund's time King John granted a charter to the Church, giving to chapters and convents the power of electing their Heads without his interpofition. And though this privilege was foon interfered with by the Pope, it feems probable that the chapter of Roche exercifed their power in the election of Reginald, for we find in the "*Fines*," before mentioned, that he was a monk of great importance in Ofmund's time, and confequently the one whom from his experience the community would wifh to have at their head.

During the abbacy of Reginald the Abbey increafed confiderably both in wealth and lands, and in 1231 a new confirmation charter was obtained from Henry III., of which the following is a tranflation :—

Confirmation of King Henry iii.

"HENRY, by the grace of God, King of England, Lord of Ireland, and Duke of Normandy, and Aquitaine, and Count of Anjou, to Archbifhops, Bifhops, Abbots, Priors, Counts, Barons, Judges, Vifcounts, Provofts, Servants, and all Bailiffs, and his faithful fubjects, health ! We have infpected over a charter which King Richard, our uncle, made with the Abbey and monks of Roche, of donations, fales and grants reafonably made to them in thefe words:—

Richard by the grace of God, &c., to Archbifhops, &c., health ! Know that we for the fafety of our foul and the fouls of all our predeceffors and succeffors have granted, and by this prefent charter have confirmed to the Abbey of Roche and the monks of the fame, ferving God according to the Ciftercian order, all donations and fales reafonably made to them, viz: the Abbey itfelf of Roche, with all its appurtenances, tenements and poffeffions which are in the counties of York, Nottingham and Lincoln, to wit, thofe which they themselves hold in the territory of Maltby and Hooton with the wood of Lyndric as it is inclosed by the ditch near the said Abbey, and as it is inclosed by the same ditch towards Bernehill, and from the said ditch towards Bernehill, and from Bernehill towards the Mill of the same monks as it is included, and all possessions which they have in the territory of Anstean (Anston,) Tathewic (Todwick,) Bramleye, Braithwell, Stainton, Tikehill, Doncaster, Cuningesburgh (Conisbro',) Stansale, Wellingleye, Wadeworth, Thirnscohot (Thurnscoe,) Mar, Newhus (Newhall,) Scalceby (Scawsby,) Askern, Wareleye, Alnelthorpe (Armthorpe,) Sandale, Barneby, Bramwick (Bramwith,) Steinford (Stainforth,) Wykersley, Tange, Sonke, Blide (Blythe,) Farwath, Tordwith (Torworth,) Ulcotes (Oldcotes,) Babry (Bawtry,) Scirap (Stirap,) Anes (Oneash,) Aexoure (Ashover,) Lyncoln, Wyvelsworth, Riseby, Wytrinton, and the grange of Rokesby (Roxby,) with all appurtenances, in granges, sheepfolds, houses, buildings, men, rents, services, vassals, lands, meadows, pastures, commons, woods, coppices, brushwoods, heaths, pools, waters, stews, fisheries, mills, saltsprings, marshes, turbaries,[a] twiggeries, with free ingress and egress, and all other possessions and liberties within cities, boroughs and towns and without, as reasonable charters or deeds of their donors, sellers, granters or exchangers testify of the possessions which they have, or which in future they may reasonably add to them, of whatsoever fee they may be. Wherefore, we will, and firmly enjoin, that the said Abbey and the monks shall have and hold all the aforesaid well and peaceably, entirely and honourably, as a free and perpetual alms, free and quit from all gilds,[b] danegilds,[c] corngilds,[d] themantale,[e] scutages,[f] scotages,[g] hidages,[h] carucages,[i] shires,[j] assises, pleas,[k] summonses of quest, armies, miscellaneous suits, counties,[l] wapentakes, trithings,[m] and from every mixed and common assise, and from fine which belongs to murder and larceny, and from aids to the sheriff and his bailiffs, and

---

[a] "Turbary," right of cutting turf. In 13, Henry III., William, son of Richard de Barneby granted to abbot Reginald, and his monks, for himself and his heirs, that whenever it should happen that he pared peats or dug turfs in his wood, with one or more of his men, it should be quite lawful for the said abbot and his successors to pare sods and dig turfs in the same place, to the extent of half the number of the said men, of one, to wit, or more, without impediment.—"FINES EBOR."

[b] "Gilds," payments.

[c] "Danegilds," Danegeld, a tribute imposed in Saxon times, to get a fund either for appeasing the Danes, or for repelling their invasions; some say for one purpose, some for another. King Egelred seems to have paid the Danes at five payments, 113,000 pounds, besides granting a yearly tribute of 48,000 pounds.

[d] "Corngilds," Horngeld, a tax on horned animals.

[e] "Themantale," or tenmentale; the Saxons divided their hundreds into tens, or tithings, the head-men of which, took oath of allegiance for the rest.

[f] "Scutages," Scutage, a tax upon every shield; that is, upon those that held lands by Knight's service.

[g] "Scotages," Scotage, a customary contribution (or shot) laid upon persons according to their several abilities.

[h] "Hidages," Hidage, a tax upon every hide of land; a sort of land tax.

[i] "Carucages," Carucate, a tax upon every plough.

[j] "Shires," the duty of attending upon the Sheriff, when he holds his courts.

[k] "Pleas," a plea. An assembly of Nobles for judicial purposes. [l] "Counties," comitatus, a county meeting.

[m] "Trithings," trithing, the proper form of riding, meaning a third part; as morthing means the moor division.

from all things to them pertaining, and from all other aids, and from the guardianſhip and working at caſtles, walls, ramparts, ſtews, pools, bridges, cauſeways, and other incloſures, and from warpenning,[a] averpenning,[b] thethingpenning,[c] hengwith,[d] flomenwith,[e] blodwith,[f] leirwith,[g] flemenfrith,[h] * * * * forſtal,[i] haimſoken,[j] and from franc-pledge,[k] laſtage,[l] ſtallage,[m] carriage,[n] parnnage,[o] and from all occaſions which relate to us. And from eſſarts,[p] and rewards, and waſtes, and inſpections,[q] and pleas of foreſt,[r] in ſuch manner however that if they ſhall cauſe any damage in our foreſts, beyond thoſe liberties conceded to them from us by our letters, we will that they be reaſonably puniſhed. We grant alſo, to them, that the ſaid monks ſhall have the liberty of holding their own court over all their lands, with ſoke,[s] and ſake,[t] toll,[u] and theam,[v] and infangthef,[w] outfangthef,[x] and every kind of forfeiture of themſelves, their lands and men in whatever place they occur. Becauſe, we will that they ſhould hold all their property and poſſeſſions as freely and quietly as any other church in all our land, which holds more freely and quietly by (than other) We enjoin, alſo, that the ſaid monks and their brethren ſhall be free and quiet from all toll,[y] paſſage,[z] pontage,[aa] and every other cuſtom which pertains to us everywhere in our power, of all things which they ſhall buy or ſell for their own uſe, or ſhall cauſe to be conveyed or carried away by land or by water. And we forbid their being placed on trial or anſwering with reſpect to any of their poſſeſſions, except before us or our Chief Juſtice or by our ſpecial mandate; and that no one ſhall oppreſs or diſquiet, vex or diſturb them, their property or poſſeſſions againſt the liberties of

---

[a] "Warpenning," money paid to the Sheriff or other Caſtellan, inſtead of actual watching and warding over camps, and keeping ſentry
[b] "Averpenning," a tax paid to be free from the duty of ſupplying beaſts of burden for the king on his travels
[c] "Thethingpenning," or tithingpenny
[d] "Hengwith," or haugwith, a fine for hanging a man out of your own juriſdiction, or for letting him go
[e] "Flomenwith," flemenwith, a fugative It is explained by Spelman as "mulcta fugetorum"
[f] "Blodwith,' a fine for ſhedding blood
[g] "Leirwith," a fine for lying with a perſon unlawfully, whether by force or otherwiſe
[h] "Flemenfrith," the ſuſtentation of exiles
[i] "Forſtal," the fine for occupying the ſtreet before another, and ſo preventing him from getting his wares to market
[j] "Haimſoken," a fine for a violation of the peace, or an aſſault, by forcible entry into a perſon's houſe
[k] "Franc-pledge," a token of freedom which the poſſeſſor had to ſhew every year
[l] "Caſtage," bottomry   [m] "Stallage," rent paid for the right of keeping a ſtall in a market
[n] ' Carriage"   [o] "Parnnage," a ſum paid for the right of feeding hogs in the king's foreſt, on acorns, &c
[p] ' Liſarts," clearing foreſts   [q] " Inſpections," periodical perambulation of foreſts   [r] " Foreſt," waſtes
[s] " Soke," the right of holding a court within your own lordſhip, for doing juſtice between your vaſſals
[t] "Sake," the lord's right of ſettling controverſies within his manor
[u] " Toll," the right of holding a market in your manor
[v] " Theam," the right of taking cognizance of bail forfeitures
[w] " Infangthef,' the right of judging a thief caught within the abbots manor
[x] " Outtangthef," the right of judging a thief caught without the manor   " Infang" when the thief is one of your own vaſſals   " Outfang," when he is not
[y] " Toll," a tax exacted by the lords from thoſe who traded in his market
[z] " Paſſage," turnpike toll   [aa] " Pantage," bridge toll

their charters on pain of forfeiture of ten pounds. Signed by Master Malgerio, of York; Master Roger Richmund; Vivian, Archdeacon of Derby; Robert of Thornsham, then Steward of Anjou; William de Rupibus; Girard de Furnivale; Girard Brochard, and many others. Given at Sufa by the hand of Master Docelin, then fulfilling the office of our chancellor, on the * * day of February, in the tenth year of our reign.

We also, holding the grant and confirmation of the aforesaid King Richard, our uncle, ratified and granted for us and our heirs, as the said charter which the said Abbey and monks of Roche have, reasonably testifies, grant and confirm the same. Witness, the venerable fathers, P. Wynton, (Winchester,) and W. Karleol, (Carlisle,) Bishops; Hugh de Bargo, in the county of Kent, Chief Justice of England, Ralph, son of Nicholas; Godfrey de Cramcumb; John, son of Philip; Ralph * * * Richard, son of Hugh; Alfred le Cauz; Henry de Chapel and others. Given by the hand of the venerable father Ralph, bishop of Chichester,* our chancellor, at Winchester, on the twenty-first day of January, in the sixteenth year of our reign."

If the reader will study carefully this important charter he will obtain pretty correct views of the possessions, privileges and powers of the monks of Roche about this time. The preceding list of ancient terms here interpreted, is very complete, and gives a good idea of the numerous taxes which were inflicted upon people in those days.

A general discontent in religious matters seems to have prevailed in England about this time, the people were dissatisfied with their priests, and the priests with the pope and the heads of the church

Jacke Upland in the name of the people was asking such questions as the following:—

"How many orders be there in earth? If Christ's rule be most perfect why rulest thou thee not thereafter? Maketh your habit you men of religion? If so, the better your habit the better your religion! What betokeneth your great hood, your scaplery, your knotted girdle and your wide cope? Why make ye you as dead men and be not dead, but more quick beggars than ye were before? Why make men believe that your golden trentall song for ten shillings or five at least will bring souls out of hell or out of purgatory? If this be truth, certes, ye might bring all souls out of pain, but ye are

---

* Ralph Owille bishop of Chichester, was appointed Chancellor A D 1226, but the seals were taken from him in the 22nd year of the King's reign though he still remained Chancellor

not, therefore ye are out of charity! Why bufy ye not to hear the fhrift of poor folk as well as rich lords and ladies, fince they muft have more plenty of fhrift fathers than poor folk have? Why make ye not your feafts to poor men and give them gifts as ye do the rich, fince poor men have more need than the rich? &c., &c."

Money was as it ever feems likely to be, the root of a great deal of evil The Church fleeced the people and the Pope fleeced the Church.

Speed gives this defcription by a monk of the governors of the Church of Rome at this time—" not feeking to winne mens fouls but their money, oppreffing the religious by punifhments, ufuries and fimonie, without any care of juftice and honefty "

The following quotations from a political fong in the time of Henry III. are alfo in the fame ftrain.—" Rome lying in the depths of turpitude, ranks virtues beneath filthy lucre." "Before the Cardinals and before the Patriarch a pound overcomes the Bible " "The archcifhop tread under feet the necks of the clergy and extort tears in order that they may be dried with gifts." "If anyone begins to complain of an injury, they immediately ftretch their ear to the caufe, and their hand to the gift "

But befides the "rivers of filver" which flowed out of England into the Pope's purfe—which the people felt feverely—there was another hardfhip, which they found it difficult to bear. They complained that "the church and kingdom of England is grieved, that the patrons of the fame cannot prefent as they wont into their church, for the Pope's letters. But the churches are given to Romans which know neither the realm nor the tongue thereof; both to the great peril of fouls and robbing away the money out of the realm." Alfo, " that in the benefices given to Italians neither the old ordinances, nor relief to the poor, nor hofpitalities, nor any preaching of God's word, nor care of men's fouls, nor fervice in the church, nor yet the walls of the church be kept up and maintained."

It can be well imagined that thefe Italians were not beloved, and that no opportunity was loft for illtreating them. In 1232 fays Fox, there was " a general fpoile of the Roman parfons in England," all their barns were wafted and the corn diftributed among the needy, the Italians hiding themfelves in monafteries and cells, thinking it better to lofe their goods than their lives.

Under a threat from the Pope, the King ordered the Archbifhop of York and others to find out and punifh thofe in the north, who had been guilty of this work of fpoliation. Among others was one

Robert Twing, "a comely young man and a talle fouldiour, who of his own voluntary accord, with five others fervitures, whom he took with him abroad to work that feat, came to the King, openly protefting himfelf to be the author of that deed doing, and faid he did it for hatred of the Pope and the Romaines; becaufe that by fentence of the Bifhop of Rome, and fraudulent circumvention of the Italians, he was bereved of the patronage of his benefice." The King recommended him to go to the Pope, and gave him letters certifying his right, and begging for him the Pope's indulgence. The Barons alfo fent letters by him complaining of their rights of prefentation being infringed. The miffion was moft fuccefsful, and he returned with a fatiffactory anfwer to the Barons, and a countermand to the Legate and Archbifhop of York, not to infift upon his former order, but to give inftitution to the clerk prefented by the faid Robert Twing.

Fortunately for the wealth of Roche Abbey, Reginald continued to hold the proctorfhip for Cardinal Stephen, of all his rents in England, which Ofmund had, and out of which payments the "fucceffion of abbots" fays the monks provided for themfelves handfomely. The office of Proctor however was anything but a pleafant one, and Reginald, though probably quite eafy as far as money matters went, muft have lived anything but the quiet life we are led to imagine in wandering through the peaceful and fecluded valley which was his home. Befides the troubles of his proctorfhip Reginald had a long feud with the Prior of the Holy Trinity of York, and the Prior of Drax, about the prefentation to the Church of Roxby. Each could produce charters fhewing his indifputable right to it, and the jury who had to determine the queftion (although Reginald made two attempts to get it settled) could not come to a decifion. It is however probable that the Prior of the Holy Trinity of York was the one who eventually made the prefentation.

The following legend is given by *Matthew Paris* as having occurred in the year 1236:—

Legend.

"About this fame time, in the month of May, near an abbacy called Roche, in the northern part of England, there appeared bands of well-armed Knights, riding on valuable horfes, with ftandards and fhields, coats of mail and helmets, and decorated with other military equipments; they iffued from the earth, as it appeared, and difappeared again into the earth. This vision lasted for several days, and attracted the eyes of those who beheld it, as if by fascination; they rode in arrayed troops, and sometimes engaged in conflict, sometimes as if at a tournament, they shivered their spears into small fragments with a crash; the inhabitants saw them, but more from a distance than near them, for they never remembered to have seen such a fight before, and many said that the occurrence was not without its presage. This occurred more plainly in Ireland and its confines, where they appeared as if coming from battle, and dragged their horses after them wounded and broken down, without a rider, and the Knights themselves were severely wounded and bloody; and what was more wonderful, their track plainly appeared impressed on the ground, and the grass was borne down and trampled on. Many people on seeing this vision fled before them in alarm, and betook themselves to the churches and castles, thinking that it was not an illusion, but a real battle. These occurrences came to our knowledge some years after they happened, from a report and true account of the event obtained from the Earl of Gloucester, and by the evidence of many other persons.[a]"

This legend is very similar to that of the spectre horsemen of Southerfell in Cumberland. Troups of horsemen were there seen, and "they seemed to come from the lower part of the fell, becoming first visible at a place called Knott; they then moved in regular order in a curvilinear path along the side of the fell, until they came opposite to Blakehills, when they went over the mountain and disappeared. The last, or last but one, in every troop, galloped to the front and then took the swift walking pace of the rest.[b]"

The same kind of apparitions are said to have been witnessed above Vallombrosa early in the fourteenth century. On the night of an extraordinary deluge, says Giovanni Villami, "a hermit, being at prayer in his hermitage above Vallombrosa, heard a furious trampling as of many horses; and crossing himself and hurrying to the wicket, saw a multitude of infernal horsemen, all black and terrible riding by at full speed. When in the name of God he demanded their purpose; one replied, 'we are going if it be His pleasure to drown the city of Florence for its wickedness.[b]'"

In Suffolk there is also a legend of this kind. At the little village of Acton the park gates were wont to fly open at midnight "withouten hands," and a carriage drawn by four spectral horses and accompanied by headless grooms and outriders, proceeded with great

---

[a] Matthew Paris, Bohn's Translation, page 33.   [b] Notes and Queries, Vol. vii., page 304, 1st Series,

rapidity from the park to a spot called "the Nursery corner" and were then lost sight of.[a]

A similar cortège to this last, used to be seen near Bury St. Edmunds. It went from the parish of Great Barton across the fields, regardless of fences, and proceeded to a deep hole called "Philis's Hole."[b]

Reginald ceased to be abbot of Roche in 1238.

[a] Notes and Queries, Vol. v., page 186.   [b] Notes and Queries, Vol. v., page 365.

Richard.

1238—1254.

FROM two old charters we find that during the reign of abbot Richard, the Abbey larder was pretty well supplied with the good things of this life, and both for feast and fast days the brethren were well cared for. The first charter was granted by the King in 1250, and was one of free warren in all their demesne lands of Roche, Armthorpe and Brancliffe. This was a privilege rarely granted to any but the lords, and the Abbot of Roche was not returned as lord of Armthorpe until 1317. The other charter was obtained from William, Earl of Warren, son of Hameline :—

Charter of William, Earl of Warren.

"WILLIAM, Earl of Warren, to his fishermen, of Brademer, health! Know that I, by an impulse of charity, have given to God and the Church of St. Mary of Roche, and to the monks, servants of God in that place, the tithe of the whole of the residue of all my eels from all my fisheries, which are of the parish of Hatfield, Thorne, and Fishlake, with the exception of the full tithe of my eels which belongs to the monks of Lewes, as a pure and perpetual charity. Wherefore, I command you, that you make them have the aforesaid tithe without any delay or difficulty, and in testimony of this thing, I send you these my letters patent. Farewell!"

In 1244 we find Richard acting as one of the executors of the will of William Percy, and undertaking to pay into the treasury "one pound, which the said William owed the King for his relief, and thirty pounds which he owed to the King for an aid granted to the King towards marrying his eldest daughter!"

We find from the "*York Fabric Rolls*"* published by the *Surtees Society* that the chantry of St. Mary Magdalen in the crypt of the

---

* Page 294.

Cathedral Church of York, was founded about 1240, for the foul of Galfrid de Norwich, late Dean of York, by Richard, abbot of Roche, Simon, precentor of York, Peter de Munkegate and Robert de St. Paul, his executors. In 1364 there was no fervice at this chantry on account of the rebuilding of the choir, and the chaplain celebrated at St. Andrew's altar.

We alfo find from the fame "*Rolls*"[a] that the abbot of Roche made a bequeft of 3s., by the hand of Thomas Sbyfon to the fabric of York Minfter, probably in fupport of the above chantry.

ROBERT, according to a deed of Sibilla de Sancta Maria now in the poffeffion of Mr. Mitchell of Sheffield, was Cellarer of Roche Abbey at this time. The deed is dated at Rotherham in 1239, and contains befides the name of Robert, that of William de Rupe, who was probably a monk of Roche.

Richard prefided over the abbey fixteen years, and died or refigned in 1254.

[a] Page 32.

Walter.

1254—1268.

WALTER, or Walter de Wadeworth, as his name is given in an old charter, was elected head of Roche in 1254, and if we may judge from the small scraps of history remaining he must have led a much more active life than his predecessor, and it might be added one of far less comfort, for we find him in 1256 applying to the Pope and obtaining from him the following bull:—

Bull of Urban iv. to the Abbot and Convent of Roche, concerning not paying usury to their Creditors, certain compacts notwithstanding.*

"URBAN, bishop, servant of the servants of God, to his beloved sons, the abbot and convent of the monastery of Roche of the Cistercian order, in the diocese of York, health and apostolical benediction! As your petition exhibited to us contained 'certain persons (traders in lucre in the cities of the diocese and the province of York) who have extorted much from you by usurious richness, asserting that you are bound to them for certain sums of money, very frequently disquiet you with regard to such moneys, by demanding payment for the same.' Wherefore, you have humbly supplicated us of our paternal care to see and take measures about these things. We therefore, yielding to your supplication by the authority of these presents grant you power to deduct from the sums of money of this kind for which you are bound to laymen, what has thus been extorted, on such sort that ye be not at all bound to make satisfaction for these (sums) themselves, or may be compelled to pay them against your will, but that the said laymen be bound to reckon them up towards the principal; that you also may be able to refuse the interests

---

* Lambeth Library: No. 654, Art. 53. (In dorso) Urbanus contra usurarios special.

promised to them, and redemand those which you have paid up to this time, even though you have granted and given over to them your own or any other person's letters for payment of these very interests to those same laymen, or anything else in lieu of them and not requiring them again. Moreover we thought fit that ye be absolved from all letters and apostolic indulgences already obtained, or yet to be obtained, also from the aid of the canonical and civil law and all exceptions whatsoever, and ye have also given your oath. Let no man therefore whatever infringe the letter of this our grant and absolution, or by rash daring go against it. But if any one should presume to attempt to do so let him know that he will incur the wrath of Almighty God and the blessed Peter and Paul his Apostles.

Given at the Old City, (Civita Vecchia) February * * in the second year of our Pontificate."

Besides this bull, which appears rather arbitrary, Walter seven years afterwards obtained the following:—

Bull of Alexander iv. to the Monastery of Roche, of the Cistercian order in the Diocese of York, to allow them to celebrate sacred offices in their cities, towns, granges and houses.[a]

"ALEXANDER, bishop, servant of the servants of God, to his beloved sons, the abbot and convent of Roche, of the Cistercian order in the Diocese of York, health and apostolical benediction for their devotion! We yielding to your prayers, by the authority of these presents grant to you, for yourselves and your households, licence to celebrate sacred offices in your cities, towns, granges and houses without incurring any penalty at law. Let no man therefore whatever infringe upon the letter of this our grant, or rashly dare to go against it. But if any one should presume to attempt to do so let him know that he will incur the wrath of Almighty God and the blessed Peter and Paul his Apostles.

Given at Latera, * * May, in the second year of our Pontificate—1263."

It does not appear that the licence granted by this bull was ever exercised. The "*Monasticon*" describes Dunscroft, one of the Abbey granges near Doncaster, as a cell of Roche, but *Mr. Hunter* is most decided in his opinion that such was not the case.

In the "*Placitorum Abbreviatio*,"[b] we find the following suggestive fragments:—

Henry III. "The abbot of Roche offered himself on the 4th

[a] Lambeth Library: No. 643, f. 8. [This bull is partially damaged.] [b] Page 130, 136.

day againſt Richard de Barneby, Hugh and Alexander his brothers, on the plea why they had *beaten, enormouſly wounded and illtreated* againſt the peace &c., Alan de Smetheton and Nicholas de Rypun his monks and brother Thomas the Granger.

And they did not come &c. And the Sheriff commanded that Richard ſhould be attached by Alexander de Stubbes and Robert Carzon; and Hugh by Thomas, ſon of Hugh de Barnby and Nicholas de Bramwith; and Alexander by Thomas Thoc and Thomas de Sandal. Thereupon they give ſufficient pledges that they will on the Octave &c.

Henry III. The abbot of Roche by his attorney &c. Againſt Richard de Barneby, Hugh and Alexander his brother, on the plea (aforeſaid.) And they did not come &c. Thereupon they were all in mercy. And let the Sheriff diſtrain upon their lands &c. So that he ſhould have their bodies &c."

What the cauſe of this quarrel was does not appear, but it was moſt likely about game. Barnby Grange was one of the firſt poſſeſſions of the monks, and remained in their hands as long as their houſe ſtood. It was given them by Gervis de Barnby.

In December, 1264, certain Biſhops, ſundry Barons, an unheard of crowd of Priors and Abbots (among whom was Walter, abbot of Roche,) and from each county two moſt loyal, upright and diſcreet Knights, and from each borough two of the more diſcreet, loyal and upright of their citizens and burgeſſes were called together by the following mandate, to conſult with Simon de Montfort, who " in all but name a king," having defeated the Royal army at Lewes held King Henry captive at the time this ſummons was iſſued:—

Summons to Parliament.

"HENRY, by the grace of God, King of England, Lord of Ireland and Duke of Aquitaine, to the venerable father in Chriſt, Walter by the ſame grace, Abbot of Roche, greeting! Foraſmuch as after ſerious conteſts and diſturbances which had long been taking place in our realm, our deareſt ſon Edward was given up and detained as a hoſtage in order to ſecure and confirm peace in our realm, and now, bleſſed be God! that the aforeſaid diſturbance is quieted, it behoves us to take meaſures for making ſecure proviſion for the liberation of the ſame, and for confirming and completing full ſecurity and tranquillity of peace, the honour of God and the benefit of our whole realm, and about certain other affairs of our realm which we are unwilling to diſpatch without your advice and that of our other prelates and magnates; we therefore fend this our mandate, defiring you by that fidelity and love in which you are bound to us, to poftpone every prefling matter and lay afide all other affairs, and be with us at London on the Octave of St. Hilary next to come, to difcufs with us and the aforefaid prelates and magnates whom we have caufed to be fummoned to the fame place, and to give your advice, and this as you love us and our honour and yours, and the common tranquillity of our realm, by no means omit.

Witnefs the King at Worcefter, December 14th."

Prior to this time parliament had confifted of only eleven prelates and twenty-three peers. Now more than one hundred of the inferior dignified clergy, two knights from each county and two reprefentatives from each borough were fummoned, an innovation which proved too popular to be laid afide when the King regained his liberty.

This parliament affembled on January 28th, 1265.

On the 28th of May of the fame year, Prince Edward efcaped from his guards and joined Mortimer. On Auguft 4th he took the field againft Simon de Montfort at Evefham, defeated and killed him and fet his father the King at liberty, notwithftanding that parliament had enacted that neither the King nor Prince Edward fhould aggrieve Montfort or his affociates for their paft conduct.

Whatever may be faid againft Simon de Montfort it fhould always be remembered that to him we owe the three eftates of parliament, king, lords and commons.

Befides attending parliament Walter would have to attend a general chapter now and then in France. In 1256 all the Englifh Ciftercian abbots were invited to attend on St. Michael's day, to confider whether they fhould grant an aid to the Pope and King Henry III., which they declined.

We may judge what a confufed and turbulent ftate the country was in at this time, by an Inquifition which was taken this fame year (1265)—"Whether Walter had intruded himfelf into the manor of Sandbec by occafion of the troubles late in England, and the jury found that he had not, but that he had been in poffeffion before the troubles, in the troubles and after the troubles."

Walter the eight abbot of Roche and the firft to fit in parliament died in 1268.

Alan, Jordan and Philip.

1268—1286.

ALL that we know of thefe three abbots is that they reigned between the above dates. Alan may have been the Alan de Smetheton, who in the laft abbot's time was one of the monks "beaten and wounded."

In 1275 we find from the "*Hundred Rolls*," that two other monks got into trouble at Armthorpe. A complaint is made againft Richard de Heydon, fenefchall to Earl Warenn who fent William de Counhal, Alan Fitz Chapel and many others, "To the grange of the Abbot of Roche at Armthorpe, beyond the liberties of the faid Earl, and took brother Richard the granger, and John the forefter of the faid Abbot, becaufe the faid John had fhot a certain animal in the aforefaid wood of the faid abbot, and had purfued it into the warren of the faid Earl, and he (Richard de Heydon) imprifoned them at Coningfbro, and detained them until the faid Abbot came and paid a fine of 40*l*. for the faid brother,—which he fully paid; but the faid John he would not let go on any account, but kept him in prifon for a whole entire year." This was indeed very hard upon John the forefter, efpecially if he were kept in that damp circular pit which is now to be feen in the keep of the Caftle of Coningfbro'. This fame Richard is alfo accufed of having practifed "diabolical and innumerable oppreffions."

The affairs of the Abbey feem to have glided quietly on about this time, the only other thing worthy of notice is that the abbot's right to free warren in Roche, Armthorpe and Brancliffe was difputed, which as we have already feen was given them in Abbot Richard's time by Henry III. The abbot came in anfwer to the fummons "And faid that he claimed free warren in Roche &c., by charter of Lord Henry the King, father of our Lord the King that now is, granted in the 35th year of his reign, which he produced and which teftified that the faid Lord the King granted to a certain abbot and convent of Roche, predeceffors of that abbot, that they and their successors for ever should have free warren in all their demesne lands of Roche, Armthorpe and Brancliffe in the county of York, &c."

Considerable possessions still continued to fall into the hands of the monks of Roche, notwithstanding the restrictions of Mortmain Act which was passed at this time, and provided that no person religious or other should buy or sell or receive under pretences of a gift or term of years, or any other title whatsoever, nor should by any art or ingenuity appropriate to himself any lands or tenements in mortmain *(in mortua manu)* upon pain that the immediate lord of the fee, or, on his default for one year, the lords paramount, and in default of all of them, the King might enter thereon as a forfeiture. This however was soon got over by the religious houses setting up a fictitious title to the land which it was intended they should have, and then bringing an action to recover it against the tenant, who by fraud and collusion made no defence, and thereby judgment was given for the religious house, which then recovered the land by a sentence of law upon a supposed prior title.

Philip ceased to be abbot in 1286.

Thomas.

1286—1287.

HOMAS profeffed canonical obedience to John Romaine, Archbifhop of York, on the 7th non. Nov., 1286, and held his abbacy a year all but a few days, but beyond that, nothing is known of the life of this abbot.

In the lift of the abbots of Roche given by Dr. Burton in his "*Monafticon Eboracense,*" no mention is made of this abbot, and the prefidency of Stephen the next abbot is made to commence a year earlier than it really did. Thomas terminated his fhort rule in 1287.

Stephen.

1287—1300.

STEPHEN profeffed canonical obedience as abbot of Roche, to John Romaine, Archbifhop of York, in 1287. The following is his form of profeffion:—" I brother Stephen, abbot of Roche promife that I will perpetually fhow fubjection, reverence and obedience as appointed by the Holy Fathers, according to the rule of the order of St. Benedict, to thee Father John, Archbifhop of York, and to thy fucceffors canonically to be fubftituted, and to the Holy See of York, fave my order, and this with my own hand I fubfcribe. Given at Thorpe, 3 non. November."*

Stephen held his abbacy during ftormy times and muft have lived any thing but a peaceful and fecluded life. When Durandus poor and unknown firft fheltered himfelf in a fecluded valley beneath fome rocks, a life of fimplicity feemed poffible, but now—with poffeffions innumerable and fcattered, with courts to prefide over and law fuits to anfwer and with chapters and parliaments to attend;—peace muft have been impoffible. However alluring it may appear in the abftract to live in undifturbed repofe, it can never be the lot of man; and Stephen perhaps was none the lefs happy in having to perform in addition to his duties as a religious fuperior, thofe of a temporal and patriotic lord.

In 1293 a Norman and an Englifh veffel met off the coaft near Bayonne and landed for water. Both crews arriving at the well at the fame time, a quarrel enfued which ended in one of the Normans being killed. To revenge this the Normans feized an Englifh fhip and having hanged at the yard-arm together with fome dogs feveral of the crew, they again abandoned the veffel. The Englifh retaliated in a like barbarous manner on all French fhips without diftinction,

---

* Reg. John Romaine, page 12.

and the French revenged themselves again in return on the English and Saxons, until the sea became a scene of piracy and murder. At length a fleet of two hundred Norman vessels sailing south for wine, and committing the usual barbarities on all the English ships they met with, so roused the ire of the English in the sea ports that they sent out sixty armed vessels to meet them on their return. An obstinate battle was the result, in which the English were victorious, and it is said that the loss of the French was 15,000 men. In consequence of this defeat, Philip the French King, demanded reparation and restitution, and cited Edward as Duke of Guienne to appear before his court in Paris, to answer for these offences. To prevent a national war, King Edward sent over to Paris his brother Edmund, to arrange matters and prevent further hostilities. But Philip would be appeased only on one condition. Edward must give him seizin and possession of the province of Guienne; he would then feel his honour satisfied, and promised to restore it immediately. Edward who was engrossed with the Scots agreed, and Philip as might have been expected, finding himself so easily in possession, again cited Edward, and for non-appearance condemned him, and Guienne by a formal sentence was declared forfeited and annexed to the crown of France. King Edward enraged and ashamed at being so over-reached determined at once to invade France, and recover his lost territories. To do this effectively he invoked the aid of every one, and even went so far as to empty the jails and make soldiers of thousands of the prisoners. Of course the abbot of Roche having interest and money had to do his share, and he received the following summons to attend a council of the clergy.

"THE King to his beloved in Christ, the abbot of Roche, greeting! In what manner the King of France has maliciously cheated us of our territory of Guienne, and has thence by fraud ejected us, unjustly detaining the same, we believe is not unknown to your fraternity. With a view therefore to recovering that territory from the hands of the said King, we rely upon your counsel and aid, as well as that of the rest of the prelates and clergy of our realm, whom this business touches equally with ourselves, being forthcoming. Therefore, we have arranged (God willing) to be in person at Westminster on the feast of St. Matthew the Apostle and Evangelist, next coming, to treat together with you and the rest of the prelates and clergy of the said realm, towards applying a remedy against this sort of malice. We command you, firmly enjoining you by the faith and love in which you are bound to us, that you be present in person at the said day and place &c.

Witness the King, at Portsmouth, August 19, 1294."

The King opened the assembly in person. After stating the necessities of the war in Guienne, he requested both their prayers and their aid. "Because, my good Lords," he continued "You see that the Earls, Barons, and Knights not only contribute their goods, but expose their lives in your defence; and as to you therefore, who cannot venture your bodies, it is fitting that you should afford some aid from your purses." After many debates the clergy voted two tenths, but the King was not satisfied with this, and at length after much threatening they consented to give what the King demanded, a moiety.

The army which Edward sent at first, met with many successes, but the advantages obtained were lost by the Governor of Podensac, who, when that small fortress was besieged by the French Commander, capitulated, and agreed to articles, which though favourable to the English, left the Gascons prisoners at discretion. The French Commander immediately hanged fifty of them, and the consequence was that the Gascons enraged at their comrades being delivered up so easily, joined the French, and the English were obliged to capitulate and return. Not content with the advantage thus obtained, Philip threatened an invasion of England, and even made a sudden attempt on Dover which he burnt.

Edward in trouble at this and fearing for the safety of his kingdom, was again in need, and asked for parliamentary supplies. Stephen therefore with others received a summons to parliament.

"THE King to his beloved in Christ, the Abbot of Roche, greeting! In what manner the King of France has fraudulently and craftily cheated us of our territory of Guienne, by unjustly detaining it from us is known to you. Now however, not content with the aforesaid fraud and malice, having got together a very large fleet and a great multitude of warriors, with which he has now in a hostile manner invaded our realm and the inhabitants of the said realm, and purposes to blot out entirely from the land the English tongue, (which God avert!) if his power correspond to the detestable intent of his iniquitous conception. Inasmuch then as foreseen darts are less injurious, and your interest as well as that of the rest of the citizens of the said realm is at stake in this matter, we command and enjoin you by the faith and love with which you are firmly bound to us, to be present on the Sunday next after the feast of St. Martin in the winter next to come, at Westminster in person." November 13, 23 Edward I.

But Edward's fears were groundless. England did not fall into the hands of the French, nor was the English language blotted out. After making an attempt upon Dover the French forces were compelled to retire.

The differences with France still remained unsettled. Abbot Stephen was summoned again to appear in person at Bury St. Edmunds on the morrow of All Souls, (November 3, 1296) for the purpose of confirming the grant of a subsidy stated to have been promised in case the King of France should refuse to conclude a truce of peace.*

A fifth was demanded from the clergy, but they refused to grant it, saying that both themselves and the King would be excommunicated if they did so, as it would be contrary to the constitution lately published by Pope Boniface VIII., forbidding the clergy to contribute anything belonging to the Church to a secular Prince. The King was pleased for the time to receive this answer, and the business was adjourned to another parliament to be held at London in the beginning of the ensuing month of January.

When the clergy reassembled pursuant to this adjournment, they again deliberated whether they could comply with the King's demands and after much discussion came to the conclusion that they could not. The King became extremely indignant at their answer and put the whole of them out of the protection of the law. "If they went abroad, in quest of maintenance, they were dismounted, robbed of their horses and clothes, abused by every ruffian, and no redress could be obtained by them for the most violent injury." The clergy were soon compelled by these vexations to yield, and the Archbishop elect of York with many others compounded. The clergy in the north yielded sooner than those in the south, as the former were in daily dread of the Scots, and were glad to pay anything for their protection.

But besides having to give money the abbot of Roche was expected to find men with horses and arms. In 1297 Edward to increase his army which he intended to direct against France, required the attendance of every proprietor of land, possessed of twenty pounds a year; and Stephen consequently received a command similar to the following from the Sheriffs of Yorkshire, Nottinghamshire and Derbyshire, in all of which counties he had property.

"ON the part of our Lord the King I have especially summoned required and firmly enjoined on all my bailly, possessing twenty pounds

---

* This summons was repeated

of land and rent per annum and more, to be at London on the Sunday next after the Octave of St. John Baptist; with horses and arms ready with the King in person to cross over to foreign parts."

Soon after this the Sheriff received another brief, and he continues,

"AFTERWARDS by another mandate which came to me afterwards, all the aforesaid are premonished to be at Nottingham at the aforesaid day and in form aforesaid, before William de Ormesby the assignee of the Earl Warrenne, to cross over into the parts of Scotland and to do there what the said William on the part of our Lord the King may enjoin upon them. To the Abbot of Roche."

From the above documents it would seem that Stephen in his time must have been a busy and an important personage. But he had yet another duty to perform.

When a royal person died the clergy were required to celebrate his or her exequies. The following is a copy of the order received by Stephen to celebrate those of Edmund, brother of King Edward; and who, as the reader has seen, was sent by the King to France, to make peace with Philip.

"KING Edward to his beloved in Christ, the abbot of Roche. The most High Creator of all things, has created human nature after his own image and similitude and has placed it, being constituted of soul and body, in this miserable world for this end, that having at his will and pleasure finished the course of this life as of some journey, that of which it is composed should be resolved into its elements, and on the return of the body to the earth from which it proceeds the spirit should return to the Lord by whom it was given. And this journey no one can perform without coming in contact with many defilements, just as the feet of travellers cannot pass along without the adhesion of dust. Wherefore those who are passing from the present world greatly stand in need of being assisted by the prayers of the living. Inasmuch therefore as that illustrious man Edmund, our most dear and only brother, who was always ready, devoted and faithful in our interests and the interest of our realm, and in whom manifold virtuous and gracious gifts shone forth, has been withdrawn from this light, as seemed good to the Creator, (on account of which withdrawal we reckon ourselves and the said realm to be rendered most desolate) which we announce to you not without grievous bitterness of soul: we earnestly require and ask your friendship now that we are solemnly and with devotion celebrating the exequies of our said brother, that you commend his soul to the most High God, with singing of masses and other aids of devout prayers, specially enjoining the same upon all and singular the religious under your charge. Witness the King at Aberdeen, * * * * 1296."

Almost the last act which Stephen performed must have been that of attending the parliament held two months before the election of the next abbot, John.

This parliament was held in London on the 6th of March, 1300, "for the safety of the crown and the welfare of the people," and the abbot of Roche was commanded to be there in person, "to advise with the other 'magnates' and 'proceres' on the affairs of the King and the kingdom."

John.

1300.

OHN'S abbacy was of ſhorter continuance than that of any other abbot of Roche. He profeſſed canonical obedience to Thos. Corbridge, Archbiſhop of York, on May 30th, 1300, and reſigned or died before December 18th of the ſame year.* This profeſſion was made in the Chapel of Lautun (Laughton), in the preſence of the Prior of Workſop and other Priors, W. de Wentworth, S. de Rotherham and many others.

John was ſummoned to attend parliament at Lincoln on September 25th, or January 20th, 1301. This ſummons had to be anſwered by the next abbot Robert. The only recorded act which it is probable was performed by John, was that of celebrating, on 25th September, by command of the King, the exequies of "that noble man Edmund, formerly Earl of Cornwall, our moſt dear couſin who was always ready, devoted and faithful to our intereſts and the intereſts of our realm &c."

* Reg. Thomas Corbridge, page 5.

Robert.

1300—1324.

ROBERT profeffed canonical obedience as abbot of Roche at Scroby, on December 18th, 1300, and held his abbacy twenty-four years. He led a life of great activity, and the troubles he had to contend with, as we fhall prefently fee, were not a few. He was in conftant attendance at parliament.

In 1301 he had to attend the parliament to which the former abbot John had been fummoned, and which was held at Lincoln, on the Octave of St. Hilary, 20th January. "Great debates arofe at this parliament refpecting the perambulation of the forefts."

In 1302 Robert was fummoned to parliament at Weftminfter, on the Octave of the Nativity of St. John the Baptift, 1ft July, in order to treat and advife on certain arduous affairs with the other prelates and nobles.

Again in 1302 he was fummoned to parliament at Weftminfter, at Michaelmas—prorogued to the morrow of St. Edward, 14th October. The Scots were once more troublefome, and abbot Robert had again to furnifh men and arms.

In 1305 he was fummoned to parliament at Weftminfter, on Tuefday, the fifteenth day after the Purification, 16th February—prorogued to the Sunday next after the Feaft of St. Matthias the Apoftle, 28th February, to confult "on certain affairs which fpecially concern the kingdom of England, and alfo the fettlement of Scotland."

In 1307 Robert was fummoned to the celebrated Parliament held at Carlifle, on the Octave of St. Hilary, 20th January. At this parliament was paffed the "Statute of Carlifle," in which all religious perfons were forbidden to fend any tax beyond the fea. "Alien fuperiors having fet divers unwonted and heavy payments, and impofitions on the monafteries in fubjection to them in England, the King can no longer fuffer fuch loffes and injuries to be winked at, and provides a fufficient remedy &c."

But besides this (which must have been a great relief to many monasteries,) very important alterations were made in the use of seals in religious houses.

"AND further, our Lord the King hath ordained and established that the abbots of the orders, Cistercianses and Premonstranses, and other religious orders, whose seal hath heretofore been used to remain only in the custody of the abbot, and not of the convent, shall hereafter have a common seal, and shall deposit the same in the custody of the prior of the monastery or house, and four of the most worthy and discreet men of the convent of the same house, to be laid up in safe-keeping under the private seal of the abbot of the same house; so that the abbot, or superior of the house which he doth govern, shall by no means be able of himself to establish any contract or obligations as heretofore he hath used to do. And if it fortune hereafter that writings of obligations, donations, purchases, sales, alienations, or of any other contracts, be found sealed with any other seal than such a common seal kept as is aforesaid, they shall be adjudged void and of no force in law."

This statute was sent with the King's letters patent to the abbots of the undermentioned places :—Egliston, St. Agatha, Jeroval, Byland, Fountains, Roche, Welbeck, Rufford, Gerwedon, and Spalding.

Why this statute was sent to so few abbots does not appear, nor why the abbot of Roche was singled out as one of the few. It however was a step of great importance, for hitherto the monks had had very little control over the management of the possessions of the monastery to which they belonged. It was to them an enfranchisement similar to the introduction of the commons into parliament.

At a council held in St. Paul's Church, at London, in 1237, before the Pope's Legate, it was decreed: "that in order to prevent the issuing of false instruments, all archbishops, bishops, abbots, priors, deans, &c., should hold seals; in the granting of the use of which, faithful and circumspect caution was to be observed; faithful, that it might be easily granted, to those who required it, and circumspect, that it might be denied to false and fraudulent persons,"

Fig. 1, Plate X. is the secretum, or private seal of the abbot of Roche. Bishops and abbots usually had oval seals. The former held the pastoral staff in the left hand, abbots in the right. Symbols were also sometimes introduced, indicating the worth and character of the abbot, In this seal the *star* is the symbol of the Epiphany.

The *crescent* signifies the increase of the gospel.

The *flowers* denote purity of life.

At the death of an abbot his seal was sometimes broken by a hammer, upon one of the steps before the altar.

Fig. 2, Plate X. is a sketch of the matrix of the private seal of the abbot of Roche, now in the possession of G. S. Foljambe, Esq., of Osberton Hall, near Worksop, in whose family it has been for several generations

The earliest common seals which were cut directly after the passing of the statute of Carlisle, bore the representation of the patron saint of the Abbey; but in later seals the abbot took the place of the saint, to whom he is represented praying. Before the reign of Edward the III. these saints and abbots were seated upon thrones, but after this time they are represented standing beneath canopies and arches.

Fig 3, Plate X. is a representation of the earliest common seal of Roche, which has yet been found. It is appended to a deed made in 1385, which is now in the possession of Mr. Mitchell, of Sheffield. This seal has never before been published.

Fig. 4, Plate X. is the last common seal of Roche. It was with this that the deed surrendering the Abbey to King Henry VIII. at the dissolution was sealed.

Besides the parliament held at Carlisle, abbot Robert was summoned in the same year, 1307, to attend a parliament at Northampton, on the 15th day after St. Michael, 13th October, in order to treat and advise concerning the celebration of the funeral of the late King, and also, about the solemnization of the espousals and coronation of the present king, Edward II.

In 1309 he was again summoned to parliament at Westminster, one month after Easter, 27th April, to consult with the King on "certain arduous affairs."

In 1311 he was summoned to parliament at London, on Sunday next before the feast of St. Laurence, 8th August. Robert is commanded to lay all other matters aside, and to appear in person before the king at the said day and place, to treat and advise with the prelates and nobles. At this parliament Piers Gaveston the king's favourite, was banished the king's dominions.

In 1312, Robert was summoned twice to attend parliament, on the 23rd of July, and on the 20th of August. The King was in trouble at home and abroad, and needed the help of all at that time. His favourite Gaveston was murdered and his enemy Robert Bruce under arms.

From this last parliament, held August 20th, Robert must have gone over to a general chapter of his order, as the following document shews:—

"THE King to the guardians of the passage of the port of Dover, health! We command you, that you freely permit our beloved in Christ, the abbot of Roche, of the Cistercian order, who is about to set out to his general chapter to be held immediately at Cisteaux, to pass in the harbour of the aforesaid to foreign parts, and to pay him for his expenses twenty marks at this time. Witness the King at Canterbury, August 21st, 1312."

In 1313 abbot Robert was summoned to attend parliament three times: on the 18th of March, the 8th of July, and the 22nd of September, "to treat on the affairs of the kingdom and the war against the Scots." He was required also to do more than give his advice on this last subject.

"THE King to his beloved in Christ, the Abbot and Convent of Roche, greeting! Inasmuch as for the purpose of making resistance to Robert de Bruce, a rebel and enemy to us, and his accomplices and adherents, who propose shortly to invade with hostile intent our Scottish Marches—as we think has already come to your notice—we have ordered certain nobles of our kingdom, with a fixed number of armed men to take their destination to the said parts, for doing which it behoves us necessarily to have a large sum of money, and since certain prelates of the province of Canterbury in our parliament convoked on the 8th of July, one by one liberally, on loan yielded and granted certain sums of money in aid of the business aforesaid, to be allowed to them at their next payments to us, whether from tenths or from military service due from them in Scotland, or otherwise; we, equally confiding in you also to exhibit your zeal for our defence, earnestly require and ask you to be willing to lend us to the extent of *fifty marks* for the exigent purpose aforesaid, according as our beloved clerk William de Melton shall deem fit to require of you on our behalf. And this by all means do, as ye love us, our honour and your own, and the preservation of the realm, receiving from the said William letters patent witnessing the receipt of the said money. Witness the King at Wyndsor, August 13th."

Besides these fifty marks he had to send horses and arms, to muster at Berwick-on-Tweed, on the 10th of June.

The King determining to put an end to the constant wars which were being carried on against Scotland assembled at this time an enormous army from Gascony, Flanders, Wales and Ireland, and with which and his English soldiers he marched into Scotland, to the fatal field of Bannockburn, where on the 25th of June, 1314, was fought "the great and decisive battle of Bannockburn, which secured the independence of Scotland, fixed Bruce on the throne of that kingdom, and may be deemed the greatest overthrow that the English nation (since the conquest) has ever received."

What was the fate of the men, horses and arms which Robert sent from the quiet valley of Roche?

But the valley of Roche was anything but peaceful a few years after this, for we find in 1322, John de Mowbray and others, with 80 men at arms and 400 footmen, adherents of Thomas, Earl of Lancaster, ravaging the whole country about Roche Abbey. They besieged the castle of Tickhill, which was successfully defended by the king's constable, William de Anne, and despoiled the town and church of Laughton, carrying away all their cattle and goods. Abbot Robert must have had a very difficult part to act during these disturbances, for while it was evidently to his interest to remain on friendly terms with the rebels that his Abbey and property might escape spoilation, at the same time the king demanded "that he should raise as many men at arms and foot as he could to march against the rebels and adherents of the Earl of Lancaster, who are destroying our people and besieging with an armed force our castle of Tickhill."

Robert received this mandate on the 16th of February, and the muster was to take place at Coventry, on February 28th, "where he proposed to be, (the Lord willing) with horses and arms, as decently and powerfully as he could." On the 16th of the next month, the battle of Boroughbridge put an end to our good abbot's troubles, and on the 23rd of March, the turbulent Earl of Lancaster was also no more.

Robert held his abbacy only two years after this period.

William.

1324—1330.

WILLIAM, the fifteenth abbot of Roche, profeffed canonical obedience to William Melton, Archbifhop of York, on the 9th of December, 1324.

In 1327, William received the following order to ftay at home, and take care of his abbey, which was in danger, in confequence of the Scots having entered England, Robert Bruce hoping to take advantage of the weak ftate of the government:—

"THE KING to his beloved in Chrift, the abbot of Roche greeting! How the Scotch, our enemies and rebels have entered our kingdom with hoftile intent, inhumanely perpetrating homicides, depredations, fires and other ills innumerable, and as we (Edward III) are in our own perfon with our army pofted in the parts of the march of Scotland, to reftrain their malicious defign, your forefight well knows; and inafmuch as it ftands ordered by ourfelves and our councils that no nobles, prelates or others, nor any perfon of note fhould go out of the fame kingdom, and efpecially from the parts on this fide Trent, fo long as the faid enemies thus ftay within our realm, and it is given us to underftand that you propofe to betake yourfelf in perfon to our general chapter, to be held at Cifteaux, we, wifhing the aforefaid order to be inviolably obferved, prohibit you under penalty of a heavy forfeiture to us, to betake yourfelf to any ftrange places beyond your own bounds, fo long as the faid enemies thus remain in our realm, under pretence of any licence by us to you previoufly granted, until we fhall have thought right to order otherwife thereupon, but that you attend more carefully than ufual to the cuftody of your Abbey, and to all other the premifes. Witnefs, the King at Stanhop, Auguft 3rd, 1327."

Twelve other abbots whofe monafteries were in the north of England, received the fame command.

William ceafed to be abbot of Roche in 1330.

Adam de Giggleswick.

1330—1349.

GIGGLESWICK is a place famous for its Well, which is said to rise and fall about eighteen inches several times a day.

"At Giggleswick where I a fountain can you show
That eight times in a day is said to ebb and flow."
Drayton's Polyolbion.

An Adam, son of Adam de Gigglefwick is mentioned in *Burton*, as having given to the Monks of Fountains Abbey "3*s*. 4*d*. per annum, to find veils for the * * * * * who came to the abbey gate to be cured." It is not impossible that Abbot Adam may have been connected with this family. It is not however necessary that an abbot should be of high origin. Monks, according to *Chaucer*, "Cominly comen of pore peple," and "Ther farthirs ride but on ther fete." But, however high or low may have been the birth of Adam de Gigglefwick, he had sufficient interest with the Monks of Roche to induce them to elect him as their abbot in 1330.

The intense religious feeling which had in the few previous centuries induced men to give up so much of their property to the church was already beginning fast to wane; and it doubtless was not without reason that complaint was made at this time to the Pope, that "The alms and devotion of all men were diminished." Religious communities would be ill able to bear any loss of income, at a time when the King, for the purpose of carrying on his wars with France, was ever demanding heavy subsidies and loans, both in wool and money.

For fifteen years Adam struggled on with these difficulties until 1345, when there came a bright and happy day for the monks of Roche. John, the last Earl of Warren, beholding the poverty of the Monastery of Roche, and admiring the beauty of its buildings, gave the monks that year "*in loco penitentiæ*," says *Mr. Hunter*, the Church of Hatfield, valued at that time at seventy marks per annum; having previously obtained a licence from the King to enable him to do so.

An imperfect copy of the charter which conveyed this gift to the monks of Roche is among *Dodsworth's MS.*, of which, as far as it could be made out, the following is a translation :—

Charter of John de Warren, Earl of Surrey.

"KNOW all men as well present as future, by these presents that we, John de Warren Earl of Surrey, beholding the scarcity of fruits, rents and possessions generally pertaining to the religious men, the Abbot and Convent of Roche, in the diocese of York, and to their monastery; also nobly grieving for the paucity of monks serving God there; and being most deeply anxious for the augmentation of divine worship, and also for increasing (by the help of God), the number of brothers in the same; have given and granted in form and manner underwritten for the causes aforesaid, and other devotions moving us thereto, as far as in us lies, and we can rightly do so, the right of the patronage or advowson of the Parish Church of Hatfield in the said diocese of York, belonging to us by hereditary right, with all rights, fruits, rents, possessions and appurtenances whatever to the said church in any way pertaining from ancient time, to the said abbot and convent and their monastery by the will, consent and assent of our Lord Edward the third, the illustrious King of England, requested by us on this behalf from the Lord King himself, and obtained, and by special licence as by letters royal, composed on occasion of the aforesaid remaining in the possession of the Abbot and Convent, evidently appears. To have and to hold the said right of patronage or advowson of the Church aforesaid, for all times to the aforesaid Abbot and Convent and their monastery aforesaid, in such manner, namely, that from the time of the appropriation of the said Church to the said religious and their monastery, being sufficiently, lawfully and strictly made, according to the requirements of the law, and in which they shall enjoy peaceable possession of the right of receiving and holding for the greater part, the fruits and rents of the tithes to the said Church belonging, free from impediment or calumny of any kind, then incontinently thereafter, with all diligence, without delay, they shall take and assume into their habit and vows beyond the number constituted in the said monastery at the time of its foundation, thirteen honest men and competently skilled in literature; and the said number thirteen beyond the said monks constituted at the time of the said foundation, the said Abbot and Convent and their successors in the said monastery shall, by immediately supplying new ones in the place of those who die or otherwise fail of the said thirteen, acknowledge, sustain and for ever find and have patiently to serve Almighty God unto their live's end * * * * all the aforesaid monks for ever, from that time in which the said number * * * shall have been (God granting) beyond * * the foundation * * * daily XIII * * * monks * * * according as * * * * was for the time, VIII. masses a day with collects * * * * for the souls of the said Lord Edward the King, and the most excellent Lady Philippa, the Queen, his consort, and William, their son, who * * * * of the said King and Queen, and also for our good state and soul, and for the souls of all our relations, and all the faithful dead, so long as * * * * other masses and the said obsequies in the said monastery * * * * shall make and pay, and shall make our death * * * * on the day of our anniversary, as well in largesses, alms, * * * * in saying masses and other customary devotions, and as for death * * * * in other monasteries * * * * in divine and other offices aforesaid is wont solemnly to be performed * * * and if they shall cease in their service (which God forbid!) the said Abbot and Convent, the said burdens interposed in the manner in which it is permitted * * * * either in part or three times, publicly admonished about performing and observing the premises by us, our heirs or executors, shall have corrected or and thenceforth * * * * the Church of Hatfield aforesaid which we our heirs or successors who for the time being shall be * * * * the aforesaid John Earl of Surrey, and our heirs will warrant and defend for ever against all people, the said right of patronage or advowson of the Church aforesaid, with all its rights and appurtenances, to the said Abbot and Convent and their monastery aforesaid, in manner and form aforesaid. In testimony whereof to this writing indented, my seal together with the common seal of the said Abbot and Convent are alternately appended. Witness, &c., given at Lewis, on the first day of December, in the tenth year of the reign of King Edward, the third since the Conquest."

The appropriation of this magnificent gift was effected by William la Zouch, Archbishop of York, reserving out of the profits an annual pension of ten marks to himself, and five for the Dean and Chapter, and ordering a proper house to be built by the Abbot of Roche, for the vicar, who was to be paid fifteen pounds a year at Easter, Michaelmas and Christmas by equal portions.

When John, Earl of Warren, died, all his lands north of the Trent went to the crown and were settled upon Edmund of Langley, a younger son of the King. But as he was only six years old, his mother, Queen Philippa, was allowed to receive the profits for the education of her children. The second son of Edward the third was born at Hatfield, and in consequence took the name of William de Hatfield. "Upon this occasion," says *Thoresby*, Queen Philippa gave five marks per annum to the Abbey of Roche, and five nobles to the monks there. This sum, however, when the Prince died, was transferred to the Church of York, where he was buried, to pray for his soul!*

Adam de Giggleswick ceased to be Abbot of Roche in 1349, and it is not improbable that he may have fallen a victim to the pestilence which raged that year, and which, *Stowe* says, "Was so vehement and sharpe that there remained not the tenth person alive throughout the realm."

* Ducatus Leodiensis pref. p. xv.

Simon de Baukewell.

1349—1358.

SIMON DE BAUKEWELL, or Bakewell, profeſſed canonical obedience on the 25th October, 1349, and on the ſame day received the benediction of William de la Zouch, Archbiſhop of York, in the chapel of his Manor of Cawood.[a]

Already monachiſm was upon the decline, and bitter ſarcaſms were in circulation. *Walter Mapes*, who had a ſtrong hatred of the clergy, and of the Ciſtercians in particular, wrote about this time ſuch ſentences as the following[b]:—

> "I saw the warkes and trade of abbots there eche one,
> Of whom their flock to leade to hell not one doth miſſe."

> "Worse than a monke there is no fende nor sprite in hell,
> Nothing so covetuose nor more strange to be knowen,
> For if you give him ought, he maie poſſeſſe it well,
> But if you aſke him ought, then nothinge is his owne."

Simon ceaſed to be abbot of Roche in 1358.

[a] Reg. William de la Zouche, p. 41.   [b] Walter Mapes, Cam. Soc., p. 279, 280.

John de Aston.

1358—1396.

JOHN DE ASTON, like several of the preceding abbots, seems to have come originally from a place not far distant from Roche. He professed canonical obedience as abbot of Roche, to John Thoresby, Archbishop of York, on 23rd of November, 1358.[a]

During the abbacy of John de Aston, the advowson of Roche Abbey changed hands from John Levet to Richard Barry, citizen and merchant of London.

In 1362, monachism received a severe blow from the author of "*Peirs Ploughman's Vision and Creed.*" In it the monks are accused of having falsified religion, and of being actuated solely by pride, covetousness, and self-love. A most remarkable prophecy may be found in the *Vision*, commencing at line 6239.

> " Ac ther shal come a Kyng,
> And confesse you religiouses,
> And beat you as the bible telleth
> For brekynge of your rule.
>
> *   *   *   *   *
>
> And thane shall the abbot of Abyngdone,[b]
> And all his issue for ever,
> Have a knok of a Kyng,
> And incurable the wounde."

John de Aston ceased to be abbot of Roche in 1396.

---

[a] Reg. John Thoresby, p. 202.
[b] Abingdon in Berkshire was the house into which monks, strictly so called, were first introduced in England, and is, therefore, very properly brought forward as the representative of English monachism.

Robert.

1396—1438.

THE name of this abbot is given on the authority of *Dr. Burton*, who, however, does not give the fource from whence he derived his information. Although the Abbeys of England had yet a hundred years to ftand, many prophecies of their ultimate fall were made about this time, the moft interefting of which is perhaps the following prophetic parable:—

"WHEN on a certayne time a byrde was brought into the worlde all bear and without fethers, the other byrdes hearing thereof, came to vifite her: and for that they fawe her to be a merveilous fayre byrde, they counfailed together how they might beft do her good, fith by no meanes without fethers, might fhe either flee or live commodioufly. They all wifhed her to live for her excellent forme and beauteis fake, in fo much that among them all there was not one, that would not graunt fome part of her own fethers to deck this byrd withall: yea, and the more true they fawe her to be, the more fethers ftill they gave unto her, fo that by this means fhe was paffing well penned and fethered and began to flee. The other byrdes that thus had adorned her with goodly fethers, beholding her to flee abroad, were merveiloufly delighted therewith. In the end, this byrde feeing herfelf fo gorgeoufly fethered, and of all the reft to be had in honour, began to wax proud and hawty, in fo much that fhe had no regard at all unto them by whom fhe was advaunced: yea, fhe punged (pierced) them with her beak, plucked them by the fkinne and fethers, and in all places hurted them. Whereupon, the byrdes fitting in councell agayne, called the matter in queftion, demanding one of another what was beft to be done touching this unkinde byrde, who they fo lovingly with their own fethers had decked and adourned: affirming, that they gave not their fethers to the intent that she thereby, puft up with pride, should contemptuously despise them all. The peacocke therefore answereth first: 'Truly,' said he, 'for that she is bravely set forth with my painted fethers, I will again take them from her.' Then, saith the falcon, 'And I, also, will have mine againe.' This sentence at length took place among them all, so that every one plucked from her those fethers which before they had given, challenging to them their own againe. Even so, oh you Cardinals, shall it happen unto you; for kings, potentates and princes have bestowed upon you goods, lands and riches, that should serve God; but you have poured it out and consumed it upon pride, all kinde of wickednefs, ryot and wantonnes."[a]

The painful foreshadowings of future trouble, seem however, not to have materially affected the health of abbot Robert. He held his abbacy forty-two years, during which time the crown of England three times changed hands.

Robert ceased to be abbot of Roche in 1438.

[a] Foxe.

John Wakefield.

1438—1465.

JOHN WAKEFIELD was elected abbot of Roche and received the benediction of Archbishop John Kemp, on June 7th, 1438.*

During his time, Roche Abbey obtained a new benefactor and founder in Matilda of York, Countess of Cambridge, who lived in the neighbouring castle of Coningsborough. The following is a translation of the part of her will referring to Roche:—

Will of the Countess of Cambridge.

"IN the name of God, Amen. On the feast of the assumption of the Blessed Virgin Mary, in the year of our Lord 1440, I, Matilda, of York, Countess of Cambridge, being of right mind and sound memory, make my will in this manner:

First, I leave and commend my soul to God and the Blessed Mary and all His saints, and my body to be buried in the monastery of Roche, in the chapel of the Blessed Mary, before her image, situate in the southern part of the church of the said monastery.

Also, I will that there lie over my grave a stone of alabaster, raised aloft after the manner of a tomb, with an effigy, after the manner which I will tell to my executors.

Also, I leave to each chaplain present at my funeral two-pence, and to each parochial clergyman, six-pence.

Also, that my executors appoint wax to be burnt about my body at the time of my funeral, according to their discretion.

Also, I will that twelve poor persons be clad in white gowns, each of whom shall bear one twisted wax taper, of the larger size, in honour of our Lord Jesus Christ and the Blessed Mary, and all

---

* Reg. John Kemp, p. 393.

His faints; and that thefe be held by them at the time of my funeral and of my mafs, and that each of them have twelve-pence.[b]

Alfo, I leave to three chaplains of honeft converfation, forty-two marks, that they may celebrate and pray for my foul, and for the foul of my lord, and for the fouls of my parents; and that one keep a fchool, if he will.

Alfo, I will that every year each of them fay onet rental of the bleffed Gregory, and daily fay in their maffes this prayer:—"*Deus qui eft summa noftræ Redemptionis, &c.*," when they can conveniently do fo.

Alfo, I leave to the monaftery of Roche one white veftment, to the intent that one monk of the fame place may celebrate for my foul for a week, and have daily one penny; and another monk for another week, and fo each in turn may feparately celebrate and pray for my foul in the faid monaftery, for the fpace of feven years complete.

Alfo, I leave to the abbot of Roche fix fhillings and eight-pence, and to each monk there, twenty-pence, on the day of my burial.

Alfo, I leave to the abbot and convent of the fame place, forty marks, on condition that if they are willing fufficiently to fhow their obligation to their *founder*, they fhall, once in each year, for ever, for my foul's health, celebrate my obit in funeral fervices, and a mafs with two wax candles burning over my body during the fame time.

Alfo, I will that my whole veftment of red colour, worked with gold, with one chalice and two crewets, two beft filver candlefticks and one filver bell, remain with my body, for the perpetual ufe of the faid church, * * * * * In witnefs whereof, I have to this prefent writing affixed my feal. Given in the monaftery of Roche, on the day and place aforefaid."[c]

Matilda, Countefs of Cambridge, was the daughter of Thomas Lord Clifford, and the fecond wife of Richard Plantaganet, ordinarily known as Richard of Coningfborough, Earl of Cambridge. She did not long furvive the making of her will. It is dated 15th Auguft, 1446, and fhe died on the 26th of the fame month. Her fucceffors were held *founders* of Roche up to the time of the diffolution.

John Wakefield died in the middle of the year 1465, and was buried at Roche with all the honours due to his ftation.[d]

---

[b] Thomas Duke of Exeter, who died in 1426, ordered fomething fimilar to this "I will that there be as many poor men as I may have lived years at my funeral, each carrying a torch, and habited in a gown and hood of white cloth, and each receiving as many pence as I have lived years, and that there be the fame number of poor women, of good character, clothed in a gown and hood of white cloth, and each receiving a penny "—"Teftamenta Vetufta," vol 1 p 208

[c] "Teftamenta Eboracenfia," Surtees Society, vol 11 p 118

[d] Reg Geo Nevil, part 1 p 11

John Gray.

1465—1479.

CONCERNING the election and benediction of John Gray, we have the following letter and memorandum, which are preserved in the Archbishop's register at York :—

Letter from the Abbot of Newminster.—

"TO the most reverend father in Christ, George, by the grace of God, Archbishop of York. Your devoted son, John, abbot of Newminster, of the Cistercian order, in the diocese of Durham, father abbot and immediate visitor of the monastery of the Blessed Mary of Roche, sends all manner of reverence and honour due to so great a father. We would signify to your most reverend paternity by the tenor of these presents, that the monastery of Roche being lately vacant by the death of the venerable father in the Lord, John de Wakefield, the last abbot; and he being dead and his body buried with the exequies due to his ecclesiastical office, the prior and convent of the aforesaid monastery of Roche, proceeding to the election of a future pastor, elected the religious man, brother John Gray, whose election, after due enquiry made into his fitness, we have confirmed. Wherefore, we pray your Lordship's pre-eminence to grant him your holy benediction. In testimony of which, our seal and the seal of the venerable father in the Lord, the abbot of Rufford, our coassessor is appended. Given in the monastery of Roche, the seventh day of August, 1465.

"Memorandum. That, on the sixth day of September, 1464, the Lord Archbishhop received the aforesaid letter, at Scrooby, and commanded Lord William Bishop of Dromore, his suffragan, to confer benediction upon brother John Gray, the aforesaid abbot elect."

It will be noticed that an interval of a month took place between the election and the benediction of this abbot.

John Gray vacated his abbacy, not by death as *Dr. Burton* has it, but by resignation, on the 5th of June, 1479.*

* Reg. Geo. Nevil, pt. i. p. 11.

William Tikil.

1479—1486.

THE letter of the abbot of Newminster to the Archbishop of York, concerning this abbot, is also preserved, and is even more interesting than the one relating to abbot John Gray.

Letter from the Abbot of Newminster.

"TO the most reverend father and lord in Christ, Lord Laurence, by the grace of God, Archbishop of York, Primate of England, the lord abbot of Newminster, of the Cistercian order, Father abbot and immediate Visitor of the monastery of the Blessed Mary of Roche, of the order aforesaid, and the aforesaid diocese, sends all manner of reverence with the honour and deference due to so great a father, to the utmost gratification of his wish. We humbly thought right to explain to your lordship's preeminence, by the tenor of these presents, that our filial monastery of Roche aforesaid, lately becoming vacant by the voluntary cession and free resignation of the religious man, Master John Gray, late abbot of the said monastery, and so resigning, we, by our paternal authority, which we exercise on this behalf, on the 5th of June, 1479, absolved and exonerated him from all jurisdiction and rule over the said monastery, and from his place and state in the chapter of the monastery; and the venerable father of Rufford, acting as our coassessor in the calling of a new pastor, in due form, according to the rules of the order there was presented, and elected the discrete man, brother William Tikil, one in morals, knowledge of temporals and experience of age, sufficiently furnished. Whom thus canonically presented and elected, we confirmed and led him into the church and installed him, and brought him back into the chapter house, and bound him by an oath, in the customary form of the order, and did all other things which are, or were requisite by the right of our order. Wherefore, we pray your lordship's pre-eminence to be graciously pleased to confer the boon of your sacred benediction upon the said person so elected and instituted. Whom, may God, the giver of all good gifts, prosper with felicity in this present vale of tears, and lead at last to the infinite joys of His heavenly kingdom. In witness whereof, we have caused to be placed to these present writings the seal of our office, together with that of our coassessor aforesaid. Given in our chapter-house of Roche aforesaid, in the month and year above expressed."

William, Tikil, (Tickhill,) was elected abbot of Roche June 5th, 1479, and he held his abbacy until the latter end of 1486.

ª Reg. Laurence Booth, p. 104.

Thomas Thurne.

1486—1488.

IN the regifter of Thomas Rotherham, Archbifhop of York, there is the copy of a letter given under his feal at Scrooby, on the 19th day of December, 1486, empowering his venerable confrere and Bifhop William Dromore, his fuffragan, to confer benediction on brother Thomas Thurne, who had been elected and confirmed abbot of Roche.*

Thomas Thurne (Thorne) ceafed to be abbot of Roche early in 1488, after having held his abbacy little more than a year.

* Reg. Thomas Rotherham, p. 234.

William Burton.

1488—1491.

ILLIAM BURTON profeſſed canonical obedience and received benediction at the hands of Biſhop William Dromore, his ſuffragan, on the laſt day of February, 1488.[a] He ceaſed to be abbot of Roche in 1491.

[a] Reg. Thos. Rotherham, p. 242.

John Morpeth.

1491—1503.

ON the eighteenth of August, 1491, Archbishop Thomas Rotherham granted a commission to William, by the grace of God Bishop of Dromore, to confer benediction on John Abbot of the monastery of Roche.[a]

We may conclude from the name of this abbot that he originally came from Newminster; Morpeth being the name of a town near that monastery.

John Morpeth ceased to be abbot of Roche in 1503.

[a] Reg. Thomas Rotherham, p. 251.

John Heslington—Henry Cundal.

1503—1538.

THE DISSOLUTION.

A wake, ye ghoftly persons! awake, awake,
B oth prieft, pope, byfhop, and cardinall,
C onsider wisely, what wayes that ye take,
D aungeroufly beyng like to have a fall,
E very where the mischiefe of you all,
F arre and neare, breaketh out very faft:
G od will needes be revenged at the laft.
H ow long have ye the world captived
I n sore bondage, of men's traditions?
K ings and Emperours ye have deprived,
L ewdly usurping theyr chiefe poffeffions:
M uch misery ye make in all regions.
N ow your fraudes be almoft at their latter caft,
O f God sore to be revenged at the laft.
P oore people to opprese, ye have no fhame,
Q uaking for feare of your double tyranny;
R ightfull juftice ye have put out of frame,
S eeking the luft of your god—the belly:
T herefore, I dare you boldly certifie,
V ery little though ye be thereof agaft,
Y et God will be revenged at the laft.[a]

A. B. C. by William Thorpe.

[a] Foxe.

THROUGHOUT the whole of the first quarter of the sixteenth century, tremblings and commotions, every day increasing in violence, were felt, and only too well recognized by the monks as the forerunners of that relentless earthquake which was to shake their fair abbeys into ruins, and to cast them forth upon the world, homeless and despised.

Monachism received its first fatal shock when Cardinal Wolsey, in order to found a College at Oxford (now Christ's Church,) and another at Ipswich, his native place, obtained leave from Pope Clement to suppress and appropriate the revenues of what he called certain poor and small monasteries, in which he acknowledged that neither God was served, nor religion kept. The abbots, seeing the danger of such a precedent, endeavoured to induce Wolsey to abstain from seizing upon the abbey lands, by offering him instead, large sums of money. The abbot of St. Mary's, York, to save his cell of Romburgh in Suffolk, offered the Cardinal three hundred marks sterling. But all these intercessions of the abbots were in vain, the work of demolition and impropriation commenced at once, and continued steadily until the desired sum had been raised, jealous Catholics here and there expressing their disapprobation in different ways. At Beggam, in Sussex, after the brethren had been turned out of their house, "a riotous company, disguised and unknowne, with painted faces and visers, came to the same monasterie, and brought with them the chanons, and put them into their place again, and promised that whensoever they rang the bell, that they would come with a great power and defend them." But resistance was in vain, the enthusiastic defenders of the religious men of Beggam and elsewhere were soon silenced and punished, and the monastic system had to carry on its existence with its foundations sapped, and its superstructure propped as well as might be. There however, is nothing which so urgently tempts interference as a prop! In the first place, one despises anything which is so dilapidated as to require such assistance, and then one immediately begins to speculate as to the probable consequences of removing it: and lastly, to prove the accuracy of these speculations, the required blow is given. We need not be surprised then, to find that there existed a party whose aim was to knock away the props which upheld monachism without themselves being at the same time buried in the ruins. King Henry VIII., after having read the Beggar's Supplication against the monks, is reported to have said "If a man should pull downe an old stone wall and begin at the lower part, the upper part thereof might chance to fall upon his head." If this be true, it would appear that the Defender of the Faith himself was of the iconoclastic party.

Volumes might be written shewing the numerous causes which had rendered the monks so unpopular, but the two following descriptions of a monastery and a monk will satisfy the reader :—

MONASTERY.—"A house of ill-fame, where men are seduced from their public duties, and fall naturally into guilt from attempting to preserve an unnatural innocence."[a]

MONK.—Treated after the Linnæan system.

"*Definitio.*—An animal, anthropomorphic, hooded, howling by night, thirsting.

"*Descriptio.*—Body erect, biped, back curved, head depressed, always hooded, and clothed in every part, covetous, fœtid, filthy, drunken, lazy, more patient of want than labour; at the rising and setting of the sun, and especially at night, they congregate, and when one cries out, all cry; run together at the sound of a bell, walk always in couples, are clothed in wool, live by rapine and plunder, assert that the world was made for them alone, carry on their amours clandestinely, do not marry, expose their young, fight with their own species, and attack their enemies unawares from ambushes.

"The female differs little from the male, except in having her head always veiled, is cleaner, less drunken, and never leaves home, which she keeps clean. When young she grasps at all sorts of play things, stares about her on all sides, and salutes the males by nodding. When older, she becomes spiteful and malignant, and when angry, agitates her jaw bones incessantly with open mouth. When called, they answer "Ave." When allowed, they chatter promiscuously, and if a bell rings are suddenly mute.

"*Differentia.*—Man speaks, reasons, wills; the *monk* is often mute, has no reason or will, is governed solely by the orders of his superiors. The head of *man* is erect, the head of a *monk* is depressed with eyes turned to the ground. *Man* seeks his bread by the sweat of his brow, the *monk* growes fat by laziness. *Man* dwells among men, the *monk* seeks solitude and hides himself, avoiding the light. Whence it follows, that the *monk* is a genus of mammalia distinct

[a] "The Tin Trumpet."

from *man*, intermediary between him and the ape, approaching nearest to the latter, from which it differs very little in voice or manner of living.

"*Usus*.—An useless burthen on the earth."[*]

The worst enemies of the monks could not wish more to be said than is contained in the foregoing lines. They contain doubtless a great amount of exaggeration, but if even a quarter of the accusations in them be true, it is not surprising that the enemies of the monks were numerous.

In 1534, the king, having been pronounced by Parliament supreme Head on earth of the Church of England, determined to exercise his right of visiting every religious community, for the purpose of finding out their real condition. He accordingly commanded his secretary, Thomas Cromwell, to issue a commission to that effect. Thomas Cromwell, was the descendent of a Lincolnshire family, and was well fitted for this work, having been employed by Wolsey in the suppression of the monasteries already referred to. He appointed three visitors, Doctors Legh, Layton, and Ap Rice; and probably towards the end of the year 1535, the two former appeared before the gate of Roche Abbey, for we find them about that time at Fountains, the abbot of which place they wrote to Cromwell was "a vara fole and a miserable ideote."

The manner in which the visitors approached an abbey, was to come upon it suddenly, summoning the brethren immediately before them. An amusing illustration of this may be found in *Dr. Layton's* letter to Cromwell, describing what he did on arriving at the Abbey of Langdon.

"Immediately discending from my horse, I sent Bartlett, your servant, with all my servants to circumcept the abbay, and surely to kepe alle bake dorres and starting hoills, etc. I my self went alone to the abbot's lodging, joynyng upon the feldes and wode, evyn lyke a cony clapper full of startyng hoilles, a goode space knokkyng at thabbottes dore, *nec vox nec sensus apparuit*, saveyng thabbottes litle doge that, within his dore faste lokked, bayede and barkede. I found a short polax standing behynde the dore, and with yt I dasshhede thabbottes dore in peisses, *ictu oculi*, and set one of my men to kepe that dore, and aboute house I go with that polax in my hande, *ne forte*, for thabbot is a daingerouse desperate knave and hardy. But for a conclusion, his gentle woman beystrrede her stumpis towards her startyng hoilles, and ther Bartlett

[*] Specimen Monachologiæ

wachying the purfuet towke the tendre damoifel, and after I had examined hir, to Dover ther to the maire to fett hir in fum cage or prifon for viii dayes, and I brought holy father abbot to Canterbury and here in Chriftes church I will leve hym in prifon. In this foden doying *ex tempore* to circumcept the houfe and to ferche, your fervant John Antonie his men mervelede what fellow I was, and fo dyde the refte of thabby, for I was unknowyn ther of alle men. At laft, I founde her apparel in thabbottes cofer. To tell howe all this commodie, but for thabbot a tragedie, hit were to long. How hit fhalle appere to gentilmen of this contrey, and other comons, that ye fhalle not deprive or vifite but upon fubftanciall groundes Surely I fuppos Gode him felf put hit in my mynde thus fodenly to make a ferche at the begynnyng, bycaufe no chanon appered in my fyght; I fuppofede rather to have founde a woman emongifte them than in thabbottes chambre. The refte off alle this knaverie I fhall differ tyll my cumyng unto you, whiche fhalbe with as muche fpede as I can poffible, doyng my affured deligence in the refte. Scribulled this Satterday, and written with the hafty hand of your affured fervant

RICHARD LAYTON.

When the vifitors had affembled the brethren together, they gave leave to every one under twenty-four years of age to go where he pleafed, and if any chofe to quit their monafteries they had a fecular drefs given them and forty fhillings, and were reftored to the full privileges of the laity.

Gifted with fuch unbounded power, it is not to be wondered at that the vifitors performed their tafks fometimes in an unfeeling manner. Dr. Ap Rice complained to Cromwell of the overbearing manner of Dr. Leigh in his vifitations,—that he was too infolent and pompatique, and handled the fathers too roughly for not meeting him at the door when they had no warning of his coming —that he had twelve men waiting on him in livery, befides his brother, which were a great tax upon the fmall monafteries,—and that he took too much money in the filling up of the vacancies which he found in abbeys.

After the King's fupremacy was eftablifhed, all thofe abbots that had formerly received confirmation of the Archbifhop, were now confirmed by him, through his Lord Vicegerent Cromwell; fo that when a vacancy occured, care was taken to allow no one to become the head of a religious houfe, unlefs he was favourable to the king. Leave to elect was given, but the name of the perfon to be chofen was firft declared. It is not unlikely that Henry Cundal, the laft abbot of Roche, was inftituted in this manner, for no record of his confirmation and benediction can be found in the Regifters of the Archbifhops of York.

What treatment the brethren of Roche experienced at the hands of Doctors Legh and Layton is not known, nor has the document defcribing the moral condition in which the monaftery was then found been preferved.

The queftions which the vifitors demanded of them were eighty-fix in number, and have been epitomized by *Burnet* as follows:—

Whether divine fervice was kept up day and night, in the right hours? and how many were commonly prefent, and who were frequently abfent?

Whether the full number, according to the foundation, was in every houfe? Who were the founders? What additions have been made fince the foundation? and what were their revenues? Whether it was ever changed from one order to another? By whom? and for what caufe?

What mortmains they had? And whether their founders were fufficiently authorized to make fuch donations?

Upon what fuggeftions and for what caufes they were exempted from their diocefans? Their local ftatutes were alfo to be feen and examined.

The election of their head was to be inquired into. The rule of every houfe was to be confidered. How many profeffed? And how many novices were in it? And at what time the novices profeffed?

Whether they knew their rule, and obferved it? Chiefly the the three vows of poverty, chaftity, and obedience? Whether any of them kept any money without the Mafter's knowledge? Whether they kept company with women within or without the monaftery? Or if there were any back-doors by which women came within the precincts? Whether they had any boys lying by them?

Whether they obferved the rules of filence, fafting, abftinence, and hair fhirts? Or by what warrant they were difpenfed with in any of thefe?

Whether they did eat, fleep, wear their habit, and ftay within the monaftery, according to their rules?

Whether the Mafter was too cruel or too remifs? And whether he ufed the brethren without partiality or malice?

Whether any of the brethren were incorrigible? Whether the Mafter made his accompts faithfully once a year?

Whether all the other officers made their accompts truly? And whether the whole revenues of the houſe were employed according to the intention of the founders?

Whether the fabric was kept up, and the plate and furniture were carefully preſerved?

Whether the convent ſeal and the writings of the houſe, were well kept? And whether leaſes were made by the maſter to his kindred and friends, to the damage of the houſe? Whether hoſpitality was kept? And whether at the receiving of novices, any money or reward was demanded or promiſed? What care was taken to inſtruct the novices?

Whether any had entered into the houſe, in hope to be once the maſter of it?

Whether in giving preſentations to livings, the Maſter had reſerved a penſion out of them? Or what ſort of bargains he made concerning them?

An account was to be taken of all the parſonages and vicarages belonging to every houſe, and how theſe benefices were diſpoſed of, and how the cure was ſerved.

Having obtained anſwers to the eighty-ſix queſtions, the Viſitors were ordered to give before departing ſeveral injunctions to the following effect:—

"That they ſhould endeavour, all that in them lay, that the act of the King's ſucceſſion ſhould be obſerved," (where it is ſaid that they had under their hands and ſeals confirmed it. This ſhows that all the religious houſes of England had acknowledged it:) "and they ſhould teach the people, that the King's power was ſupreme on earth, under God; and that the Biſhop of Rome's power was uſurped by craft and policy, and by his ill canons and decretals, which had been long tolerated by the Prince, but was now juſtly taken away.

The abbot and brethren were declared to be abſolved from any oath they had ſworn to the Pope, or to any foreign potentate; and the ſtatutes of any order, that did bind them to a foreign ſubjection, were abrogated, and ordered to be razed out of their books.

That no |monk ſhould go out of the precinct, nor any woman enter within it without leave from the King or the Viſitor; and that there ſhould be no entry to it but one.*

Some rules were given about their meals; and a chapter of the Old or New Teſtament was ordered to be read at every one. The Abbot's table was to be ſerved with common meats, and not with

---

* The ſtrictneſs of this injunction was intolerable, and was the cauſe of many giving up the monaſtic life

delicate and ſtrange diſhes; and either he or one of the ſeniors, was to be always there to entertain ſtrangers.

Some other rules follow about the diſtribution of their alms, their accommodation in health and ſickneſs One or two of every houſe were to be kept at the univerſity, that, when they were all inſtructed, they might come and teach others: and every day there was to be a lecture of divinity for a whole hour: the brethren muſt all be well employed.

The Abbot or head was every day to explain ſome part of the rule, and apply it to Chriſt's law; and to ſhow them that their ceremonies were but elements introductory to true Chriſtianity; and that religion conſiſted not in habits, or in ſuch like rites, but in cleanneſs of heart, pureneſs of living, unfeigned faith, brotherly charity, and true honouring of God in ſpirit and in truth: that therefore they muſt not reſt in their ceremonies, but aſcend by them to true religion.

Other rules are added about the revenues of the houſe, and againſt waſtes; and that none be entered into their houſe, nor admitted under twenty-four years of age.

Every prieſt in the houſe was to ſay maſs daily; and in it to pray for the King and Queen.

If any broke any of theſe injunctions, he was to be denounced to the King, or his Viſitor General.

The Viſitor had alſo authority to puniſh any whom he ſhould find guilty of any crime, and to bring the Viſitor General ſuch of their books and writings as he thought fit.

Cromwell's Viſitors having aſcertained the condition of every religious houſe, at length returned and laid upon the table of the Houſe of Commons the famous "Black Book" of the Monaſteries which ſtated that two thirds of the monks of England were living a life ſo drunken, ſo profligate, and ſo iniquitous that the details of it may not be entered into. This parliament aſſembled on the 4th of February, 1536, and be it remembered it was a Catholic one. When the contents of the "Black Book" were read out in the Parliament Houſe, the indignation produced was ſo great that the cry aroſe of "Down with them!"[a] and under the influence of this ſtrong feeling the Act for the diſſolution of the ſmaller monaſteries having a yearly income leſs than two hundred pounds, was paſſed, "by the conſent of the great and fatte abbottes" ſays *Grafton*,[b] "in hope that their great monaſterys ſhould have continued ſtill. But even at that

[a] Latimer's Sermons, p 123   [b] p 445

tyme one fayde in parliament houfe, that thefe were as thornes, but the great abbottes were putrifyed old okes, and they muft needs followe."

The preamble of this act runs as follows:—

"FORASMOCH as manifeft fynne, vicious, carnall and abomynable lyvyng, is dayly ufed and commytted amonges the lytell and fmal eabbeys, pryoryes, and other relygyous houfes of monkes, chanons, and nounes, where the congregacion of fuch relygyous perfones is under the nombre of XII perfones, whereby the gouvernours of fuch relygyous houfes and thir convent, fpoyle, deftroye, confume and utterly wafte, afwell their churches, monafteyres, pryoryes, principall houfes, fermes, granges, landes, tenementes, and heredytamentes, as the ornaments of ther churches and ther goodes and cattalle, to the high dyfpleafour of Almyghty God, flaunder of good relygyon, and to the greate infamy of the kynges highnes and the realm, if redres fhuld not be hadde therof; and albeit that many contynuall vyfytacions hath bene hertofore had by the fpace of two hundreth years and more, for an honeft and charytable reformacion of fuch unthrifty, carnall and abhomynable lyvyng, yett neverthelefle, lytell or none amendement ys hytherto hadde, but ther vycyous lyvigng fhamelefly encreaffeth and augmentith, and by a curfed cuftome is fo rooted and enfefted that a greate multytude of the relygyous perfones in fuch fmale houfes doo rather chofe to rove abrode in apoftafy than to conforme them to the obfervacions of good relygyon; foe that without fuche fmall houfes be utterly fuppreffed, and the relygyous perfons therein commytted to greate and honorable monafteries of relygyon in this realme where thei maye be compelled to lyve relygyoufly for the reformacion of their lyves, ther canne elles be noo reformacion in this behalf. In conclufion whereof the Kynge's moft Royall Majefty beyng fupreme hede on erthe under God of the church of England, dayly findyng and devyfyng the increafe advauncement and exaltation of true doctryne and vertue in the feid churche, to the onelye glorye and honor of God and the totall extirpyng and dyftruccion of vyce and fynne, havyng knowledge that the premyfes be true, as well by the comptes of his late vyfytacions as by fundry credyble informacions, confyderyng alfo that dyverce greate folempne monafteryes of this realme, wherein, thankes be to God, relygyon is right well kept and obferved, be deftytute of fuch full noumbers of relygyous perfons as they ought and maye kepe, hath thought good that a playne declaracion fhould be made of the premyfes afwell to the lordes fpirituall and temporall as to other his lovyng fubjectes the commons in this prefent parliament affembled; whereupon the feid lordes and commons by a greate deliberacion fynally be refolved, that yt ys and fhalbe moche more to the pleafour of Almyghty God and for the honor of this his realme that the poffeffions of fuch fpiritual relygyous houfes, nowe beyng fpent, fpoyled, and wafted for increafe and mayntenance of fynne, fhould be ufed and converted to better ufes, and the unthrifty relygyous perfons foo fpendyng the fame to be compellyd to reforme their lyves. And therupon moft humbly defire the kynge's highnes that yt may be enacted by auctoryte of this prefent parliament, that his majeftie fhall have and enjoy to hym and his heirs for ever all and fynguler fuche monafteryes pryoryes and other relygyous houfes of monkes, chanons, and nonnes, of what kyndes or dyverfyties of habyttes, rules, or orders foo ever ther be called or named, which have not in landes and tenements, rentes, tythes, porcions and other heredytamentes, above the clere yerely value of two hundreth pounds; and in lyke maner fhall have and enjoy all the fcytes and circuytes of every fuche relygyous houfes, and all and fynguler the manors, granges, meafes, londes, tenements, revercions, rents, fervyces, tythes, pencions, portions, churches, chapelles, advowfons, patronages, annuyties, rightes, entres, condycions, and other heredytamentes apperteynyng or belongyng to every fuche monafterye, pryory, or other relygyous houfe, not havyng as ys aforefeid above the feid clere yearly value of two hundreth poundes, in as large and ample maner as the abbottes, pryours, abbeffes, pryoreffes, or other governers, of fuche monafteryes, pryoryes, and other relygyous houfes now have or ought to have the fame in the right of ther houfes. And that alfo his highnefs fhall have to hym and to hys heires all and fynguler fuch monafteryes, abbeis, and pryoryes whiche at eny tyme, within one yere next aftre the makyng of this acte, hath be gevyn and graunted to His Majefty by any abbot, pryor, abbes or pryores, under the covent feals, or that otherwyfe hath be fuppreffed or dyfolved. And all and fynguler the manors, londes, tenementes, rentes, fervyces, revercions, tythes, pencions, portions, churches, chappelles, advowfons, patronages, rightes, entrees, condicions, and all other intereftes and hereditaments to the fame monafteryes, abbeys, and pryoryes, or to any of them, apperteynyng or belongyn. To have and to holde all and fynguler the premyffes with all ther rightes, profyttes, juryfdiccions, and commodytyes, unto the Kyng's Majeftye and to his heires and affigns for ever, to doo and ufe therwyth his and ther owen wylles to the pleafor of Almyghty God and to the honor and profytte of thys realme."[*]

[*] 27 Hen VIII cap 28

Provision is then made to render void any alienations of land or property which any abbot may have made, fearing the dissolution of his monastery. All ornaments and goods are given to the King as well as the monasteries themselves and their lands. The greater monasteries are ordered to admit the members turned out of the lesser.

The yearly income of Roche Abbey having been returned as more than two hundred pounds,[*] it was not affected by this act. It however had a very narrow escape, as the surplus income which preserved it was only twenty-two pounds.

To carry out the act of Suppression, Doctors Legh and Layton again made their unwelcome appearance in Yorkshire, and, as might be anticipated, were not more popular than they had been during their former visit. In fact it was impossible that men whose employment was one of sacrilege and destruction, could be looked upon by any but a few Puritans, with anything but dissatisfaction. Their servants also treated the monks with an insolent contempt; taking from the churches and chapels of the dissolved houses, their relics and spoils, and displaying them as they travelled from one place to another. Some made saddle-cloths of the church vestments, or wore them as garments; and some hammered the silver relic cases into sheaths for their daggers. The people seeing these things going on, began to wonder what would be the end, and a rumour soon spread that all religion was to be done away with, and that the parish churches would soon share the fate of the monasteries, or that only one for every seven or eight miles would be left, the plate of which would be confiscated, and chalices of tin supplied instead. They also thought from the enquiries which Cromwell was making about births, deaths, and marriages, that they would soon have to pay a fine to the King for every christening, burial and wedding, whereas that sagacious statesman had only the admirable intention, which he two years afterwards carried out, of instituting parish registers. In all these suspicions, the people were encouraged by the great abbots, who were now sorely taxed by the crowds of monks who arrived from the suppressed houses, and who knew well that their turn was soon coming.

At Louth, in Lincolnshire, the feeling of the priests and people had grown so strong, that it at length broke out into a formidable insurrection. Beginning on the first of October, 1536, with a few inhabitants gathered together in a knot on the green of the town, and headed by a cobbler, they in a few days numbered thousands,

[* See "Valor Ecclesiasticus."]

there being among them priests, and monks to the number of seven or eight hundred, whose words of peace were "Kill the gentlemen, if they will not join us they shall be hanged."*

On the third of October they drew up six demands which were to be made of the King. The first was that the religious houses should be restored; and the others required that they should be relieved from obnoxious taxes and persons, one of the latter of course being Cromwell. Two messengers were sent to London with these demands, and while they were detained there, sixty thousand rebels had found their way to Lincoln, but for want of provisions, could not remain there. The royal army seeing them rapidly dispersing, began to fear there would be no battle.

After some time the answers to the demands of the rebels arrived and were read in the chapter house of the Cathedral. These being more or less satisfactory, the rebel army being much demoralized, broke up, the whole rising and dispersion having occupied less than a fortnight. But the fire of insurrection only smouldered!

The Pilgrimage of Grace.

THE rebellion in Lincolnshire was immediately followed by a still more formidable rising in Yorkshire, called the "Pilgrimage of Grace." One Robert Aske, a Yorkshire gentleman and a barrister in good practice at Westminster, and who had been spending the law vacation in his native country, on his way back to his business, met with a party of the Lincolnshire rebels who demanded his name, and offered him the popular oath to be "faithful to the King, the Commonwealth, and to Holy Church." These rebels having thus "taken" him, as Aske afterwards called it, became his body-guard, and with strange rapidity, the name of Aske became the rallying cry of the rebels.

Upon the failure of the insurgents in Lincolnshire, Robert Aske left that country and returned into Yorkshire, and there he grew still more famous. The fire of insurrection re-kindled, and the stuff of the Yorkshire rebels proved to be even more inflammable than that of the Lincolnshire Bells and beacon-fires were clanging and burning all over the country, and addresses bearing the name of Robert Aske, which he afterwards declared to be forgeries, were handed about and posted on every church door, requesting the people to assemble "to preserve the Churche of God frome spoylyng &c."

* Froude, vol III, p 114

Upon hearing of the infurrection, the King wrote to Lord Darcy to fupprefs it, but that nobleman fhut himfelf up in his Caftle of Pomfret, and would not mufter his men.

On the 14th of October, the rebel force collected on Weighton Common, where Afke was chofen commander-in-chief. This army appears to have been a very formidable one, as the men were ftrong and well armed. They were grouped, according to their parifhes, in companies, the priefts bearing the croffes of their churches before them. On their banners they had a crucifix with the five wounds and a chalice; and every one wore on his fleeve as the badge of the party an emblem of the five wounds of Chrift, with the name Jefus wrought in the midft.[a]

Before this force, Hull, Pomfret, and York foon furrendered, and in all the places where they were victorious, the monks were reinftated in their monafteries, and "though it were never fo late when they returned," writes the Earl of Oxford to Cromwell, "the friars fang matins the fame night."

On the 21ft of October, the rebel army had its head quarters at Pomfret, in the caftle of which place "the great captain" Afke fat at the head of the rebel council, together with the Archbifhop of York, Lord Darcy, and others. Here he received "with a cruel and ineftimable proud countenance," the Lancafter Herald, who had been fent with a royal proclamation, and which proclamation, in fpite of the entreaties of the Herald, he would on no account allow to be read.

On the 24th of October, the royal army under the Duke of Norfolk and Lord Shrewfbury, was at Doncafter, to which place the rebels alfo marched from Pomfret, thirty thoufand ftrong, the royalift army numbering no more than eight thoufand.

Having arrived, they deployed along the banks of the river, which was much fwollen, from Ferribridge to Doncafter; and thus with the river dividing them, the two armies lay watching each other for two days; the heads of each party, in the meanwhile endeavouring to come to fome arrangement which might prevent bloodfhed.

At length, on the 26th of October, it was agreed that a conference fhould be held upon the bridge, when nine gentlemen from either fide met, and Sir Thomas Hilton, on behalf of the rebels, explained their demands. Thefe were arranged into twenty-four articles.[b] The portions of thefe articles which more particularly relate to our fubject, were that "the abbeys fuppreffed be reftored—

---

[a] Burnet, vol. i. p. 416.   [b] Froude, vol. iii., p. 136.

houses lands and goods." "That the Lord Cromwell have condign punishment as a subverter of the good laws of the realm." "That Dr. Legh and Dr. Layton have condign punishment for their extortions in the time of their visitation of the religious houses, and other their abominable acts by them committed and done."

This conference lasted the whole day, and in the darkness of night it was agreed that Sir Robert Bowes and Sir Ralph Ellercar, accompanied by the Duke of Norfolk, as an intercessor, should carry the articles to the King. It was also arranged that there should be an armistice, and that the mustered on both sides should be disbanded.

On the 29th of October, the King received the messengers graciously, and in order to gain time, detained them a fortnight; in the meanwhile sending messengers north to endeavour to combat the delusions of the people.

On the 14th of November, Bowes and Ellercar were dismissed "with general instructions of comfort," and a promise that a final reply should be given in a month. But when at length this answer arrived, it did not suit the insurgents, and after a hasty council, held at York, Aske again collected his army. The royal army also reoccupied the line of the Don, and had its head-quarters at Rotherham. And yet only one thing kept up the insurrection. The King would not grant a complete pardon to the rebels. He would have five or six of the worst offenders.

This obstacle at length, however, was removed, the King granting, by the advice of his privy-council, a general pardon, and on the 2nd of November, an agreement was come to at Doncaster, the rebels believing that their entire petition had been granted. At the close of this meeting, Aske knelt down in the presence of the Lords, and having desired that he should no more be called "captain," with others, pulled off their badges crossed with the five wounds, all of them saying "we will wear no badge or figure but the badge of our sovereign Lord."

It had been well if the "Pilgrimage of Grace" had thus ended, but the people growing suspicious that the King's promises would not all be fulfilled, again rose under Sir Francis Bigod. George the eldest son of Lord Lumley, tried to take Scarborough and failed. Hallam attempted Hull with the same result. Bigod succeeded in taking Beverley, but was soon obliged to fly.

The King enraged at this new rebellion, sent down orders to execute a large number of the insurgents in every town and village, and make such a "fearful spectacle" as shall be a warning to others, and "Finally, forasmuch as all their troubles have ensued by the folicitation and traitorous confpiracies of the monks and canons of thofe parts, we defire you at fuch places as they have confpired or kept their houfes with force fince the appointment at Doncafter, you fhall, without pity or circumftance, caufe all the monks and canons that be in any wife faulty, to be tied up without further delay or ceremony. "The Duke of Norfolk obeyed this order and hanged feventy-four perfons. The Abbot of Kirkftead, the Abbot of Barlings, and feventeen others were alfo hanged at Lincoln. The Abbot of Fountains, the Abbot of Jervaulx, the Abbot of Rievaulx, the Prior of Bridlington, Bigod and others were hanged at Tyburn. Lord Darcy and Afke were alfo arrefted and accufed of having been concerned in this frefh attack. On the arreft of Afke, " his fervant, Robert Wall, did caft himfelf upon his bed and cried 'Oh, my mafter! Oh, my mafter! they will draw him, and hang him, and and quarter him;' and therewith he did die for forrow." The prophecy of this faithful one was only too true. In July, 1537, Robert Afke was drawn through the ftreets of York on a hurdle, and afterwards hanged, from the top of a high tower, his laft requeft being granted "Let me be full dead or that I be difmembered, that I may pioufly give my fpirit to God, without more pain." Lord Darcy was executed on Tower Hill. And thus, at laft, drowned in its own blood, rebellion died!

The demolition of the religious houfes which had been checked for awhile by the rebellion, again commenced, and went on rapidly. And the King knowing that he had nothing now to fear, began to make arrangements for the fuppreffion of the greater monafteries.

In the fummer of 1537, a new vifitation of the religious houfes was ordered. Dr. Legh and Dr. Layton being again appointed Vifitors for the North of England. They were ordered to examine the monks ftrictly in all things that related either to their affection to the King and the fupremacy, or to their fuperftition, in their feveral houfes; to difcover what cheats and impoftures there were either in their images, relics or other miraculous things, by which they had drawn people to their houfes on pilgrimages, and gotten from them any great prefents. Alfo to try how they were affected during the late commotions; and to difcover every thing that was amifs in them, and report it to the Lord Vicegerent.[a]

In anfwer to thefe queftions we have the following document relating to Roche, two copies of which exift. One in the Rolls

[a] Burnet.

House, "*Historical and other documents*, No. 761, p. 8." and the other in the British Museum, "*Lansdowne MSS.*, 988 fol. 4."

"The compendium of the discoveries made by Dr. Legh and Dr. Layton in the visitation of the royal province of York in the Bishoprics of Coventry, Lichfield and others, in the time of Henry VIII.

Rupa alias Roche.

Sodomites. { William Hela / John Wheland / Robert Reine / Henry Wilson / John Doddesworth.

Suspected of Treason. { John Robinson, suspected of the crime of treason and imprisoned at York.

Superstition. { Pilgrimage is made hither to an Image of the Crucifix, found (as it is believed) on a rock, and is held in veneration.

Founder. { The Earl of Cumberland.

The annual account, 170*l*.
The House owes 20*l*."[a]

There are many points of interest in the foregoing writing. Of the five monks who are said to have been guilty of an unnatural crime, two, John Wheland and Robert Rein had left the monastery before the dissolution, which took place a year afterwards.

John Robinson, who at the time of the visitation was confined in York Castle, suspected of treason, was probably not guilty, as we find him liberated and receiving his pension in the reign of Queen Mary.

The search for objects of superstition seem not to have been very successful at Roche, as only the Image of the Crucifix on a Rock[b] is recorded; but at other Houses most extraordinary objects were found. Relics innumerable. The parings of St. Edmund's toes;

---

[a] Memorandum (in a modern hand) "This filthy Book of Calumnies was invented by the Commissioners for the purpose of justifying the suppression of the religious houses, and the robbery of the Church. It is referred to in 'Burton's Anatomy of Melancholy,' Part 3, Sec 2, number 1."
Another memorandum says "The whole of the visitation is of this description."

[b] I have sought in vain for any traces of this curious object. The Visitors had instructions to deface and utterly destroy everything of an useless or superstitious character, and they seem to have done their work thoroughly here

the pen-knife and boots of St. Thomas a Becket; pieces of the true crofs, enough to build a fhip; a piece of St. Andrew's finger, in pledge for 40*l*, but which the Vifitor will not redeem at the price. In fact every reliquary feems to have been

"Icrammed ful of cloutes and bones"

each one fuppofed to have its own peculiar power. There were relics againft bad weather, againft weeds, againft difeafe and pain, and there were relics which would bring you every bleffing,

"So that he offer pense or elles grotes."

But what brought the monks into ill favour more than thefe relics was their images. The moft popular of thefe was the Crucifix of Boxley Abbey, in Kent, which went by the name of "*the rood of grace.*" The eyes of this Image on fit occafions "did ftir like a lively thing," the body bowed, the forehead frowned, and the lower lip dropped as if about to fpeak. The people of Kent believed in this rood above all others, and the offerings to it were enormous. At length, however, a fceptical commiffioner arrived, and nothing awed, examined the figure clofely. The refult of this infpection was the difcovery of a fufficient amount of mechanifm to produce the forementioned actions. The Image was immediately taken down and publicly exhibited. It was fhewn at Maidftone. It performed before the court at Whitehall, and finally, it went through its motions at Paul's Crofs, where the Bifhop of Rochefter lectured upon it, and when the indignation of the people was at its higheft, it was given to them, and in a few moments it was torn in pieces. Celebrated Images from Walfingham, Ipfwich, Doncafter, and Penrice, were alfo brought to Smithfield, and burnt together.

When the people faw how they had for centuries been deceived and tricked out of their money, a ftrong reaction took place, and inftead of the feeling of fear and devotion which had fo long chained them, a recklefs and barbarous inconoclafm now poffeffed their minds; and they were ready when a religious houfe was fuppreffed, to pull down, fpoil and pilfer, and to defecrate even the churches in which only a few days before they had worfhipped!

But to recur to the difcoveries of Dr. Legh and Dr. Layton at Roche. The Earl of Cumberland is returned as the Founder. This was Henry Clifford, the firft earl and the defcendant of Thomas de Clifford, the fixth lord, whofe daughter, Matilda, Countefs of Cambridge, became founder of Roche in 1446. (See page 59.)

It will alfo be feen that the yearly income had fallen in a year from 222*l* to 170*l*, and that the Houfe had run into debt 20*l*. This falling off in the yearly value, laid Roche Abbey under the power of the act for the suppression of the lesser monasteries, and looks as if Henry Cundal, the last abbot, like the abbots of other Houses, had made away with the property to enrich himself before being driven out.

A year after this second visitation of the monasteries, Roche Abbey was surrendered to the Crown.

Surrender Deed of Roche Abbey.

"TO all the faithful in Christ, to whom the present writing may come, Henry (Cundal) Abbot of the Monastery or Abbey of the Blessed Mary the Virgin, of Roche, in the diocese of York, of the Cistercian order, and the Convent of the same place, eternal salvation in the Lord!

KNOW YE that We, the aforesaid Abbot and Convent by unanimous assent and consent, after due deliberation in our minds, of our certain knowledge, and by our own pure act, for certain just and reasonable causes specially moving our minds and consciences thereto of our own accord and will, have given and granted and by these presents do give and grant, yield and consign to our Most Illustrious Prince and Lord, Henry VIII, by the grace of God, of England and France, King, Defender of the Faith, Lord of Ireland, and on Earth Supreme Head of the English Church, the whole of our said Monastery or Abbey of Roche and all the site, groundplot, circuit and precinct of the said Monastery of Roche aforesaid. Also all and singular manors, demesnes, messuages, gardens, backyards, tofts, lands and tenements, meadows, pastures, woods, rents, reversions and services, mills, transit fees, military fees, wards, marriage fees, born villeins with their belongings, commons, liberties, frankpledges, jurisdictions, offices, courtleets, hundreds, views of frankpledge, fairs, markets, parks, warrens, vineyards, waters, fisheries, ways, paths, empty homesteads, advowsons, nominations, appointments, donations of churches, vicarages, chapels, chantries, hospitals and other ecclesiastical benefices whatever, rectories, vicarages, chantries, pensions, portions, annuities, tithes, oblations, and all and singular our emoluments, profits, possessions, hereditaments, and rights whatever, as well within the said County of York as within the Counties of Lincoln, Derby and Nottingham or elsewhere within the realm of England, Wales and the marches thereof, whatever way belonging, regarding, appending or devolving upon the same Monastery or

Abbey of Roche aforesaid; and all our charters, evidences, writings, and muniments of every kind in any way regarding or concerning the said Monastery or Abbey, its manors, lands and tenements and the rest of the premises with the appurtenances, or any parcel thereof; TO HAVE, hold and enjoy the said Monastery or Abbey, its site, groundplot, circuit, and precinct of Roche aforesaid; also all and singular domains, manors, lands, tenements, rectories, pensions and the rest of the premises with all and singular their appurtenances, to the aforesaid our most Invincible Prince and Lord King Henry, his heirs and assigns, to whom for all effect of law in this behalf which may or can follow therefrom, we subject and submit as in duty bound, ourselves and the said Monastery or Abbey of Roche aforesaid, and all rights in whatever way by us acquired, giving and granting, as by these presents we do give and grant to the said Royal Majesty, his heirs and assigns, all and every manner of full and free faculty, authority and power to dispose of us and all the Monasteries of Roche aforesaid, together with all and singular manors, tenements, lands, rents, pensions, services and singular the aforesaid, with their rights and appurtenances, and at his Royal pleasure and will to alienate, give, convert and transfer to any uses whatever, according to his Majesty's pleasure, and such disposals, alienations, donations, conversions and translations by his said Majesty in what manner soever to be made, we promise by these presents that we will consider that they ought from that time forth to be ratified, and will hold them ratified, granted and for ever confirmed. And that all and singular the premises may have due effect, we have moreover of our own free choice, for ourselves and our successors, openly, publicly, expressly, with sure knowledge and willing minds, renounced and ceased from all quarrels, provocations, appeals, actions, litigations and instances whatever on our part which in any way seek or may hereafter seek for remedies and benefits for us and our successors in that behalf under pretext of disposal, alienation, translation and conversion aforesaid and the rest of the premises, all mistakes arising from fraud, fear, ignorance, or any other matter having without dispute, exception, objection or allegation, been entirely removed and laid aside, as by these presents we do renounce and cease from, and in this writing give up our interest in the same. AND WE the aforesaid Abbot and Convent and our successors will warrant against all people by these presents, the said Monastery, precinct, site, mansion and Church of Roche aforesaid, and all and singular the manors, demesnes, messuages, gardens, backyards, tofts, meadows, feedings, pastures, woods, underwoods, lands, tenements

86   ROCHE ABBEY.

and all and singular the rest of the premises with the appurtenances to the said Lord the King his heirs and assigns for ever. In testimony whereof We the aforesaid Abbot and Convent have caused to be placed to this writing our common Seal.[a] Given in our Chapter House on the 23rd day of the month of June, in the 30th year of the reign of King Henry aforesaid."[b] (1538.)

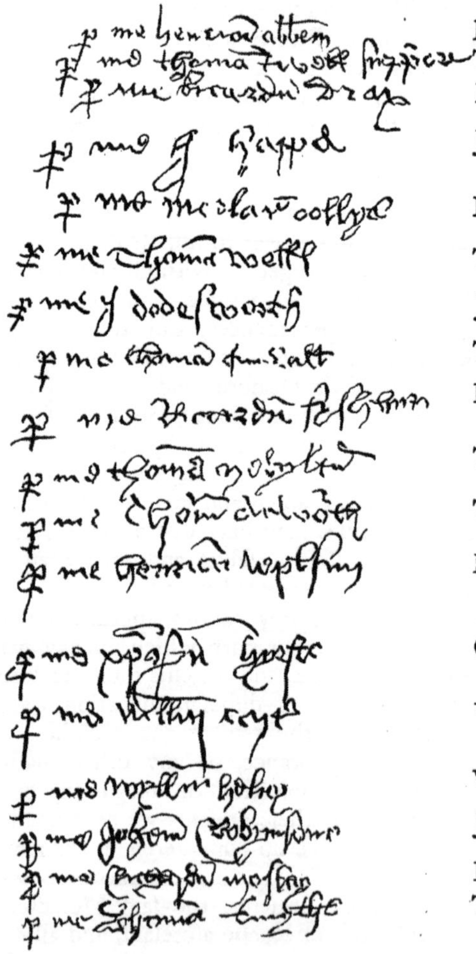

Henry, Abbot
Thomas Twell, Subprior
Richard Drax

J. Happa

Nicholas Collys

Thomas Wells

J. Dodsworth

Thomas Cundall

Richard Fyshburn

Thomas Medyltun

Thomas Acworth

Henry Wylson

Christopher Hyrste

William Carter

William Helay

John Robynsone

Richard Moslay
Thomas Smythe

[a] See Plate X., Fig. 4.   [b] From the Augmentation Office.

THE DISSOLUTION.

This Deed was executed before Doctor William Petre, a Clerk of Chancery, (afterwards Secretary of State) at the time[a] and place above mentioned.

The fignatures of the Abbot and Monks, fac-fimiles of which are here given, are written upon the margin of the deed and are becoming very obfcure.

Of the after hiftory of the monks who figned the Surrender Deed little is known beyond what may be gathered from the contents of the following document:

Roche.

"The Abbot (Henry Cundal) for penfion XXXIII li VIs. VIIId.
The Sub-prior (Thomas Twell) VI li XIIIs. IIIId.[b]
The Bourfer (John Dodfworth) VI li [c]
XI prefts Monks every V li——LV li.
IIII Novices every LXVIs. VIIId.——XIII li VIs. VIIId.
The Abbot to have his books and the IIIIth parte of the plate the Cattal the houfehold ftuf a Challis and Veftment and XXX li in money at his departure with a contentment porcion of Corn att difcreation.

Every Monk to have at his departure his haulf years porcion by waye of Rewarde and XXs. befides towardes his apparail.

Every to have his porcion feparite and free.

Every fervaunt by waye of Reward his haulf yeres wages.

The Kynges Majeftie to pay the debts of the Houfe."[d]

From the handfome provifion made for the Abbot, it may be taken for granted that he refigned his abbacy with a good grace, and gave the commiffioners very little trouble.

In 1553, fifteen years after the diffolution, twelve of the eighteen who figned the Surrender, ftill enjoyed their penfions.[e]

---

[a] The date of the furrender of Roche Abbey, has by all who have written on the fubject hitherto, been given as 1539. The 30th year of Henry VIII begins April 22nd, 1538, and ends April 21ft, 1539. The 23rd of June, 30 Henry VIII muft therefore be in 1538.

[b] Thomas Twell feems to have remained in the neighbourhood of Roche after the diffolution. Mr. Hunter's keen eye which omits nothing, firft difcovered this interefting fact, from the two following entries in the accounts of the Sheffield Church Burgeffes,—"Hallamfhire," p. 140.

ITEM. P[d] to the ryngers y[t] dyd ryng for Sr. Thomas Twell, at the recevynge of certen ftuf gevyn by hym to the Church, wth p[d] to the preftes and clerk for dyrge XVId.

ITEM. P[d] for the cofts and charges for feching Sr. Thomas Twell will from Blythe IIs.

[c] The Burfar was the treafurer of the Houfe. He received the rents, paid the wages, and difcharged all the debts of the Abbey.

[d] Chapter Houfe Ebor. Bag. 25.   [e] Bibl. Bodl. 8º D. 50. 51. Jur.

	£	s.	d.		£	s.	d.
Henry Cundal	33	6	8	Thomas Medyltun	5	0	0
Thomas Twell	6	13	4	Henry Wilfun	5	0	0
John Dodefworth	6	0	0	William Carter	5	0	0
Richard Fyfhburn	5	0	0	Thomas Welles	5	0	0
Thomas Harryfonne (?)	5	0	0	John Robynfone	3	6	8
Nicholas Collys	5	0	0	Richard Moflay	3	6	8

The following is an account of the plate, cattle, corn, &c., which the the Abbey had at the diffolution. The quantity of plate is fufpicioufly fmall. Had Henry Cundal, like other abbots, provided for the future, by felling part of it?[a] The fact of a tabernacle being in pledge for 40*l* does not allay the doubt.

The Inventory.

"This is the inventorye of all the lands and gudes perteyneing to the Monafterye of Roche by eftimacion.

Imprimes, Landes and tenementes perteyneing to the fame Monafterye in divers plafis fome CCXXII li or thereaboutes by eftimacion.

  Item. Plate in the fame Monafterye.
      A croffe w^t a fhanke parcell gilte.
  Item. VII Chalice where of one lentt.
  Item. One croche[b] parcel gilte.
  Item. A tabarnacle wyche lyes in plege for XL li.
  Item. II faltes gilte w^t one covering.
  Item. One ftandinge Cupe w^t cover parcell gilte.
  Item. One whitt bolle.
  Item. A Alte Cupe parcell gilte.
  Item. Mafers[c] VI.
  Item. Spoones XXXII.[d]
  Item. Catle perteneing to the fame.
  Item. *Imprimis.* IIII fcore oxen kyen and yonge beftis.
  Item. V cartte horse.

---

[a] The Abbot of Fountains at midnight caufed his chaplain to fteel the fexton's keys, and took out a jewell and a crofs of gold with ftones. One Warren, a Goldfmith of the Chepe, made the Abbot believe a ruby was a garnet, and otherwife cheated the venerable Father, he being "a vara fole, and a miferable ideote." "Suppreffion of Monafteries p. 100."

[b] Crofier [c] Wooden Bowls or Goblets. These mafers are called "Anafers" in the Mon. Ang.

[d] The Vifitors were commanded to take away with them all fuperfluous plate. It would appear from the above fufpicioufly fmall lift that the Abbot of Roche, like the Abbot of Fountains had become aware of the fact, and had made a timely difpofal of part of it.

THE DISSOLUTION.

Item. II mears one folte and one ſtagge.[a]
Item. VI ſcore ſhepe yonge and olde.
Item. XL ſwyne yonge and olde.
Item. XI feder bedes w^t all other thenges belonging.
Item. In Whitt and Malte IIII ſcore quarter.

(In the oppoſite column.)

Ffeis payed of the ſame lands and tenementes as after foluis:—
The Corrody of John Keeper and his wife Cs.
Item, imprimis to my lord of Hampton for the Stewardſhipe of Armthorpe ſomme XXVs VIIId.
Item. To Thomas Greene for kepeing of the courtes pertening to the ſame Monaſterii, ſomme XXXs.
Item. To the balye of Rokeby, ſomme XIIIs. IIIId. w^t a lyverye cotte.
Item. To the balye of Armthorpe ſomme XIIIs. IIIId., with a liverye cotte.
Item. To James Bankes for Receiving of Rents at Sannbeke and Hawton, and other plaifes ſomme XXs.[b]

Theſe be the detts y^t ys owing to the ſame Monaſterye:—
Imprimis. Maſter Roberd * * * ſomme XVIII li.

Theſe be the detts that the ſaid monaſterye doth owe :—
Imprimis. To Maſter Robert' Stelle ſomme XL li.
Item. To William Hellingworth ſomme XX li.
Item. To Willyam Halle of the newe mylne ſomme VI li XIIIs. IIIId.[c]"

It is rather a ſingular fact that the following intereſting letter ſhould have eſcaped the notice of all previous writers on Roche. It is ſuppoſed to have been written by Cuthbert Shirebrook, a dignified eccleſiaſtic, who was born near Roche Abbey, and educated at the free ſchool of Rotherham, and whoſe uncle was preſent at the ſuppreſſion of Roche.

Letter on the Suppression of Roche Abbey.

"IN the plucking down of religious houſes for the moſt part this order was taken: that the viſitors ſhould come ſuddenly upon every houſe and unawares, to the end to take them napping, as

---

[a] A Horſe under three years old.
[b] This is not a complete liſt of the officers employed by the Abbot of Roche. There was beſides theſe a ſteward and a bailiff at Thurſtonland, a bailiff at Streethorpe, a ſteward at Roxby, and a receiver at Barnby.
[c] Chapter Houſe, Ebor. Bag. 25.

the proverb is, left if they fhould have had fo much as any inkling of their coming, they would have made conveyance of fome part of their own goods to help themfelves withal, when they were turned forth of their houfes, and both reafon and nature might well have moved them fo to have done, although it will be faid all was given to the King before by Act of Parliament; and fo they had neither goods, houfes, nor poffeffions. And then they had to give the King great thanks, yea pray for him upon their black beads, that he was fo gracious a prince to them, to fuffer them to ftay fo long after that all was given from them. And therefore if the vifitors being the King's officers and commiffioners in that behalf, took their dinner with them, and then turned them forth to feek their lodging at night, or at the furtheft the next day in the morning, where they could find it (as it was done indeed,) they did no wrong; nor truly no great right: for fo foon as the vifitors were entered within the gates, they called the abbot and other officers of the houfe, and caufed them to deliver up to them all their keys and took an inventory of all their goods, both within doors and without: for all fuch beafts, horfes, fheep, and fuch cattle as were abroad in paftures or grange places, the vifitors caufed to be brought into their prefence: and when they had fo done, turned the abbot with all his convent and houfehold forth of the doors.

"Which thing was not a little grief to the convent, and all the fervants of the houfe departing one from another, and efpecially fuch as with their confcience could not break their profeffion: for it would have made an heart of flint to have melted and wept to have feen the breaking up of the houfe and their forrowful departing; and the fudden fpoil that fell the fame day of their departure from the houfe. And every perfon had every thing good cheap; except the poor monks, friars, and nuns, that had no money to beftow of any thing: as it appeared by the fuppreffion of an abbey, hard by me, called the ROCHE ABBEY; a houfe of white monks: a very fair builded houfe, all of freeftone; and every houfe vaulted with freeftone, and covered with lead (as the abbeys was in England, as well as the churches be.) At the breaking up whereof an uncle of mine was prefent, being well acquainted with certain of the monks there; and when they were put forth of the houfe, one of the monks, his friend, told him that every one of the convent had given to him his cell* wherein he lied: wherein was not anything of price, but his bed and apparel, which was but fimple and of fmall price: which

---

* Dr. London on fuppreffing the Charter Houfe gave "to every brodor his celle."—Sir Hy. Ellis', "Orig. Letters," 3rd Series, vol. iii. page 183.

monk willed my uncle to buy something of him; who said, I see nothing that is worth money to my use: No, said he; give me ijd. for my cell door, which was never made with Vs. No, said my uncle, I know not what to do with it. (For he was a young man unmarried, and then neither stood in need of houses nor doors.)* But such persons as afterwards brought their corn and hay or such like, found all the doors either open, or the locks and shackles plucked away, or the floor itself taken away, went in and took what what they found, filched it away.

"Some took the service books (of parchment?) that lied in the church, and laid them upon their waine coppes (waggon copes) to piece the same: some took windows of the Hayleith and hid them in their hay; and likewise they did of many other things: for some pulled forth the iron hooks out of the walls that bought none, when the yeomen and gentlemen of the country had bought the timber of the church. For the church was the first thing that was put to the spoil; and then the abbot's lodging, dortor, (dormitory) and frater (refectory) with the cloister and all the buildings thereabout, within the abbey walls, for nothing was spared but the ox-houses and swinecoats, and such other houses of office, that stood without the walls;ᵇ which had more favour showed them than the very church itself; which was done by the advice of Cromwell, as Fox reporteth in his book of "*Acts and Monuments*." It would have pitied any heart to see what tearing up of the lead there was, and plucking up of boards, and throwing down of the sparres; and when the lead was torn off and cast down into the church, and the tombs in the church all broken (for in most abbeys were divers noble men and women, yea and in some abbeys kings, whose tombs were regarded no more than the tombs of all other inferior persons: for to what end should they stand, when the church over them

---

* The monks seem to have been very anxious to make the most of the occasion to realize as much as possible Dr Layton, writing from Bilham Abbey, says —"When we were makyng salle of the olde vestments within the chapitre house, the monks cryede a newe marte in the cloister, every man bringing his cowle caste upon his nec to be solde, and solde them indede —" Ellis, 3rd Series, vol iii, page 267"

I am indebted to the Rev J Eastwood for the following interesting entry from the Churchwardens accounts at Ecclesfield, which shews that the vestments were sold at Roche

"1542 Sir Robert Cobcroft, ten shillings, which he paid for vestments at Roche"

ᵇ John Freeman writing to the Lord Privy Seal about the razing of the Abbeys in Lincolnshire says,—"The King's Commission commandeth me to pull down to the grounde all the walls of the Churches, stepulls, cloysters, fraterys, dorters, chapter howfys, with all other howfys, saveyng them that be necessary for a farmer," the charge of doing this would be so great he continues that he thinks it would be best to take down the bells and lead and pull down the roofs and batulments and stairs, and "lete the wallis stande, and charge som with them as a quarre of ston to make salys of as they that hathe nede will fetche "—Sir Hy Ellis' "Orig Letters,' 3rd Series, vol iii, page 269

was not spared for their cause,) and all things of price either spoiled, carped away, or defaced to the uttermost.[a]

"The persons that cast the lead into fodders, plucked up all the seats in the choir, wherein the monks sat when they said service; which were like to the seats in minsters, and burned them, and melted the lead there withall: although there was wood plenty within a flight shot of them[b] for the abbey stood among the woods and the rocks of stone: in which rocks was pewter vessels found that was conveyed away and there hid: so that it seemeth that every person bent himself to filch and spoil what he could: yea even such persons were content to spoil them, that seemed not two days before to allow their religion, and do great worship and reverence at their mattins, masses and other service, and all other their doings: which is a strange thing to say, that they could this day think it to be the house of God, and the next day the house of the devil: or else they would not have been so ready to have it spoiled.

"For the better proof of this my saying, I demanded of my father, thirty years after the suppression, which had bought part of the timber of the church, and all the timber in the steeple, with the bell-frame, with others his partners therein, (in the which steeple hung viij. yea ix. bells; whereof the least but one could not be bought at this day for XXli., which bells I did see hang there myself more than a year after the suppression,) whether he thought well of the religious persons and of the religion then used? And he told me, yea: for, said he, I did see no cause to the contrary. Well, said I, then how came it to pass you was so ready to destroy and spoil the thing that you thought well of? What should I do? said he. Might I not as well as others have some profit of the spoil of the abbey? for I did see all would away; and therefore I did as others did.[c]

"Thus you may see that as well they that thought well of the religion then used, as they which thought otherwise could agree

---

[a] The Commissioners seem to have taken their workmen with them. John Portman writing to Cromwell, from Lewes, in Sussex, (the monks of which place had their part with the monks of Roche of the eels caught in the fisheries belonging to Earl Warren, at Hatfield, &c.,) says,—" We brought from London xvii persons, 3 carpentars, 2 smyths, 2 plummars, and one that kepith the fornace (for melting the lead.) Every of these attendith to hys own office: x of them hewed the walles abowte, among the whych ther wer 3 carpentars, thiere made proctes (props) to undersette wher the other cutte away, thother brake and cutte the waules."—"Suppression of Monasteries," page 181.

[b] At Fountains Abbey heaps of ashes were found when the nave was excavated, which Mr. Walbran thinks must be the remains of the stalls and screens of that abbey, but we know that all the wood work of the monasteries had not this fate.

[c] Dr. London writing from Warwick, says,—" The power people thorowly in every place be so gredy upon thee Howlys when they be suppressed that by night and daye, nott only of the townys, but also of the country, they do contynually resorte as longe as any dore, wyndor, yren, or glass, or lowse ledde remaynythe in any of them. In every place I kepe wacche as longe as I tary and prison those that do thus abuse them selvys, and yet other will not refrayne."—Sir Hy. Ellis' "Orig. Letters," 3rd Series, vol. iii., page 139.

well enough, and too well, to fpoil them. Such a devil is covetoufnefs and mammon! and fuch is the providence of God to punifh finners, in making themfelves inftruments to punifh themfelves, and all their pofterity from generation to generation! For no doubt there hath been millions that have repented the thing fince; but all too late. And thus much upon my own knowledge touching the fall of the faid Roche Abbey."[a]

The following verfes give in a few words the rife and fall of monachifm: They are entitled "A Tale of Robin Hoode dialoguewife, between Watt and Jeffry;[b]" and, like the foregoing letter, they defcribe the eagernefs and greed with which the people feized upon the property of the monks when the abbeys were diffolved:—

"Adam Bell[c] was ware and wise
When hee firft began to rise,
As the bee in summer's prime
Sucks the marigold and thyme,
Sucks the rose and daffodill,
Leaving, taking what fhe will,
And from flower to flower doth glide,
Sweetly by the river fide;
Where chryftal ftreams delightfull runninge,
Are ever sweetened with his cumminge.
Such was Adam in his prime,
In the flower of his time,
Soe he taftes every sweete
Till with fatt he fell afleepe;
As he flumbered in the dale,
Spread upon the gentle vale,
A famifhed Lion[d] came that way,
Hungry, panting for his pray,
In his grasping pawes he bent him,
And in pieces all to rent him;
Yet his cabin doth remaine
Beaten with the winds and raine,
Spoyled of all the paffers by
Whose huge frame doth terrify;
All that wondrous monument
All the world's aftonifhment.
When the wolves[e] and foxes[f] saw
Adam in the Lion's paw;
Ours is Robin's ftrength they cried,
And sett him round on every fide."

[a] MS Cole vol xii p 1—49
[b] MS Harl. 367 f 150.   [c] Monachifm   [d] King Henry VIII   [e] Puritans.   [f] Politicians.

But although Cundal had furrendered his Abbey to the King, the Commiffioners, on furveying the lands, found their value to be over 200*l* per annum. It did not therefore yet come under the power of the Act. And this being the cafe with many other abbeys, a new Act was called for, and paffed in 1539, for the fuppreffion of the greater monafteries. By it all the religious houfes of whatever value, which had been or fhould be fuppreffed, were given to the King and his fucceffors for ever. A fweeping fentence! Almoft enough to make Richard de Bufli and Richard Fitz Turgis, who had given their lands to the monks "*for ever,*" rife from their graves in remonftrance!

But the money of the peaceful monks was required for other and far different purpofes. The introduction of artillery had rendered all our ports and harbours liable to attack and deftruction; every expofed pofition therefore, had to be guarded by earthworks, and forts, and numerous batteries had to be erected. To accomplifh this the fpoils of the Church were ufed. The clear yearly value of all the fuppreffed houfes is ftated to have been 131,607*l*. 6*s*. 4*d*, but the true value was at leaft *ten times* as much,[a] 18,000*l* of this money the King defigned to convert into a revenue for eighteen[b] Bifhopricks but this number dwindled down to fix.

Of the inmates of Roche there is little more to fay. A monk of Roche compiled a hiftory of the Manor of Todwick, from the Conqueft to the reign of Henry III. It is printed in the "*Monafticon.*" Another of the monks fhortly before the diffolution went about making notes of the churches in Yorkfhire.[c] It is to be regretted that that both his name and MS. are loft, and that all attempts to recover them have been fruitlefs. Extracts from the MS. were made by Mr. de la Pryme, which are now in the Britifh Mufeum with the reft of that gentleman's collection. When he faw it it was bound up with other manufcript matter, and in the poffeffion of Mr. Canby, of Thorne.

In judging of the value of the monaftic inftitution, the diffolution of which has now been defcribed, it is not fair to give undue prominence to that period when decay was faft approaching, left gazing on the decrepitude of age, we may chance to forget that the healthy vigour of manhood ever exifted. It is eafy to join the popular cry,

---

[a] Burnet, Vol 1, p 488

[b] Workfop was to have been one of the eighteen —"Suppreffion of Monafteries, p 264.

[c] Mr Hunter has ufed thefe notes in his "Deanery of Doncafter," Vol 1 pp 41, 188

> "O aye, the monks, the monks, they did the mischief
> Theirs all the grossness, all the superstition
> Of a most gross and superstitious age!"

But there doubtless was a time when the monks did good service in England, and

> "We will as soon believe with kind Sir Roger
> That old Moll White took wing with cat and broomstick
> And raised the last night's thunder,"

as that the inmates of the monasteries were the cheating pestilent knaves which some historians have represented them to have been.

Let us remember that for centuries they were the sole keepers of the records of religion philosophy and antiquity; that to them we are indebted for a great portion of the early history of this country; and that they were the promoters of science and art. They were lawyers, doctors, architects, chemists, artists, poets and practical farmers. The good they did by settling down in waste places and reducing them to a state of cultivation must have been very great. In wild and solitary places they made roads, cut drains, and otherwise rendered them habitable.

> "Be courteous, Commerce—there are bridges high,
> Ranging their salient angles o'er the strand,
> Which the monks reared; where some proud dwellings lie,
> A fane exorcised agues from the land."

There can be no doubt also that the monks spent a large sum of money in entertaining strangers and way-farers, and in alms to the poor. A sufficient proof of this may be found in the draft of an Act of Parliament, prepared after the dissolution of some of the monasteries for the purpose of enforcing the practice of hospitality upon those who bought the abbey lands. In the MS. the following passage is underlined:—

"NEVERTHELESS, the experience which we have had by those houses that are already suppressed, sheweth plainly unto us that a great hurt and decay is thereby come, and hereafter shall come, to this realm, and great impoverishing of many the poor subjects thereof, for lack of hospitality and good houseHolding that were wont in them to be kept, to the great relief of the poor people of all the counties adjoining the said monasteries beside the maintaining of many smiths, husbandmen and labourers that were kept in the said houses.

It should therefore be enacted that all persons taking the lands of the suppressed houses must duly reside upon the said lands, and must keep hospitality; and that it be so ordered in the leases.*

Besides the hospitality which the monasteries offered they were also the refuge and the sanctuary of those victims of ceaseless tyranny which in the vicinity of a baronial castle were ever to be found.

Let us not then condemn monachism, because when it had accomplished its work, it became the parent of ignorance, bigotry, and licentiousness; but let us rather recall the period when it was " the guardian of learning, the author of civilization and the propagator of humble and peaceful religion."

> " The sacred taper's light is gone,
> Grey moss has clad the altar-stone,
> The holy image is overthrown,
>   The bell has ceased to toll.
>
> The long ribbed aisles are burst and shrunk;
> The holy shrine to ruin sunk,
> Departed is the pious monk,
>   God's blessing on his soul!"

* Rolls House MSS., 1st Series, p. 900.

The Possessions.

THE POSSESSIONS.

HE landed poffeffions of Roche Abbey were for the moft part fituated in the Weft Riding of Yorkfhire, and within a few miles of the fpot on which the Abbey was built; but other lands of importance were in the neighbouring counties of Nottingham, Lincoln, Derby, and Lancafter. In the defcriptions of the following places, when no County is mentioned, it muft be underftood that they were fituated in Yorkfhire.

Abdy.—The Abbot of Roche had property in this hamlet, which is fituated five miles north of Rotherham, but what it was or who gave it is not known. It probably came into the hands of the monks after the year 1232, and could not have been of great value, as, in 1535, it and three other places were together eftimated at only 33s. 9d. per annum.

Aggcroft.—The grange of this place was, with its appurtenances, given by the Founders, and confirmed to the monks by Alice, Countefs of Eu, in 1219.[a]

Alverley.—Whatever property the monks had here could not long have continued in their poffeffion, for it is not named in the lift of the places mentioned in the confirmation of Henry III. 1232, and between the years 1238 and 1254 it was exchanged for some lands in Slade Hooton, belonging to Robert de Ripariis. *(See Loverfal.)*

In 1277, William, fon of John Vavafor, quitclaimed all right in wards, efcheats, &c., in this place.

Anes see **Oncafh.**

Anston.—Nicholas de Saint Paul gave an oxgang[b] of land with

---

[a] See page 77.
[b] As much land as an ox can plough in a year, varying in quantity from fix to forty acres.

a toft[a] and croft here, and confirmed to the monks what had been given to them by Leo de Manvers, and Michael, his fon. He alfo gave them all the woods and rents which he had recovered from the faid Leo and his fon. *(See Brancliffe.)*

The monks held land in Lumby and Afton in 1535, for which they paid 1½d. to the heirs of Weftnis (Wafteneys).

Armthorpe.—This place, which in old charters is written Arneldthorpe and Arnethorpe, was a moft important part of the poffeffions of the monks. The grange was given them by Thomas de Arnethorpe before 1186.

Roger, fon of Hugh Fitz Walter, gave two oxgangs of land with a toft and croft here, and a culture called Gunhale, with the North-wood in this territory, which Agnes, daughter of Robert de Brunington, quitclaimed.

William, fon of Henry de Marifco, in 1246 quitclaimed all his rights in the inclofures here.

Adam, fon of Ralph de Armthorpe, gave one oxgang of land here.

Henry de Armthorpe of Pollington, fon and heir of Adam de Armthorpe, quitclaimed all his rights in the manor of Armthorpe in 1330.

Jeremiah, the parfon of Roffington, with his corpfe, gave all his meadow in the fouth part of the wood here, called South-wood.

It appears by "*Kirby's Inqueft*" that the monks held Armthorpe as one Knight's fee[b] of the King *in capite* in pure and perpetual alms the gift of Richard I.

In 35 Henry III. the Abbot of Roche had a grant of free warren here. This grant was difputed in the time of Edward I., and the abbot was fummoned to fhow by what warrant he claimed free warren. In anfwer the abbot produced the charter of Henry III., which fhewed his right.[c]

In 9 Edward II. the Abbot of Roche was returned Lord of Armthorpe. He had in his employ a Steward, a Bailiff,[d] a Forefter, and a Granger, who was a monk.[e]

---

[a] A houfe, or rather a place where a houfe ftood, which is decayed.

[b] A Knight's fee is fo much inheritance as is fufficient to maintain a Knight, which in Henry the Third's time was fifteen pounds, or two hundred acres.—Bailey.

[c] In 1535, Sir William Fitz William was fteward of Armthorpe, and Miles Wyn bailiff; the former receiving 40s. and the latter 20s. per annum.

[d] See page 89. [e] See page 34.

The yearly income derived from Armthorpe is given in the "*Valor*" as £23 10*s*., this sum being made up of rents, falls of wood, profits of court, rents of assize, &c.

At the Dissolution all the property which the monks had here went to the crown, and in 33 Henry VIII., the King, wishing to extend the limits of Hatfield chase, added Armthorpe to it. Not so much, however, with the intention of increasing the space for his deer as to ensure their safe keeping by placing it under the authority of the officers of the chase; for we find that the manor of Armthorpe was granted in 1551 to the Duke of Northumberland. It had been let from the dissolution until the date of this grant in two portions, one at £2 16*s*. 4¾*d*. and the other at £21 19*s*. 2*d*. per annum, out of which 13*s*. 4*d*. was paid to the collector of the rents, making the clear yearly value £24 2*s*. 2¾*d*.[a]

Arncliffe.—It would appear from *Tanner's* references that the monks held a tenement in this place, but the reference given is incorrect, as it has been found to refer to property formerly belonging to the Abbot of Westminster. It is certain, however, that the monks of Roche had possessions in the neighbourhood of Arncliffe, and it is not unlikely that they also had the tenement referred to by *Tanner*.

Ashenbeech see **Rochdale**.

Ashover.—Property in this place, which is also called Aexoure, in Derbyshire, was given to the monks before the year 1186, by Simon de Plesley. It was still in their hands in 1232, but seems to have been disposed of before the dissolution.

Askern.—In the Confirmation of Henry III. the monks are returned as having property in this place. At the dissolution it still remained in their hands.

Baine.—Henry, son of Maurice de Askern, gave one oxgang of land here, but it does not seem to have remained long in the hands of the monks.

Barnby.—The grange of this place was given to the monks before the year 1186, by Gervas de Barnby; and in 1245, Benedict, the Rector of Barnby, gave them the tithe of the grange also.

In 10 John, there was a fine between William Fitz Thomas and Alice his wife, and Osmund the Abbot of Roche, in which a verdict

---

[a] Particulars for grants 5 Ed. VI. sect. e.

was returned for the abbot of one bovate of land with the appurtenances in Barnby.

In 13 Henry III., there was a fine between the Abbot of Roche and William, fon of Richard de Barnby, in which the faid William acknowledged and granted for himfelf and his heirs that the aforefaid abbot and his fucceffors fhould, as is fitting, have common right of pafture for the whole year, for every kind of beafts from the grange of the faid abbot, except goats, everywhere in the wood of the faid William de Barnby; and that they fhould have pigs of the actual breeding of the faid grange in the fame wood, free from pannage[a] for ever. And, moreover, the faid William granted for himfelf and his heirs, that the aforefaid abbot and his fucceffors fhould have and receive every year from the aforefaid wood, fix cartloads of wood for ever, to wit, two cartloads of good building timber, of oaks not fhaped, and two cartloads of wood for burning, and other two for fencing. And in like manner the faid William granted for himfelf and his heirs that whenever it fhould happen that he pared fods or dug turfs with one or more of his men in the faid wood, it fhould be quite lawful for the faid abbot and his fucceffors to pare fods or dig turfs in the fame place, to the extent of half the number of the fame men, without impediment.

The Abbot of Roche rented land in Barnby of the Lord of Sprotburgh.

At the diffolution the yearly value of Barnby grange was given as £7 10s. 8d. The monks had alfo a rent-charge of £1 10s. 1d. and rent and a farm valued at 13s. 9d., and perquifites of court, 1s. 4d., in all £9 15s. 10d. John Green, bailiff and receiver of Barnby,[b] had 10s. per annum at the diffolution.

In 36 Henry VIII., the manor of Barnby, late parcel of the poffeffions of Roche, was granted to Richard Turke, citizen of London. The quantity and value of the timber growing upon the manor of Barnby and Bramwith at this time may be learnt from the following entry:—"There be growing aboute the fcytuation of the fayd mannor and V tenementes there, and in the hedges inclofyng the landes apperteyning to the fame, CXL. okes and afhes of LX. and LXXX. yeres growth, moft parte ufually cropped and fhred, whereof LX. referved for tymber for houfboote to repayre the houfes ftanding uppon the fcyte and for ftakes for hedgeboote to repayre and maynteyne the faid hedges and fences and LXX. refydue valued at VId. the tree whiche is in the holl XLs."[c]

---

[a] Money paid for licenfe to feed fwine upon maft (i. e. the fruit of wild trees) in the woods.
[b] Brother Thomas was granger at Barnby in the time of Henry III., and in trouble. See page 32.
[c] Particulars for grants. Mifcellaneous No. 61, Rolls House.

Barnoldswick.—The grange here is mentioned in King Henry's "*Valor*" as one of the poffeffions of the monks of Roche, and is valued at £8 per annum. It does not feem to have belonged to them in 1232, as no mention is made of it in the confirmation of Henry III. It was here that the monks of Kirkftall firft fettled in 1147.

Bawtry.—The Abbot of Roche had property here in 1232, but of what it confifted and who gave it is not known. It had been difpofed of before the diffolution.

Bilham.—In the reign of King John, William de Barvile gave to the monks of Roche four oxgangs in this place and quitclaimed his right in four other oxgangs, which Henry de Worthley unjuftly detained. *Dodfworth* fays that he gave the monks *all* his lands in Bilham.

Blitheshaw see **Thirnscoe.**

Blyth.—John de Kyveton, parfon of the church of Radcliffe-on-Trent, made a fine with the King of twenty fhillings for licenfe to affign one meffuage, thirty-fix acres of land, three acres and twenty-four fhillings of rent, with the appurtenances in Blythe and Torworth, to the Abbot of Roche and the convent of the faid place. *(See Kiveton.)*

In the time of Edward III., the Abbot of Roche was fummoned to anfwer to the King "by what warrant" he claimed to hold certain lands and tenements in Blyth in perpetual alms, free and quit from all taxes, &c., in anfwer to which the abbot produced the charter of Henry III.,[a] which he faid the prefent King had confirmed at Clipfton in his fecond year. In anfwer as to how the abbot and his predeceffors had ufed their liberties, twelve jurors on their oath faid that they had ufed them well. That they were always amerced with others in the country, and as to pontage, they faid that the abbot ought not to be quit from making and repairing the bridge of Nottingham, called the "Town Bridge."

In the Regifter of Blyth Priory, fol. 103, there is a compofition between the prior and convent of that place, and the prior of Roche, acting for the abbot, concerning tithes here.

In Edward II. the Prior of Blyth held of the Honour of Tickhill the whole town of Blyth in demefne in pure alms, except 40s. which the Abbot of Roche held in that town in exchange for the mill of Serlby in Nottinghamfhire.

[a] See page 20.

Botildewelletwang see **Todwick**.

Braithwell.—The monks seem to have had no property here until the beginning of the thirteenth century. An oxgang of land with pasture for eighty sheep was granted them by Thomas, son of Artrop de Braithwell, who also confirmed all that his ancestors had given, and Richard, his brother, confirmed the same.

William, son of Gerbode gave ten acres of land in the fields of this town, with pasture for sixty sheep, and Robert, his brother, gave twenty acres of land in the same fields, with pasture for six score sheep.

The monks of Roche had therefore the right of pasture here for two hundred and eighty sheep.

Before the dissolution the monks paid one quarter of corn yearly at the mill of Coningsborough from the land which they held in Braithwell. After the dissolution the house and land of the abbot, together with some property called Bellstring Lands, were let to W. Wilson at £1 6s. 2d. per annum, paying thence to the crown 24s., and to Lord Hundesdon at his manor of Coningsborough one quarter of wheat. In 1563 all this property was granted to Charles Jackson, of Firbeck, Co. Notts., gent., at thirty-two years' purchase (£16 17s. 4d.). The moiety of the money to be paid in hand and the rest within fourteen days. The wood and underwood were sold the next year to Charles Jackson and Wm. Mason, for forty marks.*

Bramley.—Mabilia, the widow of Ote de Tilli, the seneschal of Coningsborough, gave two oxgangs of land with a toft and croft here, of her own patrimony, or according to *Dodsworth*, "her lord-ship of Bramley," but the monks were not to have common of pasture for more than a hundred sheep. She also confirmed three oxgangs in the same place.

The monks first had property here about the year 1190.

The abbot paid seven-pence rent to Roger Fretwell for land in Bramley.

Mr. *Hunter* says, that the grange of the Abbot of Roche here, after the dissolution, became the seat of a family of Spencer, who acquired much of the property that had been in the hands of the *religious*.

Bramwith.—Gervis de Barnby gave the grange here, before the year 1186.

William, son of William de Bladesworth, gave and confirmed

* Particulars for grants.

what he had here, and what the monks held of the fee of Allen de Hooton in this place.

In 3 King John, there was a fine between William de Infula and Ofmund, Abbot of Roche, tenant of two carucates of land with the appurtenances in Bramwith. Verdict to William. And William granted to the aforefaid Abbot and his fucceffors all the aforefaid land with the appurtenances, to hold of him and his heirs at the fervice of two marks per annum, fave foreign fervice.

In 10 Henry III., there was a fine between Adam of Halyhton and Jane his wife, Robert, fon of Richard, and Sufanna his wife, plaintiffs; and Richard (? Reginald) Abbot of Roche, tenant of one bovate of land and half a fishery, with the appurtenances in Bramwith.

The rents of affize and cuftomary tenements here were valued in 34 Henry VIII. at £3 15s. 9½d.

The manor of Bramwith at the diffolution was granted to Richard Turke, citizen of London.

Brantcliffe.—This grange was given to the monks before 1186 by Leo de Manvers. In 35 Henry III. they had a charter of free warren here.

At the diffolution, the Abbot's land here, which is called "The farm of the grange," was valued at £20. In 36 Henry VIII. it was granted to William Butler and others.

In the lane leading from this grange to the Sheffield and Workfop road, there is ftill a bridge which goes by the name of the "monks' bridge."

Bridlington.—The property of the monks feems to have extended to this well-known place, which is fituated in the Eaft Riding. Odenell, fon of Nicholas d'Aubeney, gave one mark per annum out of his mill at Bridlington. There is no mention of this gift in the lift of the poffeffions of Roche at the diffolution; it had probably therefore been difpofed of before that time.

Brookhouse.—This place is fituated in the parish of Laughton, and appears in the "*Valor Ecclefiafticus*" of Henry VIII. as one of the places belonging to Roche.

Broom Riddings.—This place lies about a mile and a half on the road from Rotherham to Roche Abbey. Robert de Herthwic, for the good of the foul of Beatrix his wife, gave two acres of land here, abutting upon Gofeker, with the meadow lying at the head of the faid acres. The monks feem to have difpofed of this property before the diffolution.

Bugthorpe.—This place is situated in the East Riding, near Pocklington. Idonea, wife of Nicholas de Bugthorpe, gave two acres of land here. No mention is made of it at the dissolution.

Brathmere see **Hatfield.**

Callinglow.—This place is near Oneash grange, and formed part of the property which the monks had in Derbyshire at the dissolution.

From the "*Particulars for Grants*" we learn that "the farm of the grange in the Peak, called Calengelawe, with all lands, meadows, pastures, &c., parcel of the possessions of the late monastery of Roche, freely resigned, were in 1540 demised to John Leke, Esq., at 40s. per annum."

Campsal.—The monks had something here at the dissolution.

Carlton.—From the "*Hundred Rolls*" we find the following history of the manner in which this place came into the hands of the monks.

The ancestors of the King (4 Edward I.) had one manor in Carlton, belonging to the Crown, which was wont to yield £10 per annum, of which, King John gave to one Eustachius de Ludham and his heirs 30s. yearly. And King Henry III. gave the residue of the said rent, to one Algret, the Cross-bow man by his charter, and the said Algret gave that rent to the Abbot of Roche, who then held it, and paid the King 6d. yearly.

From the same source we learn that the Abbot had here twenty acres of meadow of the fee of Tickhill.

Sarah, relict of Richard de Bawtry, quitclaimed all her right in one oxgang of land here.

In 31 Henry III., the Abbot of Roche obtained a charter of confirmation of liberties and privileges in the manor of Carlton-in-Lindric, in Nottinghamshire, which was some time the King's demesne.

The monks did not hold this property long, as we find from the following charter :—

Royal Charter.

"The King to all whom, &c., greeting. Inasmuch as we have learnt by an inquisition which we have caused to be made by Hugo de Rodmerchewyet, in the county of Notts., that it is not to the

---

* Rolls House. Miscellaneous, No. 24.

injury or prejudice of ourſelf or others if we grant to our beloved in Chriſt, the Abbot and Convent of Roche, power for them to give and grant ten librates* of land and rents with the appurtenances in Carlton-in-Lindrik, which the ſaid Abbot and Convent hold of us by the ſervice of a pair of gilt ſpurs or ſixpence per annum for all ſervice, to our beloved and faithful Richard de Furneys to have and to hold to the ſaid Richard and his heirs of us and our heirs by the ſervice aforeſaid for ever, we wiſhing to do the ſaid Abbot and Convent a ſpecial favour in this behalf have given licenſe as far as in us lies for them to be able to give and grant the aforeſaid ten librates of land and rents with the appurtenances to the ſaid Richard, to have and to hold to him and his heirs of us and our heirs as aforeſaid, and to the ſame Richard we in like manner grant as a ſpecial favour by theſe preſents power to receive the ſaid ten librates of land and rents from the aforeſaid Abbot and Convent, being unwilling that the ſaid Abbot and Convent or their ſucceſſors by reaſon of the donation and grant of the ſaid ten librates of land and rent, or the aforeſaid Richard or his heirs by reaſon of the reception of the ſame ſhould by us or any of our heirs whatever be diſturbed, moleſted, or in any way aggrieved. Teſted at Canterbury the firſt day of October, 1295."[b]

Carr.—At the diſſolution the yearly rents of Slade Hooton and Carr were valued at £9 8s. 1d.

Caſtleſhaw ſee **Norþdale.**

Catwick.—William, ſon of Gilbert de Catwick gave in 1263 one eſſart of land with a toft in this place.

Chatſworth.—Adam de Edinſor gave twenty acres of land upon Stanhege, in the territory of Chatsworth in Derbyſhire, with paſture for two hundred ſheep and ſixty cattle, forty hogs and ſix ſaddle horſes, with their produce of two years of age.

Coningsborough.—Although many of the benefactors of Roche lived here, the monks never ſeem to have had large poſſeſſions in Coningſborough.

Robert, ſon of Glai, gave the land and wood of this place as far as White Well, between the road and the river. The grant was confirmed by Pope Urban in 1186: It was in their hands in 1232, but had been diſpoſed of before the diſſolution, at which time, however, they paid 2s. 6d. rent for the mill of Coningſborough.

---

[a] A librate of land is, according to Cowel, four oxgangs of fifteen acres each. Bailey ſays fifty-two acres.
[b] Pat. Rot. 23 Edw. I. M. 5.

Cudworth.—About the middle of the thirteenth century, Thomas, fon of Robert, of Eccleffield, quitclaimed to the Abbot and Convent of Roche, for ever, all right and claim that ever he had in four bovates of land with the appurtenances in Cudworth, which Henry of Selefai gave them; the Abbot for the quitclaim paying two marks of filver. The monks had no property here at the diffolution.

Cumberworth.—From the following charter we find that the monks had property here at a very early period:—

Charter of William Earl Warren.

"To all the faithful in Chrift whom this prefent charter may come, William Earl Warren, greeting in the Lord. Know that I have granted, and by this my prefent charter confirmed to God and the Bleffed Mary and the monks of the Rock, for the welfare of my soul and thofe of my anceftors, all the land of "Cumbrewode," with the meffuages and all the appurtenances which Matthew de Shepley gave and confirmed to them by his charters, to hold in perpetual alms according to the tenor of the charter of Matthew. Thefe being witneffes: William fon of William, Malveifin de Herfy, Richard de Memers, Baldwin de Herfy, Robert de Brettvile, Ralph de Eccleshale, John de Wakling, *clerk;* John Wakefield, *clerk;* Reginald Coc."[*]

The property which the monks had in this place is now called Upper Cumberworth Half.

Deepcar.—This place, with Rawmarfh, Abdy, and Haugh, was valued at the diffolution at 33*s.* 9*d.*

Denshaw see **Rochdale.**

Doncaster.—The two following charters give a diftinct account of the property of the monks in this town:—

Charter of William de Roffington.

"KNOWE YE that I, William, fon of Wulfagh, of Roffington, have granted and given, and by this my charter confirmed to God, the Bleffed Mary, and the Monks of Roche, for the welfare of my foul and that of Leuufa, my wife, my toft in Doncafter, with the appurtenances in which I abode, which I held of Ralph, fon of William Albus, near the church of St. George, to have and to

---

[*] Morehoufe's Hiftory of Kirkburton.

hold for ever, freely and quietly. Paying thrice yearly to the said Ralph, son of William Albus, and his heirs, two shillings for all service and demand, at the four stated terms (of the year) in Doncaster. Moreover, I have granted and given to the said monks that land which I held of Walter, son of Leon, to have and to hold for ever, freely and quietly, paying thrice yearly to the said Walter or his assigns four-pence for all service and demand, at the four statute terms in Doncaster. Moreover, I have granted and given to the said monks four-pence in my lifetime, yearly, to be paid at the four statute terms in Doncaster. Witnesses: Jeremiah de Rossington, William, his brother, Hugh de Langethwait, Peter de Waddeworth, Reginald, the bailiff, Henry de Marsh, John, son of Eudo de Bruntot."

Charter of Amabill de Brampton.

"KNOW &c., that I, Amabill, daughter of Robert de Brampton, formerly wife of Roger, son of William Strie, in my widowhood and free power have granted and quitclaimed of me and my heirs for ever to Michael de Brampton, my brother, and his heirs, to give and assign to whomsoever and at whatever time he may please, all the right and claim which I had or might have had under the name of dowry, or in any manner or occasion, in all that land with the buildings and the appurtenances in the town of Doncaster, which William de Warmsworth, chaplain, conferred upon the Abbot and Convent of Roche, to wit, that which lies between the land which Gena de Castello held, and the lane which extends from Francis street towards the Church of St. George, in length and breadth, as William Albus, my grandfather, held it, without any reservation. In such manner, to wit, as that neither I nor any of my heirs shall be able henceforth to place or require any right, or claim, or challenge in the said land, nor in the buildings, nor in the appurtenances; and that this my grant and quitclaim may remain ratified and firm, I have confirmed this present charter with my seal. Witnesses: Peter de Waddeworth, Reginald de Ketelbergh, Peter de Rosington, Richard, son of Hugh, Adam de Scawsby, John Bruntat, (?) Robert, his brother, Reginald, the tailor, Reginald, son of Reginald, and others."[a]

The Abbot of Roche had property here at the dissolution, at which time they paid elevenpence three farthings rent to the provost of the Lord the King of Coningsborough, issuing from the land in Doncaster with its members.

[a] For these charters I am indebted to Dr. Sykes, of Doncaster, who possesses the originals.

William de Warmsworth, chaplain of this place, also gave the monks a piece of land with certain buildings here.

Dunscroft.—The Abbot of Roche erected a grange here for the management of his possessions at Hatfield, from which place it is about half a mile distant.

The "*Monasticon Anglicanum*" gives Dunscroft as a Cell to Roche Abbey, and refers to a seal published by Edward Rowe Mores, Esq., as the seal of the Cell.

Mr. Hunter says, the legend of this seal is not Dunscroft, and that no Cell ever existed here.[a]

Pope Alexander IV. granted permission in 1263, to the Abbot of Roche, to celebrate sacred offices in his granges, &c.; but there seems no reason to believe that Dunscroft grange ever held a higher position than any other of the abbey granges.[b]

Eilrichthorpe.—This place, which adjoined the abbey grounds, was given to the monks soon after the foundation, by Richard de Busli, the son of the Founder.[c]

Ewes.—Walter, son of John de Wolvethwait, gave all his land here. This place is called Ehus by *Dr. Burton*. From a charter before me, it appears that the property of the monks at Ewes, called Holtheng, was given at the dissolution to Robert Thornhill, of Walkeringham, and Hugo his brother, who in 1547 granted it to John Sanderson.

Ennuse.—In 1248, the Abbot of Roche gave the King Henry III. five marks for having seizen of the mill of Ernuse in the county of Nottingham.[d]

Farworth see **Harworth**.

---

[a] South Yorkshire, vol. i. page 187.

Through the kindness of Dr. Hunter I have learnt that the opinion of the venerable historian of South Yorkshire respecting this question remained unaltered. In answer to my inquiries he wrote:—"I had been long suspicious that there was some mistake about Dunscroft, when I met with Rowe Mores' engraving of the seal. The legend is imperfect, but there is enough to shew that the name of the place is not Dunscroft, to which he erroneously, as I believe, ascribed it.

If there had been really any Cell there, I must have met with something more decisive than the report of the Antiquarian of the time of Torr,—some deed or document of the time when it was in existence, or at least, some mention of it in such Surveys as the "Valor" of King Henry VIII.

I have seen nothing to distrust the opinion expressed in the S. Y. that it was the grange at which resided the person who attended to the interest of the monastery at Armthorpe, and in the Level, a superior one, as the officer was probably a person of a superior class to the ordinary grangiarii.

I should not have expressed myself so strongly had I had the least doubt about the misreading of the legend on the seal."—M.S. letter, April 13th, 1860.

[b] See page 31. [c] See page 9.

[d] I can find no place of this name. My information is derived from the "Abbreviatio Rotulorum Originalium."

Firbeck.—Walter, son and heir of John de Wolvethwaite, gave an annuity of sixpence out of a toft in this place. The monks had property here at the dissolution.

Fishlake.—William, Earl of Warren, gave the tithe of the eels caught in his fisheries at this place.[a]

Flixburgh.—William, son of Henry de Arcy gave the monks a sufficient carriage road between North and South Stather, near the bank of the Trent, in Lincolnshire, with a convenient place at which to load and unload ships or vessels in this place.

In the survey of the lands of Roche after the dissolution, the meadow in Flixburgh is valued at 10s. per annum.

Gildingwells.—In this place which is situated in the parish of Laughton, the monks possessed something at the dissolution.

Goderic-Riding.—This property lay between Wadworth and Wellingly, and was the gift of John de Chaworth. It is described by *Dr. Burton* as "all his demesne in this part." William Chaworth, mentioned in the following charter, was one of the lords of Wadworth in 1236.

Charter of William de Chaworth.

"To all the sons of Holy Mother Church present and future, William de Chaworth greeting. Know all of you that I have given, granted, and by this my charter confirmed to God and St. Mary and the Monks of Roche, for the welfare of my soul and that of my father and mother, and for the welfare of the soul of John my brother, and my heirs and all my relations, all that part which I had in my domain in 'Godrikeriding.' To wit, the land at West, which the aforesaid John gave to them, and I in like manner have given to the said monks all the brush which lies between the land of Eudo (de Wadworth) and the brook which runs toward the grange of Wellingly in pure and perpetual alms, free and quit from all service and from all which belongs to the land. And I and my heirs will warrant to the aforesaid monks the aforenamed land and brush, and quit it against all men. Witnesses: Ralph, priest of Wadworth, Henry de Chaworth, Robert, son of Payn, Robert, son of Gebod, William, son of Eudo, Godfrey de Wadworth, Robert, son of William."[b]

---
[a] See page 28.
[b] Dodsworth's M.S., vol. VIII. fol. 319 B.

Harworth.—The monks had property in this place as early as the end of the twelfth century. It is situated in the North-west corner of Nottinghamshire, about two miles East of Tickhill. Its old name was Farwath.

Gamellus de Harworth gave one oxgang of land here which he held of the fee of Robert, son of Ralph de Styrrup.

Robert de Styrrup gave one toft at the west end of the town of Harworth, with one acre of land near it, and pasture for a hundred and twenty sheep.

This property had gone out of the hands of the monks before the dissolution

Hatfield.—William, Earl of Warren, gave the tithe of his eels here after the monks of Lewis had taken their tithe.[a]

John, Earl of Warren, " Beholding the scarcity of fruits, rents, and possessions generally pertaining to the religious men, the Abbot and Convent of Roche, in the diocese of York, and to their monastery, *and admiring the magnificence of the stone work as well in the buildings of the said Abbot and Convent as in their monastery;*[b] also, nobly grieving for the paucity of monks serving God there, gave for the support of thirteen additional monks the advowson of the Church of Hatfield, then valued at seventy marks per annum." In 1345, King Edward III granted licence to the Earl to effect this gift.

Royal Charter.

" The King to all whom, &c , greeting. Know that inasmuch as our beloved cousin and liege, John de Warenn, Earl of Surrey, holds the manor of Haytfield with the appurtenances for his whole life, by the gift and grant of Lord Edward, lately King of England, our father, in such a manner that after the death of the said earl the said manor with the appurtenances, with remainder to Matilda de Feyrford for the term of her life, and after the death of the said Matilda, to John de Warenn, son of the said Matilda, and the heirs male of his body issuing, and after the discease of the said John, if he die without heir male of his body issuing, to Thomas, brother of the said John and the heirs male of his body issuing, and after the discease of the said Thomas, if he die without heir male of his body issuing, to the heirs of the body of the said earl issuing, and if the said earl die without heir of his body issuing, then the said manor,

---
[a] See page 28
[b] This sentence in italics has been omitted in the charter which is printed at page 51

with the appurtenances, to revert entirely to our said father and his heirs, as in the letters patent of our said father, thereupon executed more fully is contained; and now the said earl has besought us that (inasmuch as the said Matilda is dead, and the aforesaid John, son of Matilda, and Thomas have taken the habit of religion in the order of the brothers of the Hospital of John of Jerusalem, in England, at Clerkenwell, and in the said order are professed,) we will grant to the said earl power to give and grant the advowson belonging to the Church of Haytfeld, which he holds from us in chief, as it is said, which said church is worth seventy marks per annum, to our beloved in Christ the Abbot and Convent of Roche, to possess to them and their successors for the whole life of the said earl, we yielding graciously to the request of the said earl, have granted and given licence for us and our heirs, as far as in us lies, to the said earl that he may give and grant to the Abbot and Convent to have and to hold to themselves and successors from us and our heirs for the term of the life of the said earl, and to the said Abbot and Convent by the tenor of these presents we, in like manner, have given special licence to receive the said advowson from the said earl, and to hold to them and their successors in form aforesaid, the statute enacted about not placing land and tenements in mortmain notwithstanding. We will, moreover, and of our more abundant grace, grant for us and our heirs to the said Abbot and Convent that they may have and hold the said advowson (which ought from the causes aforesaid to revert to us and our heirs after the death of the said earl) to them and their successors from us and our heirs in pure and perpetual alms for ever, and that they may have power to appropriate the said church after the said gift and grant of the advowson aforesaid by the said earl to them made, when they see expedient, and may hold it thus appropriated to their own uses to them and their successors for finding thirteen monks chaplains to celebrate for ever divine offices in the Abbey of Roche for us, Philippa Queen of England, our Consort, and our dearest children, and for the said earl, also for the soul of William our son, who *nuper humanitus contigit* in the said manor, and for the souls of our progenitors and those of the said earl and all the faithful defunct: the statute aforesaid or any right which might belong to us after the death of the said earl, if he die without heir from his body issuing, or by reason of the profession of the said John, son of Matilda, and Thomas in the aforesaid order while they are living, or after their death, without heirs male of their bodies, notwithstanding; wishing that neither the said earl nor the said Abbot and Convent, nor the successors of the said

Abbot and Convent, by reason of the premises or statute aforesaid, or because the said advowson ought to revert to us and our heirs (as parcel of the manor aforesaid which is held of us in chief, as is said) together with the said manor after the death of the said earl in form aforesaid, or from any other causes whatever, be by us or our heirs, justices, escheators, sheriffs, or other our bailiffs, or servants whatever, hindered, molested, or in any way aggrieved. Witness, the King at Westminster, November 22nd, 1345."

The appropriation was effected by William la Zouch, Archbishop of York, he reserving certain rights.[a]

In 1348, three years after they had obtained this important gift, the Abbot and Convent of Roche, parsons of the Church of Hatfield, set forth in petition to parliament that they ought to have each year an oak in the park or woods of Hatfield; and instead of tithe of herbage, sixty large beasts running in the park or wood throughout the year. And also instead of tithe of pannage, to have all their pigs which are fed in the parsonage, running in the same woods without paying anything for pannage; and further for the tithe of the fishery of Brathmere and Neuflet, a bynde[b] of eels every year to be taken as the right of the Church of Hatfield. The Earl of Warren being dead, and the manor in the hands of Queen Philippa, they prayed that certain impediments might be removed. They were referred to the chancellor, who was to call all parties together and to do justice amongst them.

In 1355, on the day of Pentecost, an indenture was made between the Abbot and Convent of Roche, on the one part, and Thomas Rillington, John Fitz Peter, Thomas Margens, Alan del Cotes, John, his brother, John del Parkes, John Fitz Peter de Stainford, parishioners of the Church of Hatfield, on the other part, that the said Abbot of Roche, having the Church of Hatfield appropriated, granted and permitted that the said parishioners, and other the inhabitants of the town of Stainford, might, by the archbishop's license, maintain at their own cost a chaplain to celebrate divine service in the Chapel of Stainford, newly builded, for the space of three years daily, excepting on Sundays and other great festivals, whereon they were to repair to the parish church of Hatfield. This agreement was confirmed by the archbishop's vicar-general on the 17th November, 1535.

[a] See page 52.
[b] A Bind of Eels according to KENNETT, consisted of two hundred and fifty.

In 1535, the profits of the rectory received by the Abbot were as follows:—

	£	s.	d.
Mansion there (the Vicarage)	0	8	8
Glebe	1	13	4
Close and Pasture	0	5	0
Tithe of herbage of the park with pasture for 24 beasts	0	18	0
Tithe of pannage of hogs there	0	1	0
Tithe of wood, viz., one fuel tree to be delivered by the bailiff	0	1	0
Tithe of grain at Hatfield	8	0	0
Tithe of grain at Thorne	7	0	0
Tithe of grain at Stainford	5	0	0
Tithe of hay	1	10	0
Wool and lamb	2	0	0
Oblations	2	0	0
Minute and privy tithes	12	0	0
Mortuaries	0	6	8
Tithe of eels of Bràthmere	0	11	0
	£41	14	8

REPRISALS.

	£	s.	d.			
To the Vicar	15	0	0			
To the Archbishop	7	10	4			
To the King's bailiff	0	7	9			
				22	18	1
Clear yearly value				£18	16	7

At the dissolution the interest which the monks had in this place again reverted to the crown.

Haugh.—The monks had property at Haugh, near Rawmarsh, at the dissolution.

Hellaby.—Mauger, son of Roger de Stokes, confirmed the grant of six oxgangs of land here made by Geffery Fitz Payne, of Newerth. The property here and at Bramley was valued at the dissolution at £9 18s. 8d.

Hesley.—This place is situated near Roffington, in the county of Nottingham. The monks owned property here at the dissolution.

𝕳𝖊𝖘𝖙𝖜𝖊𝖑𝖑.—The monks had property here, the gift of William the Fleming, which was confirmed by Pope Urban III. in 1186.*

𝕳𝖎𝖑𝖑𝖇𝖗𝖎𝖌𝖙𝖍𝖔𝖗𝖕𝖊 see 𝕽𝖔𝖈𝖍𝖉𝖆𝖑𝖊.

𝕳𝖔𝖑𝖒𝖊.—Peter de Roffington gave the monks a wood here, now called "Holmes Carr Wood."

𝕳𝖔𝖑𝖒𝖊 see 𝕮𝖍𝖚𝖗𝖚𝖘𝖈𝖔𝖊.

𝕳𝖔𝖔𝖙𝖔𝖓-𝕷𝖊𝖛𝖊𝖙.—In 1249, Manfelyn, of Doncafter, Manfelyn, of Brodfworth, and Elias, fon-in-law of the faid Manfelyn, releafed to the Abbot and Convent of Roche all lands, rents, and tenements which they had of Hamond de Levet, in the territory of Hooton-Levet, from the beginning of the world to the world's end. For better fecurity they had put to *their Hebrew letter* with their feal. This feems to have been an interference on the part of the monaftery between Hamond de Levet and the Jew money lenders, fimilar to that mentioned in page 13.

Hamond, fon of William Levet, gave one oxgang of land, with a toft and croft in this place.

Richard, fon of William Levet, gave half of the mill here, with the pool and free water courfe from Maltby mill to the Monk's mill, with the fuit of the faid moiety, referving a right to himfelf, his heirs and affigns, to grind all their corn that fhall grow upon four oxgangs in this territory, at a multure of the fixteenth bowl.

Jordan, fon of Jordan de Infula, and Elizabeth his wife, gave all their land at Hooton-Levet.

Adam, fon of Simon de la Roche, and Joan his wife, daughter of Robert de Wickerfly, gave one oxgang of land here, with a toft and croft, which gift Sir Robert de Wickerfley, knight, confirmed.

Henry de Lacy granted and confirmed the donation which Richard de Wickerfley, and Roger and Jordan Hooton, made to the monks of Roche of common pafture of all the territory of Hooton.

The property here was valued at the diffolution at £4 19s. 2d. per annum.

𝕳𝖔𝖔𝖙𝖔𝖓-𝕽𝖔𝖇𝖊𝖗𝖙𝖘.—The monks had a farm at this place which was valued at the diffolution at 1s. per annum. *(See Slade Hooton.)*

𝕳𝖔𝖕𝖊.—*(Derbyfhire.)*—The monks poffeffed fomething here at the diffolution.

* See page 16.

Ichells.—It is not known from whom the monks derived this property. It is described in 1552 as "a close called Ichells, lying near the dyke leading from Haugh to Wentworth on the east, in the tenure of Thomas Wentworthe, Esq., at the will of the Lord the King from year to year, paying at the terms of St. Martin in winter and Pentecost equally nine shillings per annum." It was at this time granted to Admiral Lord Clinton.[a]

Ickles.—The Monks had two mills in Ickles, near Rotherham. *(See Templeborough.)*

Ingbirchworth.—From the following interesting charter we find that the monks had property here at an early date:—

Charter of Henry de Shelley.

"Know all men, present and future, that I, Henry de Shelley, son of Robert, have given, granted, and by this my charter confirmed for the welfare of my soul and of all my ancestors and heirs, to the Abbot and Monks of St. Mary of Roche, the homage and service of John, son of Robert del Ker (Car) which he owed to me and to my heirs or assigns for two bovates of land with the appurtenances in Bircheworth, and the homage and service of John, son of Adam, which he owed to me and my heirs and assigns for one bovate of land with the appurtenances in the same vill, and two bovates of land with the appurtenances which Richard and Joan held of me in the same vill, and the said Richard and Joan with all their progeny, and the said Robert and Adam with all their progeny, and one bovate of land with the appurtenances which Gilbert, the chaplain, held of me in the same vill, which is called Wetelay, to have and to hold in perpetual alms, free and quiet from all service to me and to my heirs belonging, save foreign service, as far as pertains to one carucate of land, nine carucates of which make one knight's fee. And I and my heirs will warrant all the aforesaid land with the appurtenances to the aforesaid Abbot and Monks of Roche for ever against all men. These being witnesses: Dom. Henry, parson of Rothell; Hugh de Urnethorp, then steward of Pontefract; Robert de Stapleton, Henry Walent, Robert, son of Adam; Thomas de Littel, Alan, son of Robert de Smeaton; Robert, son of Gilbert; Simon, son of * * * Alan, son of Alan."[b]

Innseby.—Simon Fitz Simon, gave land in this place, which Pope Urban III. confirmed.

---
[a] Particulars for grants 6 Ed. VI. sect. 6.   [b] Morehouse's History of Kirkburton.

Kilnhurst.—In 1385, the Abbot and Convent of Roche granted in fee to John Montforth, of Kilnhurst, one messuage, four acres of meadow and six acres of land in the town and territory of Kilnhurst, four acres of which lie near the wood of Rawmarsh, on the east side, stretching north and south; one acre abutting on Walkerfall, and one acre abutting on the town of Kilnhurst, all which they had of the gift of Roger de Kilnhurst: and that * * * which extends itself to the north field of his toft aforesaid. Also one half acre of meadow which they had of the gift of Thomas de Kilnhurst, reserving therefrom thirteen shillings and four pence rent, and a double payment from every tenant at his first entry, which if not paid within forty days, should give the Abbot the right to re-enter and seize upon the tenements again.

The earliest common seal of the Abbey is appended to the deed from which the above information is obtained. See plate x., fig. 3.

The profits of this place together with those of Ickles and Hooton-Roberts, were at the dissolution £1 7s. 8d.

Kiveton.—No remains of "the Chapel of the Holy Trinity of Kyveton," mentioned in the following charter, are now to be found.

Royal Charter.

"The King, to all to whom, &c., greeting. Know that, inasmuch as Lord Edward, lately King of England, our grandfather, by his letters patent granted and gave licence for himself and his heirs to John de Kyveton, parson of the Church of Radeclyf-on-Trent, to give and assign one messuage, thirty-six acres of land, three acres of meadow, and twenty-four shillings worth of rent, with the appurtenances in Blithe and Torworth, to the Abbot and Convent of Roche, to have and to hold to them and their successors for finding a certain secular chaplain to celebrate divine offices for the soul of the said John and the souls of his father, mother, and his ancestors and all the faithful departed, in the Chapel of the Holy Trinity of Kyveton every day, and also the same our grandfather granted and gave licence for himself and his heirs to the aforesaid Abbot and Convent to give and grant to the aforesaid John for the tenements aforesaid a certain corrody, to be received from the said Abbey to him and his heirs for the sustenance of the said chaplain and his successors for ever, and to the said John having received the said corrody and being seized thereof, to give and assign the said corrody to the said chaplain to have for himself and his successors who were to celebrate in the said chapel as aforesaid for their sustenance for ever, as in the letters patent of our grandfather aforesaid, thereupon made more fully is contained; and the aforesaid John did afterwards also give and assign, according to the force and effect of the licenfe of the King aforesaid, as we have learnt, to the aforesaid Abbot and Convent and their successors, the said messuage, land, meadow, and rent, with the appurtenances, and to the aforesaid chaplain and his successors the corrody which he obtained by the gift and grant of the aforesaid Abbot and Convent and their successors. We now, at the request both of our beloved in Christ the present Abbot and Convent of Roche, who hold the messuage, land, meadow, and rent aforesaid, and of the present chaplain of the chapel aforesaid, who receives the said corrody from the Abbey aforesaid, and for two marks which the said Abbot and Convent have paid to us, have granted and given licenfe for us and our heirs, as far as in us lies, to the said Abbot and Convent to give and assign the messuage, land, meadow, and rent aforesaid with the appurtenances to the said present chaplain, to have and to hold for himself and his successors in exchange for the corrody aforesaid being given, assigned, surrendered, and released for ever to the said Abbot and Convent and their successors by the said chaplain, and to the same chaplain both to receive the said messuages, land, meadow, and rent with the appurtenances to hold to himself and his successors for ever from the said Abbot and Convent, and to give, assign, surrender, and release the said corrody to the said Abbot and Convent and their successors in exchange aforesaid for ever; by the tenour of these presents we have in like manner given special licenfe, the statute passed about not putting lands and tenements into mortmain notwithstanding, willing that neither the said Abbot and Convent or their successors, nor the said chaplain or his successors, by reason of the statute aforesaid, therein be hindered or in any way aggrieved by us or our heirs or servants, save however the services due and accustomed from the said messuage, land, meadow, and rent. Witness, the King, at Westminster, July 8th, 1401."

Lambcote Grange.—This place is situated in the parish of Stainton. Its original name was Lambcroft, as it is so written in the *Confirmation of Pope Urban III.* in 1186, from which document we also learn that it was given the monks by Richard de Busli and Hugh de Drigwrt.

In 1563 "Lamcottes," which had formerly been in the tenure of Robert and Agnes Hewet, was let by indenture under the common seal of the late monastery of Roche to John Wilkynson, at 60s. per annum at the terms of St. Martin in the Winter and Pentecost equally. It was at this time granted by the crown to Charles Jackson.[a]

Laughton.—Nicholas, the Clerk of this place, gave a toft lying on the south side of St. John's Church, with six acres of land, now called Throapham, and which the monks held at the dissolution.

In the time of Abbot Osmund, Cardinal Stephen gave the monks the prebend of Laughton.

From the "*Hundred Rolls*" we learn that the Abbot of Roche held thirty bovates of land in the barony of Laughton in 1276.

In 1558 the possessions in this place, lately belonging to the monastery of Roche, were on the 20th of October rated to Thomas Stephenson.

Lincoln.—In 1275 the Abbot of Roche held a mansion in this city, which was then valued at 10s. per annum. At the dissolution its annual value was only 4s.

Lindrick.—King Henry II. gave one hundred acres in Lindrick near the abbey, now called King's Wood. Many have thought from the name Lindrick that this property must have been in Nottinghamshire, but erroneously, for Lindrick, near Tickhill, and Lindrick Common, Lindrick Dale, and Lindrick Brook, near South Anston, are all in Yorkshire.

Alice, Countess of Eu, confirmed to the monks the wood of Lindrick in 1219.[b]

At the dissolution the annual falls of wood and underwood were valued *communibus annis* at 40s.

Loversall.—Reginald Gurvy quitclaimed to the monks the mill in this place.

About the middle of the thirteenth century the monks of Roche gave what they had here, at Wadworth and at Alverley, to Robert de Ripariis, in exchange for his lands at Slade Hooton, two pieces of meadow in Walkeringham, and £100 in money.

Lumby.—The monks had land, &c., in this place, which they demised to Richard Burton, Esq., and Catherine his wife, on the 20th of October, 20 Henry VI. (1441.)

Maltby.—Besides what Richard de Busli (one of the founders) gave,[c] Alan, the parson of Maltby, gave his right of common in two

---
[a] Particulars for grants.
[b] See page 17.   [c] See page 4.

acres of land lying in Summer-road, in this territory. The ruins of the Abbey stand upon the southern border of this parish. *(See Roche.)*

Marr.—Jordan, son of Philip de Marr, gave all his wood in this place with four tofts, two oxgangs of land and the fourth part of an oxgang in this town and fields. By a charter dated at Woodhall, on the vigil of St. Nicholas, 1253, Thomas Fitz William confirmed to the monks all lands in Marr, of his fee, which they had of the gift of Jordan, son of Philip de Marr, and his ancestors.

John, son of Jordan de Marr, gave to the monks of Roche nine acres of land here with their capital messuage in the town, and homage and service of free men, rendering ten shillings annually and scutage. This was also confirmed by Thomas Fitz William in a charter dated at Sprotborough, Nonas Martii, 1260.

Richard, son of Hugh de Langethwaite, gave an annuity of six shillings out of a toft, and twelve acres of land in this place.

In "*Kirby's Inquest*" the Abbot of Roche is said to have held eleven bovates of the fee of Thomas Fitz William, who held the Castle of Tickhill.

The possessions at Marr and Bilham were valued at the dissolution at £8 18s. 6d.

Marr Grange was granted in 1544 to John Bere.

Micklebring.—Eugenia, relict of Gilbert de Micklebring, with the consent of Peter de Rhodes, his lord, gave four acres in this place.

Monk Bretton.—In 1285 the Abbot and Convent of Roche sold their claim to the manor and advowson of the Church of Monk Bretton to the Prior and Convent of this place for 20s. sterling.

Monyash.—John, son of Matthew de Eston, *for the support of a light at the high altar,* gave the multure[a] of twelve oxgangs of land in Monyash, Derbyshire, the tenants of which were to grind at the mills of the Monk's Grange, at Oneash, paying the twentieth bowl.

Morley.—This place is situated near Greasborough. William Bacon with his corpse gave nine acres of land here. The Prior of Nostel held four bovates of land in Morley.

[a] The toll or fee which a miller takes for grinding corn.

Charter of Abbot Walter.

"Know, &c., that we, Walter Abbot and the Convent of Roche, have granted and by our present charter have confirmed to Lord Thomas de Bellew and his heirs or assigns all the service which Robert Barker, of Swinton, and his heirs have been accustomed to do for us for the land of Morley, with all things that can accrue to us from the said land for ever, at an annual rent therefrom to us and our successors of sixteen pence at Pentecost, and to the House of St. Oswald in our name eight pence at the feast of St. Martin in the Winter for the said land of Morley. And we and our successors will warrant to the said Thomas and his heirs or assigns all the aforesaid service with all its appurtenances, so long as our donors shall have warranted it to us. Witness, the Lords Ralph de Horbiry, Ralph de Normanville, John de Staynton, knights; Ralph Haket, Robert Brinton, Roger de Bergh, James de Lyvet, Richard his brother, Raynder de Swinton, William de Roche, William de Swinton."

Newhall.—On November 28th, 1552, the farm of one close lying in Newhall, containing six acres of pasture, in the occupation of Joane Cousen, widow, by indenture, as it is said, for a term of years, yielding therefrom at the feasts of Pentecost and St. Martin in the Winter equally per annum 13s. 4d., and lately in the possession of the monasteries of Roche, was granted for divers considerations to the Right Honourable Lord Clinton, High Admiral of England.[a]

Newland.—This bill made the 20th of September in the 37th year of Henry VIII. witnesseth that we John Bellewe, Esq., and John Bloxolme, gent., have paid to Sir John Williams, knight, treasurer of the Augmentation of the Revenues of the King's Crown, the sum of * * * due to the King for the gift, grant, and clear purchase of "one mansion or tenemente in the parishe of St. Stephen in Newlánd, late parcell of Roche, togither with all and singular the woodes and underwode growinge in and upon the premises."[b]

Newsome.—Robert de Scalcebi, Adam de Newmarch, and Roger de Marr gave the monks the grange at this place. The two first of these were witnesses to the Foundation Charter of the Abbey.

Nottingham.—Philip de Oldcotes gave the monks a toft in this town and the service of another toft.

---

[a] Particulars for Grants. Sect. 8.   [b] Monasticon Ang. Appendix, p. 1643.

Oldcotes.—This place is situated in Nottinghamshire, about two miles from the Abbey. The monks had property here in the time of King Richard I.

Oneash.—*(Derbyshire.)*—The grange at this place was given to the monks soon after the foundation of the Abbey by William Avenal, Lord of Haddon. .

Richard de Vernun, with the consent of Avice, his wife, and of William his son and heir, confirmed all the land and pasture of his fee in this place, which William Avenal gave; and William Bassett, grandson of William Avenal, confirmed the same.

Richard, son of William de Verum, confirmed the above, and also what the monks had in Sterndale, with the minerals, they paying to him and his heirs 15*s*. per annum, at his manor of Haddon. He also confirmed the tenement here which William Avenal gave. Pope Urban III. also confirmed what the monks held here.

William, Earl of Ferrars, with the consent of Agnes his wife, before 1229 confirmed to the monks that way for their sheep and cattle going from their grange here, over the moor of Hartington and Heathcote, which William his father had granted to them, with some meadow; they paying to him one mark per annum.

We learn from the Taxation of Pope Nicholas, about 1291, that the possessions of the monks here, consisting of four bovates of land, a mill, mines, &c., were valued at £8 8*s*. 8*d*. per annum.

We learn from the following document that at the time of the dissolution this grange was let to Thomas Sheldon.

"In the 32nd year of the reign of the most excellent Prince Henry VIII. the farm of the grange of Oneash, parcel of the possessions of the late monastery of Roche, freely resigned, with all lands, meadows, feedings, pastures, moors, &c., from old time belonging, is thus demised to Edw. Beresford, of the County of Derby, gent., by indenture under the common seal of the late monastery at 113*s*. 4*d*. per annum, to be paid at the terms of St. Martin and Pentecost equally, viz., for the farm of the said grange £4 6*s*. 8*d*., and for tithes thereto belonging 26*s*. 8*d*., besides 6*s*. paid to the cathedral church of Lichfield for an ancient pension for tithes of all kind of the said grange; also 30*s*. paid to the manor of Haddon always at the feast of St. Martin in the Winter yearly, until it shall be adjudged by law that half the sum ought to suffice; also 13*s*. 4*d*. for having common of pasture in the moor of Middleton. And that the said farmer at the end of the term aforesaid or whenever he shall quit it shall leave four sextaries and twenty-four quarters of good and well cleaned oats behind him for the use of the aforesaid lord the King and his successors. Now on the same terms in the tenure of Thomas Sheldon.[a]

Oustrop.—William, son of William de Bladsworth, confirmed all the fishery in this place.

Overste.—William, son of John de Vavasor, quitclaimed all his right in ward, escheat, &c.

Ravensfield.—The monks had property here, the gift of Simon, son of Ralph de Tickhill. At the dissolution they paid 2s. per annum to the Hostle of St. Leonard at York, from land here.

Rawmarsh.—Adam de Sancta Maria with his corpse gave the monks free common in this place with a toft in Haugh, also a toft and croft, two acres of land, and his wood lying between the road to Abdy and Fildingale, leading to the fields of Swinton, with liberty to enclose the same.

Charter of John and Hugh Brun.[b]

"Know all present and future that we, John and Hugh, sons of Adam Brun, have remised and quitclaimed to God and the Blessed Mary and the Monks of Roche for the welfare of our souls and those of all our ancestors and heirs all right and claim which we had or might have had in all the land of Etheles, some of which Adam Brun our father held of Adam de Sancta Maria in the territory of Rawmarsh, with homages, wards, reliefs, escheats, and with all other profits which can in any way accrue to us or our heirs or assigns. Also, that neither we nor any other in our name can demand hereafter any right or claim in the said land with its appurtenances. In testimony of which we have to this writing placed our seals. Witness, Robert de Wath, clerk; Hugh de Brome, Thomas de Haby, Thomas de Lindric, Adam Depeker, Hugh de Wikesop, and many others."

The property which the monks had in Rawmarsh, Deepcar, Abdy, and Haugh was valued at the dissolution at £1 13s. 9d. per annum.

Risby.—*(Lincolnshire.)*—Walter de Falcunbridge confirmed the grant of two oxgangs of land in this place made by Walter de Kadburne. The monks held this property as early as the year 1198.

---

[a] Particulars for Grants. No. 24. [b] Dodsworth's M.S, vol. VIII. fol. 80, 81.

Roche.—Some have thought that Roche Abbey derived its name from St. Roche, the Lombardy saint, others have traced its origin to the roach fish, but from the original title ("monachi de rupe") which the monks adopted, we learn without doubt the true source. It should be noticed that the monks of Roche did not use the plural as the monks of Fountains did; they simply styled themselves "Monks of the Rock." What the particular rock was has already been pointed out.[a] "De rupe" was soon changed into "De la Roche," and when the French word Roche became anglicized the monastery began to be called Roche Abbey. Had it lasted till now it would in all probability ere this have been called Rock Abbey. The actual precincts of Roche Abbey enclosed a space of thirty-one acres. It was of a triangular shape, and was surrounded by a high substantial wall, the greater part of which may still be traced in a more or less ruined condition.[b] This land was the gift of Richard de Busli and Richard Fitz Turgis.[c] It was confirmed to the monks by John de Busli[d], by Alice Countess of Eu[e], by Pope Urban III[f]., and by many of the Kings of England. Henry III. granted the monks free warren here.

In the time of Edward I. we find the Abbot of Roche summoned to answer to our Lord the King on a plea by what warrant he claimed to have free warren in all his demesne lands of Roche, Brantcliffe, Armthorpe, and Hillbrigthorpe, without the licence and will of the King and his progenitors, &c. And the Abbot appeared and said that he claimed free warren in Roche, Armthorpe, and Brantcliffe by charter of the Lord Henry the King, granted in the 35th year (1250) of his reign, which he produced and which testified that the said Lord the King granted to a certain Abbot and Convent of Roche, predecessors of that Abbot, that they and their successors for ever should have free warren in all their demesne lands of Roche, Armthorpe, and Brantcliffe, in the county of York, &c.[g]

Charter of Adam Fitz Burnell.[h]

"To all the faithful in Christ to whom the present writing may come, Adam Fitz Burnell, of Elmishall, greeting. Know all that the Abbot and Convent of Roche are quit towards me and my heirs of five marks which they owed to my father in his charter, which is in safe custody with the holy men of Hampol, and of all debts

---

[a] See page 82. [b] See Plan of the Abbey Grounds. [c] See Charters, pages 4 and 5. [d] See page 11.
[e] See page 17. [f] See page 15.
[g] Roll. 5. D. [h] Dodsworth's MS., vol. VIII. fol. 245 D.

which they ever owed to the said Burnell my father, in such sort, however, that I Adam and my heirs shall be able to demand hereafter nothing from the said Abbot and monks by reason of any debt which they at any time owed to my father. But if any one shall bring forward in the name of my father any charter to demand any debt from the said Abbot and monks, I and my heirs with all our might will faithfully aid them. Witness, Jeremia, Parson of Rossington; William and John his brothers, Hugh de Langethwaite, Thomas de Sandal, Hugh de Bilham, John de Skellew, Reginald, Presbyter de Doncaster."

(Seal, a Lion passant.)

Elmsall lies not far distant from the property which the monks held at Thurnscoe, Bilham, Skellow, Campsall, &c. It is not unlikely that the monks bought some part of one of these of the Burnell family.

Advowson.

The advowson of Roche Abbey belonged for some time alternately to the two founders Richard de Busli and Richard Fitz Turgis or de Wickersley and their successors, and the value of it appears by one of the Clifford Inquisitions, to have been £40 each vacancy.

The right of presentation held by Richard Fitz Turgis went at his death to his son Roger de Wickersley, and from him it passed to Constantia his daughter, who married William de Levet. It then continued in the Levet family until 1377, when John Levet granted it to Richard Barry by the following charter.

Charter of John Levet.

"Be it known to all men present and future that I, John Levet, son and heir of William Levet, of Hooton Levet, have given, granted, and by this my present charter confirmed to Richard Barry, citizen and merchant of London, the whole of my estate which I have or my ancestors have ever had in the foundation of the Abbey of Roche, in the county of York, together with the patronage and advowson of the same Abbey when it may have become vacant, and with the whole of my lordship which I have or which my aforesaid ancestors ever had in the aforesaid Abbey by reason of the foundation of the same or of any other title. I also give and grant to the same Richard a certain rent of two shillings and sixpence proceeding from all those lands and tenements with their appurtenances which were given by my aforesaid ancestors for the foundation of the abbey aforesaid, along with a half-penny of rent with the appurtenances proceeding from a certain *fulling mill situated in the aforesaid Abbey*, granted as parcell of the foundation of the same abbey, which said rent had been reserved, by my anceſtors aforeſaid and their heirs for ever, from the lands and tenements aforeſaid and from the mill aforeſaid with their appurtenances over and above the donation of theſe lands along with the tenements and mill aforeſaid for the foundation of the abbey aforeſaid. I alſo give and grant to the ſame Richard all other my ſervices with all temporal and ſpiritual advantages, with all profits and appurtenances which I have or in any way ought to have of the aforeſaid abbey on account of any reſervation reſpecting the foundation of the abbey aforeſaid. To have and to hold all the aforeſaid, to wit, my eſtate in the foundation aforeſaid along with the patronage and advowſon aforeſaid, and with all my lordſhip aforeſaid, and rent aforeſaid, with all other things aforenamed and all their appurtenances by the aforeſaid Richard and his heirs and aſſigns as freely, entirely, and quietly as I or any of my anceſtors ever had any eſtate in the ſame or may have had for ever. To receive the aforeſaid rents in the form aforeſaid, to wit, the aforeſaid two ſhillings and ſixpence from all the lands and tenements aforeſaid, except from the mill aforeſaid and the half-penny rent from the ſame mill at the uſual terms: and I the aforeſaid John and my heirs will warrant and for ever defend my whole eſtate in the foundation aforeſaid, together with the patronage and advowſon aforeſaid and with all my lordſhip above mentioned and payments aforeſaid with all other ſervices and temporal and ſpiritual profits above mentioned and all their appurtenances and all other things aforenamed contained in this my preſent gift to the aforeſaid Richard and his heirs and aſſigns in the form aforeſaid againſt all people. In teſtimony of which I have affixed to this my preſent charter my ſeal. Witneſſes: Lord John Fitzwilliam, William de Meleton, Thomas de Meteham, knights; Henry de Grendon, Henry de Haloghby, Robert de Merſſh, and others. Given at Hooton on the twentieth day of February in the fifty-firſt year of the reign of King Edward, the third after the conqueſt.

In 1420 there was a fine between William Garth, John Multhorpe, and Thomas Stokes, plaintiffs; and William Levet of Hooton Levet, and Elizabeth his wife, deforciants, of the advowſon of the Abbey of Roche. The right to William, John, and Thomas. Soon after this the moiety of the Fitz Turgis family ſeems to have become united with that of the De Buſli, for in 1446 we find Maud, Counteſs of Cambridge, ſtyling herſelf "founder" of Roche, and at the diſſolution only one founder is returned, Henry Clifford, Earl of Cumberland. At the diſſolution the ſite of the Abbey and the demesne lands seem to have been let to the Earl of Cumberland, in whose hands they remained until they were sold.

Of what these consisted, their value, &c., may be learnt from the following "*Particulars for Grants,*" supplied to William Ramsden and Henry Tyrrell:—

Particulars for Grants, 37 *Hen. VIII. sect.* 2. *Memb.* 53.
William Ramsden, Grantee.

Parcel of the Possessions of the late Monastery of Roche, freely resigned, in the County of York.

The rent of the site of the said late monastery together with all houses, buildings, dovecotes, fruit gardens, orchards, gardens, ponds, and other conveniences within the precinct of the said late monastery and with the demesne land to the same belonging underwritten, as they lately were in the tenure of the late Abbot and Convent of the said late monastery, in value, to wit :—

	s.	d.
The rent of the site of the said late monastery with one dovecote and seven orchards, two of which are on the eastern side with the cemetry and the waste of Girewood, containing by estimation 2 acres, 3*s.* 4*d.* Two orchards with two little ponds on the south side and two orchards on the west side, containing among them by estimation 5 roods of land, 20*d.*; and one orchard called the High Orchard, with one great pond and the waste in the same, containing by estimation 2½ acres, 4*s.* 2*d.*	15	10
For the rent of one water mill called Barkehouse Mill .	10	0
For the rent of the grange to the same site adjacent and belonging, with three small crofts containing by estimation 3 acres	5	0
Of one pasture called Hygh Hardsall, containing 60 acres of pasture there and 50 acres of arable land, with a sheepcote there	40	0
Of one close there called Grange Wood, containing by estimation 8 acres	4	0
Of one little close called the Launde, with the waste there containing by estimation 6 acres of arable land . . .	6	0
Of one meadow called Wallehouse Meadow, with the waste there containing by estimation 4 acres . . .	6	8
Of one little common called Hellegreen, with the Waste Craggs, containing by estimation 5 acres	0	20

THE POSSESSIONS.

	s.	d.
Of one clofe called Cote Croft, containing by eftimation 3 acres of arable land	0	18
Of one field called Hellewood flat, with the wafte there, containing by eftimation 26 acres of arable land . .	13	0
Of one croft on the fouth fide of the faid field, containing by eftimation half an acre of arable land	0	6
Of one clofe called Belleflette, with the wafte ground there, containing by eftimation 6 acres	2	0
Of one field called Longfield, lying *near the high crofs leading towards Blythe*, containing by eftimation 30 acres	15	0
Of one field called Milnefield, abutting on the New Milne Dam, containing by eftimation 20 acres of arable land	13	4
Of three little crofts of meadow called Barkhoufe Meadow, abutting towards a certain houfe called the Stone, containing by eftimation 2 acres	3	4
Of a certain pafture called Oxclofe, next the Milnefield aforefaid, containing by eftimation 7 acres of pafture	2	4
Of one common called Barkehoufe Green, with the wafte ground there, by eftimation 2 acres	0	8
Of one meadow lying within the vill of Sandbeck, with the wafte, containing by eftimation 10 acres . . .	16	8
Of one little carr of wafte ground called Stirrope Car, containing by eftimation 20 acres	10	0
Of one meadow called Dooles Meadow, near the White Water next Blythe, containing by eftimation 10 acres	5	0

The whole thus demifed to Lord Hy. Clifford, Earl of Cumberland, by indenture under feal of the Court of Augmentation of the Crown, revenue of the faid lord King, as is faid, but as yet not fhewn, to be paid at the feaft of the Annunciation of St. Mary the Virgin and St. Michael the Archangel equally per annum.

No reprifals.

Upon the edge of this parchment, which is very much decayed with damp, is the following :—

£8 12s. 5d. tithe, 17s. 3d. clear. In £7 15s. 3d. at 20 years' purchafe, £155 5s. Wood, £46 17s. Total, £202 2s.—In hand, £68 15s. 4d.; at Eafter next 100 marks, at Chriftmas next 100 marks.

Memorandum. That the fame is a thing of itfelf and no parcel of any other manor, farm, or grange to the faid late Monaftery appertaining. Item. What fine or fines hath been at any time given for the fame I do not know. Item. As concerning any fpiritual promotions to the fame appertaining I know none. Item. The fame is diftant from any of the King's Majefties' manors, forefts, parks, or chaces referved for his Highnefs by a keeper, v or vi miles as I am informed. Item. I have made former particulars of the fame to the above named Lord Henry the Earl of Cumberland, by virtue of Mr. Moyle's warrant, and I know none other but the bringer defirous to purchafe the fame.'

Examined by Hugh Fuller, Auditor.

Particulars for Grants, 37 Hen. VIII. sect. 2. Memb. 54., for Henry Tyrrell, gent., Feb. 20.

The yerely value of the fcite and demeanes of the faid late Monafterie of Roche, in the countie of Yorke, is viii^{li} xii^s vi^d, whereof deducted for the tenthe xvii^s iii^d, and fo remayneth clere vii^{li} xv^s iii^d, whiche rated at xx yeres purchas amounteth to the fome of clv^{li} v^s.; adde therunto for the woddes xlvi^{li} xvii^s and fo the hole fome is ccii^{li} ii^s, whereof in hand lxviii^{li} xv^s iiii^d, at Eafter nexte lxvi^{li} xiii^s iiii^d, and at Chriftmas then nexte lxvi^{li} xiii^s iiii^d.

The King's Majeftie is pleafed and contente to difcharge the premifes of all incumbrances except leaffes and the xth before, and except fuch charges as the fermors are bound to beare and paie by force of their indentures.

M^d. to excepte and referve all the leade, belles, and belle mettall being in and upon the premifes, togither withe all fuche fuperfluous buyldinges, tymbre, ftone, iron, glaffe, and other thinges as ben excepted oute of the fermor's leaffe.

Irr. per Wm. Burnell.   Edw. North.

Countye of Yorke.

The fcyte and demeans of the late monaftery of Roche in the feyd countye, withe one mylne called Bakehoufe Mylne, in the fame countye, parcell of the poffeffions of the feyd late monaftery.

Norwood conteyneth xx acres	
Helwood Copp. conteyneth iv acres	
Backhoufe Copp. otherwife called	lx acres.
Fryth Copp. conteyneth xvi acres	
Hylclyff Copp. conteyneth xx acres	

Whereof xvi acres of viii, x, and xii yeres growthe refervid to Sr. Henrye Clyfford, Knight, Erle of Cumbrelande, for his fyre boote and hedgeboote.

---

[a] As thefe particulars are partly in Latin and partly in contracted Englifh they have been modernized.

THE POSSESSIONS.

	s.	d.	£	s.
One acre of one yeres growthe	0	6		
One acre of ii yeres growthe	0	12		
One acre of iii yeres growthe	0	18		
One acre of iiii yeres growthe	2	0		
One acre of v yeres growthe	2	6		
x acres of vii yeres growthe	35	0		
x acres of ix yeres growthe	45	0		
vii acres of xi yeres growthe	38	6		
vi acres of xiii yeres growthe	39	0		
vi acres refydue of xiiii yeres growthe	42	0		
The wood every acre aforefeyd, valued as apperyth, wych ys in the holle			10	7
The fprynge of the wood or ground of xvi acres aforefeyd, not valuyed bycaufe they be refervid, and of xliiii acres refydue, rated yerely at vi^d the acre, wych ys yerely in the holle xxii^s, and amounteth after xx yeres purchafe to			22	0
In the feyd woodes about the fcytuation of the feyd late monaftery, and in the feyd demeans be growinge dccc okes and afhes of lx and lxxx yeres growthe, parte tymbre and parte ufually cropped and fhred, wherof ccclx refervid for tymbre to repayre the houfes ftanding upon the fcyte of the feyd late monaftery, and for ploughboote, cartboote, and ftakes for hedgeboote for the feyd fermor cxl valued at xii^d the tree, and ccc refydue at vi^d the tree, which ys in the holle			14	10
Ex^r. per me David Clayton.	Total		£46	17

The fite and demefne lands of Roche were firft granted to William Ramfden, in 37 Hen. VIII., but they did not continue in his poffeffion long. They changed hands rapidly from Ramfden to Tyrrell, then to Banke, Hewett, Hunt, Frankland, and finally to the family whofe noble reprefentative ftill owns them.

Rochedale.—The monks acquired confiderable property in this parifh at an early date from Lord Robert de Stapelton. His great grandfon confirmed it to them by the following charter:—

Charter of Warinus de Scargill.

"To all true Chriftian people to whom thefe prefents fhall come, Warinus de Scargill fendeth greeting in our Lord. Know that I, for the falvation of my foul and of all my anceftors and heirs, have granted and confirmed to God and the Bleffed Virgin Mary and the Abbot and Convent of Roche and their fucceffors all the gifts and grants which Lord Robert, fon of William de Stapelton, my great grandfather, whofe heir I am, made to them. All that land and tenements which are called Hillbrigthorpe, by thefe boundaries: by the way which leadeth from Stone Edge to Knot Hill and paffeth the water of Tame and fo upwards to the other Knot Hill, and all that Knot Hill even unto Woodward Hill, eaft, weft, and north fo far as my land reacheth, with all buildings, woods, meadows, feedings, waters, paftures, and all appurtenances and other things under the earth and above the earth, with the whole foreft and all other liberties to the faid foreft belonging. I have alfo granted to the faid Abbot and Convent and their fucceffors for me and my heirs full power to enclofe all the faid tenements by the boundaries aforefaid altogether as walled and the walls if thrown down to make up and renew as often and when they may pleafe, and to keep the fame enclofed without hindrance or reproach of me or my heirs or affigns. And alfo common of pafture from the great way which leadeth from Stone Edge to the Bridgewater of Tame toward the north to the boundary aforefaid; and from Knot Hill to Woodward Hill, as the water departs towards the wood of Tame. To have and to hold all the faid tenements and paftures in free and perpetual alms, fafe and quiet from all fecular fervice, claims and demands for ever, fo that the faid Abbot and Convent of Roche and their fucceffors may do what they will with all that is contained within their faid enclofed tenements without contradiction of me or my heirs and without plea of foreft. And I, the faid Warinus, and my heirs will warrant, acquit, and for ever defend all the faid tenements and paftures and their appurtenances to the faid Abbot and Convent and their fucceffors againft all men, in teftimony of which as well my feal as the common feal of the faid Abbot and Convent to this writing indented are feverally affixed, thefe being witneffes, Lord Edmund de Waftenayes, Lord Thomas de Schofelde, Lord John de Doncaftre, knights; John of the chamber of Stapelton, William my fon, and others. Dated at Roche, on Sunday, in the feaft of the Converfion of St. Paul, in the year of Grace one thoufand three hundred and fourteen."[a]

This property was fituated in the townfhip of Quick,[b] and in the divifion called Friar Mere.

[a] I am indebted to G. Shaw, Efq., of Saddleworth, for this charter.
[b] In the confirmation of Hen. III., printed at page 21, "Quicke" fhould be read, inftead of "Sonke."

In 1310 the Abbots of Roche and Whalley feem to have had fome difpute about tithes.

Composition between the Abbots of Whalley and Roche.

"By the tenor of thefe prefents it is manifeft to all, that inafmuch as a controverfy has arifen between the religious men, the Abbot of Whalley with his convent, rector of the Church of Rochedale, on the one part, and the Abbot of Roche on the other, upon the exaction of tithes of Hillbrigthorpe, fituated within the limits of the faid parifh; the difpute has at length by the counfel and direction of the lords Abbots of Ryevall and Bildewas, judges affigned by a general chapter of the order in the faid caufe, alfo with the confent and free will of the faid parties being fettled in this manner, viz., that the faid Abbot of Roche pay every year to the aforefaid Abbot of Whalley or his certified proctor at Hillbrigthorpe forty pence of filver and one pound of wax and one pound of frankincenfe at the two terms of the year, viz., twenty pence and one pound of wax at the feaft of St. Martin in the Winter, and twenty pence and one pound of frankincenfe at Pentecoft for all tithes of garbs of all lands cultivated and to be cultivated pertaining to the faid place of Hillbrigthorpe, according to the command of the bull of Lord Boniface VIII., Pope. And becaufe in the agreement of this convention there was a doubt whether the tithe hay ought to be reckoned with the greater tithes of garbs or with the leffer, it was agreed by the parties that the faid doubt fhould be decided by a faithful inquifition of rectors, vicars of that country, fufpected by neither party, before the ordinaries of that archdeaconry in the province of the parties, and that what fhould be found by the faid inquifition fhould be held good, and the prefent compofition about tithes of garbs with the addition of the tithe of hay, either as greater or leffer tithes, as the faid inquifition fhall decree to be affigned after the faid inquifition be renewed and corroborated by the common feals of each chapter, to remain for all time. In witnefs of which the parties have placed the feals which they ufe to this ordinance bipartite. Given at Wakefield, Friday next after the feaft of St. Barnabas the Apoftle, A.D. 1310."

In 1293 the Abbot of Roche was fummoned to anfwer by what warrant he claimed to have free warren in his lands of Hillbrigthorpe. He maintained a bailiff here at a yearly income of twenty fhillings. The laft perfon who held this office was Henry Whitehead.

The rents and farms at Hillbrigthorpe were valued at the

dissolution at £20 0s. 8d., and from the following extract from the *Manchester Guardian* we are enabled to learn more in detail of what the property consisted, and also what was its ultimate destination:—

"A copy has been brought us of a Royal grant of the 35th Henry VIII. to Arthur Assheton in consideration of £361 7s. 4d. paid by him into the Court of Augmentations of the revenues of the Crown—of estates, lands, buildings, and tenements, &c., of the late Monastery of Rupe, otherwise Roche Abbey, formerly belonging and appertaining. Amongst these there are a tenement called Ashenbeech, otherwise Thoome, in the town of Saddleworth, in the parish of Ryche Dale, otherwise Rattesdale, in the occupation of Ralph and Christopher Chetham and John Wrigley, with the houses, lands, tenements, meadows, feedings, pastures, rents, revisions, services, &c., thereto belonging; the farm of Denshaw, in Saddleworth, with the mills, houses, &c.; all the lands, &c., of the grange called Castleshaw; one fourth part of the customs or services called 'boons,' to the late monastery formerly belonging; the farm of Swaincroft, in Saddleworth; the pastures called Knott-hill; the tenement in the territory of Hilbrighthorpe (now called Grange) in Saddleworth; the pastures called the Delf; all that mine of stones called Blackstondelf, in Saddleworth; various yearly rents of 16s. 4d., &c.; common pasture, turbary, &c., in Saddleworth; and the reversions of all the premises with their appurtenances; all the rents, revenues, and other yearly profits reserved in any demises of the premises; all the woods, underwoods, and trees growing upon the premises. Arthur Assheaton, his heirs, &c., to hold and enjoy all the premises, &c., as fully and entirely and in as ample manner and form as the last Abbot and late Convent of the same late Monastery at any time before its dissolution. All the issues, rents, reversions, and profits of the said granges, farms, messuages, lands, &c., are granted to Arthur Assheaton from the feast of the Annunciation of the Blessed Virgin Mary last past. (March 25th, 1543.) And lastly the King grants these letters patent under the great seal, without fine or fee, great or small, to us in our hanaper or elsewhere, to our use in anywise to be rendered, paid, or done. Witness the King at Westminster, the 5th of June. By writ of privy seal, &c."

Norby.—The Abbot of Roche derived a large portion of his revenue from the property which he held in this place. It is situated in the northern part of Lincolnshire. There exists a ready mode of communication between it and Roche by the rivers Trent and Idle, which the monks made use of, for we have already seen that they had a convenient place at which to load and unload ships on the banks of the Trent at Flixburgh, a place only a few miles off. They also had a landing place at York; so by water carriage they could easily get the produce of their land here into a good market.

About the year 1180 Hugh de Wadworth, the fourth Abbot of Roche, bought the grange of Roxby, having borrowed money from the Jews of York for that purpose.

Before the year 1186 the Abbot obtained a magnificent gift from Walter de Scoteni, called in the confirmation of Pope Urban III. "Roxby, with its appurtenances."

About the year 1200 the Abbot of Roche, in consequence of this gift, claimed the advowson of the Church of St. Mary, of Roxby. We find the following entries relating to this subject on the Roll of Pleas in the Easter term of the second year of King John:—

"*Lincolnshire.*—The Abbot of Roche sues against the Prior of the Holy Trinity of York and the Convent of the same place, that they permit him to present a fit person to the Church of Roxby, which is vacant and is of their gift, as they say, &c. The Prior says that the church is their right, as that which Ralph Paynell gave to them by charter, which they produced, which testifies this fact and the confirmation of his heirs. And the Abbot says that the same Prior never had seizin thereof, nor had he presented the last parson, but Walter de Scoteni, who gave to him the whole of the land which they have in Roxby, with the church of the same vill, by his charter which he produced, and which testifies this fact, and thereof prays a jury. And because Walter was not present, and it appertains to him to act in regard of the presentation, the Prior withdraws without a day, &c."

"*Lincolnshire.*—In assize of *darrein presentment* to the Church of Roxby, the advowson of which the Abbot of Roche claims against the Prior of Drax, and against the Prior of the Holy Trinity of York.

And the Prior of Drax comes and says that there ought not to be an assize thereof, because William Painell, of whose right and inheritance that church had been, gave the Church of Roxby to God and St. Nicholas, and to the canons serving in the territory of Drax by this charter, which he produces and which testifies this fact. He also proffers the charter of Richard de Courcy, who had to wife the daughter of the same William, confirming the gift of the same William and the charter of Robert de Gaunt, who had the same daughter to wife, confirming the same gift, and the charter of Walter de Scoteni, to whom the same Robert and his wife, heiress of the aforesaid William, had given that land where the church is situate, which testifies that Walter de Scoteni gave and by his charter confirmed to the Church of St. Nicholas and to the canons of Drax, whatsoever William had granted to the same canons in the vill of Roxby, namely, the Church of Roxby with all its appurtenances. But the Prior of the Holy Trinity produces the charter of Ralph Painell, father of the aforesaid William, who came at the conquest of England, and who gave to his church that church, and the charters of Alexander, Jordan, and William, his sons, confirming his gift, and the charter of Robert, then Bishop of Lincoln, and the confirmation of King Henry, great grandfather of the then King, and both Priors hold themselves to one answer. It was adjudged that Walter should be distrained to be present to manifest hereafter whether he be willing to warrant to the Abbot of Roche his charter or to the Prior of Drax the charter which he had made to him in the last instance, and in the meanwhile the jury to remain."

It is certain that Walter de Scoteni did not warrant the grant of the advowson to the Abbey of Roche, for the rectory continued in medieties respectively in the patronage of the two priories of the Holy Trinity and of Drax until the year 1292; but subsequently Robert the Prior and the Convent of the Holy Trinity granted their mediety of this church to the Prior and Convent of Drax.

An agreement was made before 1227 between Reginald Abbot of Roche and Alan Prior of Drax, viz., that the former granted to the latter two oxgangs of land with a toft in Roxby, for which the latter was to pay an annual rent of five shillings, and the Prior gave to the Abbot the water mill of Roxby with the pool and watercourse; and the Prior had liberty to have a horse mill within their own court to grind their own proper corn, but not that of his men, who should be obliged to do suit at their water-mill.

Philip Abbot of Roche released Thomas Prior of Drax from all suits at his court for what the latter had in Roxby.

Walter de Scoteni quitclaimed the annuity of £1 which the Abbot of Roche used to pay him.

According to an inquisition made at Lincoln before the justiciaries of the lord the King, namely, Sir William de St. Omer and Sir Warine de Chaucomb, in 1275, by twelve jurors of the wapentake of Manley, we find the following:—" Also they say that the Abbot of Roche holds one barony in Roxby for three knight's fees, which he had of the gift of Walter de Scotenai in the time of the lord King John, father of Henry last deceased, seventy years elapsed;

which barony, to wit, the said Walter held of Hugh Painel, and the same Hugh of Andrew Luterel, and the same Andrew of the lord the King in chief, and it is worth yearly one hundred marks, &c."

In 1287 John Paynel sought against the Abbot of Roche sixteen tofts and one carucate and a half of land, with the appurtenances in Roxby, which he claimed as his right by plea in court.

According to the "*Taxation of Pope Nicholas*," made about 1291, what the monks owned in Roxby was valued at £29 12s. 8d. per annum.

In 1292 John Paynel, by judgment of court, recovered against the Abbot of Roche one messuage and thirty-two bovates of land with the appurtenances in Roxby next to Stather, which the Abbot attempted to set at nought on account of errors therein alleged. This is also more fully recorded, as follows:—" John Paynell recovered before the justices of the Bench, first by default of the Abbot of Roche, one messuage and thirty-two bovates of land in Roxby, which judgement was confirmed by the justiciars before the King's counsel. And now both judgements are confirmed by the auditors of complaints, before whom the said Abbot complained of William de Brumpton, a justiciar of the Bench, that he had promulged the said first judgement in favour of and for the sake of upholding John de Kyrkeby, Bishop of Ely. In this judgement, because the Abbot said that in the time of the first judgement the first Abbot, his predecessor, who made default was dead, our lord the King enjoined that enquiry should be made by oath about his death. And the first said John proves by religious men, knights, and serving men worthy of credit, that the said Abbot who made default was alive when he made default. And the Abbot proves by his monks and other members of his community that he was dead. And it is said the said John gave the better proof, because the monks did not make their depositions as well as those whom John produced."

It will be seen by the following charters that the Abbot regained this property by purchase from Philip, brother and heir of John Paynel:—

Royal Charter.

"The King, to all &c., greeting. Inasmuch as it has been testified before us and our council that John Paynel, formerly in our court before our Justices of the Bench, by the award of our said court, recovered against Walter, formerly Abbot of Roche, one messuage and thirty-two bovates of land with the appurtenances in Roxby, by default which the said Abbot made in the suit that was between them in our aforesaid court by our brief *de recto* about the tenements aforesaid, *by which the estate of the said house is become much depressed;* we with the common council of our realm have determined this, that it be not allowed to religious men or others to enter upon any one's fee so that it come to a dead hand, without our licence and that of the chief lord from whom the thing is immediately held. Wishing therefore to do a special favour to Philip Paynel, brother and heir of the said John, we have given him licence, as far as in us lies, that he may give and assign that messuage and the aforesaid thirty-two bovates of land, with the appurtenances in Roxby, to our beloved in Christ, Stephen, now Abbot of Roche, and the Convent of the same place, to have and to hold to them and their successors for ever; and to the said Abbot and Convent that they may receive the said messuage and land with the appurtenances from the said Philip by the tenor of the presents, we grant a special favour in like manner, being unwilling that the said John, or his heirs, or the said Abbot and Convent, or their successors, by reason of the statute aforesaid by us or our heirs should receive annoyance therefrom or in any way be oppressed, save, however, the services therefrom due and accustomed to the chief lord of the fee. In testimony, &c., witness the King at Westminster on the twentieth day of June."[a]

Charter of Philip Paynel.[b]

"To all the faithful in Christ who shall see or hear the present letters, Philip Paynel, lord of Westrasen, greeting in the Lord. Know that I have received and had of the religious men, the Abbot and Convent of Roche, six hundred marks of good and lawful sterling money, in which they were bound to me for the surrender of the Manor of Roxby by a certain recognizance made in the court of our lord the King, A.D. 1293, and in like manner by divers writings made nevertheless between me and the said religious, concerning the said six hundred marks, of which six hundred marks fully and entirely within five years, as is contained in particular writings which they have in their possession, I call myself well and entirely paid and contented, and so I render the said monks quit of all expenses and losses for myself and my heirs and executors by these presents for ever; and the recognizance of six hundred marks and all writings whatever in any manner or time, however made, concerning them or part of them, I condemn and annul by these presents. And I and my heirs or executors will preserve the said religious free from harm against all men with respect to the said six hundred

[a] Patent Rolls. 21 Edw. I. Memb. 9.   [b] Dodsworth's MSS., vol. VIII. fol. 288 A.

marks, or from having any damages in respect of them for ever on pain of forfeiture of all our goods present and future. And be it known that the said Abbot and Convent have particular writings of the said payments in their possession and this writing of acquittance in full notwithstanding, so that it may not be understood by any one that I have twice levied the said six hundred marks. In testimony of which I have to the present letters placed my seal, and in testimony of the apposition of my seal I have procured the seal of the lord Prior of Drax and of Stephen * * * likewise to be placed to it. Given at the house of Drax * * * St. John Baptist, A.D. 1297."

In 1299 the King gave licence to Robert de Rothewell to give and assign to the Abbot of Roche two bovates of land with the appurtenances in Roxby; and to Ralph Brown of Roxby the same licence to give, &c., one bovate of land with the appurtenances in the same town to the said Abbot.[a]

In 1313 the King granted licence to Henry de Cokewald to give and assign to the Abbot of Roche one messuage, twenty acres of land, and two acres of meadow in Roxby, and to Hugh de le Wyk the same licence to give, &c., one toft and two acres and a half of land in Roxby, which said messuages, tofts, land, and meadow were of the fee of the said Abbot, and worth 23s. per annum.[b]

In 1339 the King granted licence, by a fine of forty marks, to John de Chaucumbe to give and assign to the Abbot of Roche one bovate and four acres of land with the appurtenances in Roxby, which were held from the aforesaid Abbot, and worth 6s. 8d. per annum.[c]

Hugh de le Wyk of Roxby gave the monks two acres of land in the same place in the South Field.

Thomas, the clerk of Flixburgh, and William de Coleton released the monks from the payment of two marks which they used to pay to them.

At the dissolution the annual income derived by the Abbot from Roxby, in rents, perquisites of court, &c., was £37 0s. 7d.; out of this the following fees were paid: £6 6s. 8d. to Thomas Lord Burgh, seneschal of Roxby; and £1 to Robert Thornabye, bailiff of Roxby.

𝕾𝖆𝖓𝖉𝖆𝖑.—In 1232 King Henry III. confirmed what the monks held in this place.

[a] Pat Rolls 28 Ed I M 73 [b] Pat Rolls 7 Edw II pt 1 Memb 8
[c] Pat. Rolls 13 Edw II Memb 44

Sandbec.—On St. Giles' day, 1241, the monks obtained their first property in this place by the following charter:—

Charter of Idonea de Vipont.

"Know, all present and future, that I, Idonea de Vipont, in my widowhood and in free power over my body, have given, conceded, and by this my present charter have confirmed to God and the Blessed Mary and the monks of the Rock, the whole of my manor of Sandbec with my corpse, with the homages and services, as well of free men as of copyholders, and with all commons, liberties, and easements pertaining to the same manor everywhere within and without the said vill of Sandbec without hindrance, to be held and had for a pure and perpetual alms free and quiet from all services, customs, exactions, and demands. And I, Idonea, and my heirs will warrant the said manor of Sandbec with its appurtenances to the said monks, and will acquit and defend it for ever against all men. Moreover, for greater security I have affixed my seal to this writing. Witnesses: John de Croyton, Thomas de Bug, John de Stainton, Richard de Horbiry, Robert de Wickersley, knights; Walter, seneschal in the castle of Tickhill, Peter de Wadworth, William de Stainton, John de Monteby, Hugh de Scelhall, John de Wlvethwait."

(Seal, Idonea at full length, with a hawk upon her left hand.)

The right of the Abbot to this manor was disputed by Robert de Vipont, the second grandson of Idonea, as may be learnt from the following:—

Testification of Richard de Boyvill.

"To all who shall see or hear these letters, and especially to the twelve knights elected to make the great assize between the Abbot of Roche and Robert de Vipont, Richard de Boyvill in the Lord eternal health. Wishing to inform you upon the oath which is about to be made to you being present, I testify in truth by God, and by the baptism with which I have been baptized, and by the knighthood with which I have been dubbed, that on the day of St. Giles, in the year of our Lord 1241, my lady Idonea de Busli, of her own free will and full power of her body, with great deliberation of mind, gave to the Church of Roche the whole manor of Sandbec, with the ploughs and all other things pertaining to it, in the presence of many of her friends and faithful servants then and there present, Sir John de Croxton, Sir Thomas de Bury, Sir R. de Boyvill, knights; and Sir J. de Monby. On the morrow of St. Giles the charter of this donation was written and sealed with the great feal and private feal of the lady on the morrow of the nativity of the Bleffed Mary next following."

The right of the Abbot to this property was again queftioned in 1265, when an inquifition was taken by Robert de Ullay, &c., at Anfton, the jurors being William de Rhodes, Adam de Monte Acuto, &c., to examine whether the Abbot of Roche had intruded himfelf into the manor of Sandbec, which belonged to Robert de Vipont, by occafion of the troubles late had in England, when the jury found that the Abbot had not intruded himfelf, but was in feizin before the troubles, in the troubles, and after the troubles.

John, fon of Gilbert de Ewes, gave the monks fix acres and a half of land in Sandbec.

Hugh, Marfhal de Sywardthorp, gave his mill in Sandbec with the pool and watercourfe.

In 1535 the annual value of the property which the Abbot held in Sandbec was valued at £14 1s.; out of this he had to pay to the Hofpital of St. Leonard at York one fhilling, and to the Prior of Blythe, for a parcel of land in Sandbec, one fhilling per annum.

The following is an account of the timber belonging to the Abbot at Sandbec at the diffolution:—

County of York.[a]

"The manor of Sandbeck, in the fayd Countye, parcell of the poffeffyons of the late monafterye of Roche, in the fame countye:

"Trees growing aboute the fcyte of the feyd manor and in the hedges inclofing the lands perteyning to the fame wyll barly fuffyce to repayr the houfes ftanding uppon the fcyte of the feyd mannor and the feid hedges and fences, therefore not valued.

Ex^{r.} per me David Clayton."

At the diffolution the manor of Sandbec was granted to Richard Turke, gentleman, citizen of London, and in 3 Edw. VI. he had licenfe to alienate it to Robert Saunderfon and his heirs.

Scawsby.—In 1198 King Richard I. confirmed whatever the monks had in this place. At the diffolution they had property here, but of no great confequence, as it with three other places was only valued at 11s. 5d. per annum.

Serlby.—Matilda de Moles, before the year 1208, gave the monks all the lands which the men of Blythe held of Hugh de Moles, her brother, and afterwards of her in the fields of Serlby in the county of Nottingham.—*(See Torworth.)*

[a] Particulars for Grants. Mifcellaneous, No. 60.

Hugh de Moles with his body gave his mills in this place with the suit thereof. *(See Blythe.)* He also gave a fishery above and below the mills, with one oxgang of land and the service of 1*s.* from Alan de Clifton and his heirs, for one oxgang of land in the same territory; and of Norman, son of Robert, for another oxgang. The monks had no property here at the dissolution.

Sezacres.—From the confirmation of Pope Urban III. we find that William de Moles and William Fitz Gerard gave Sezacres with its appurtenances.

Shelley see **Thurstonland.**

Shepwick see **Walkeringham.**

Slade Hooton.—The Abbot of Roche obtained what he had here from Robert de Ripers in exchange for other lands, &c., as is shewn by the following:—

Charter of Abbot Richard and Robert de Ripers.

"Know, present and future, that it is thus agreed between Richard Abbot of Roche and the monks of the same place, on the one part; and Robert de Ripers on the other; viz., that the aforesaid Richard the Abbot and the monks, for themselves and for their successors, have given, conceded, and by this present charter confirmed to the aforesaid Robert de Ripers, for his homage and service, and for the exchange of his land of Slade Hooton, in addition to six marks of yearly rent, and for the exchange of two pieces of meadow in Walkeringham which the same Robert held, and for £100 sterling which he gave to the same with his own proper hands, their lands and meadows which they had in Wadworth and Alverley, and in Loversal, with the wood which they had in Wadworth, with the farm of the same wood and the mill, their mill, with the site and pools and waters, and with all kinds of suits everywhere pertaining to the aforesaid mill within the aforesaid vills and without, to be held and had by the same Robert and his heir and assigns and their heirs for ever, viz., in homages, in services of free men, in villanages with the villains and their suits and chattels, in wards, in relieves and escheats freely, peacefully, and hereditarily with all commons, liberties, easements, advantages, and with all other things and with all other pertenances to the aforesaid lands, meadows, mills, pools, and waters, and wood and wood farm everywhere pertaining within the said vills and without, without any hindrance. Saving, nevertheless, to the said Abbot and Monks and their successors their land in Wellingley, with its pertenances. But the aforesaid Robert and his heirs or assigns, or their heirs, render the aforesaid Richard and the monks and their successors only 27 pence per annum, to wit, 12 pence at the feast of St. Martin in the Winter, and 15 pence at Whitsuntide, for all services, exactions, and demands which respect or can respect the said Abbot Richard and Monks and their successors. There shall be done, nevertheless, by the aforesaid Abbot Richard and the Monks and their successors foreign services which pertain to the aforesaid tenements. But the aforesaid Richard and Monks, &c., shall not make or erect, nor by means of any of them cause to be made or erected, nor shall allow Peter de Wadworth nor his heir nor assigns, nor their heirs nor any of theirs, to make or erect any mill, to wit, neither water-mill nor wind-mill in the territory of Wadworth to the hurt or detriment or grievance of the aforesaid Robert or his heirs or his assigns, or their heirs. But the said Peter de Wadworth and his heirs shall have free mulcture of the whole of their malt and corn of their own proper homestead in the aforesaid mills for ever without let from any one, as is contained in the charter which the aforesaid Richard and the monks have of the aforesaid Peter. And the aforesaid Richard Abbot and his Monks, &c., all the aforesaid lands and mills, and pools and waters, and sites of the mills, and the wood and the wood farm, and the meadows, with all things and suits, easements, and with all pertenances to them everywhere pertaining, as was aforesaid against all people for the aforesaid service will warrant, acquit, and defend for ever. Now, for this donation, concession, confirmation, and exchange, the aforesaid Robert has given to the aforesaid Richard Abbot and Monks, &c., all his land which he had in Slade Hooton, with the villains and their goods and chattels and villanages and services of free men, with all pertenances as is aforesaid, without any restraint, and his meadow which he had in Walkeringham, and £100 sterling by rendering for the land of Slade Hooton to the lords of Tickhill 6*d.* per annum at Easter, and to Arnold Bisset and his heirs the services which pertain to the aforesaid land, as is contained in the charter which the aforesaid Robert had of the aforesaid Arnold, and which the same Robert freed to the aforesaid Abbot and Monks for the warrants and security of their agreement, and by rendering Adam, son of William de Walkeringham, for the aforesaid meadow 1*d.* per annum at the feast of St. Mary Magdalen, for all services. And that all the things which are contained in this writing may remain ratified, firm, and stable, as well the said Richard Abbot and Monks as the aforesaid Robert, the present writing made after the manner of a deed have with the impreffion of their feals corroborated. Witneffes: Simon de Heden, Robert de Wlrington, Richard le Blund of Blythe, Robert de Mifterton, Hugh de Moles, Henry de Darley, Richard de Louweder, Herbert de Wlrington, Gerard de Hedon, Jeffery de Turmifton, Nicholas, fon of Jeffery de Erdefale, Thomas de Wlrington, and others."

The date of this charter is between 1238 and 1254.

Among the "*Particulars for Grants*"[a] we find the following:—

County of York.

"The manor of Hutton Slade, with Carre, Hutton Leveyt, and Hutton Robert, in the fayd Countye, parcell of the poffeffyons of the late mon. of Roche, in the fame countye."

"There be growing about the fcytuations of xii tenements and cotages there and in the hedges inclofing the landes perteyning to the fame lxxx okes and afhes of lx and lxxx yeres growth, whereof lxv refervyd for tymber to repayre the fayd tenements and cotages and one corn myln there, and for ftakes for hedgeboote to repayre and maynteyne the fayd hedges and fences. And xx refydue valuyd at iiij^d. the tree, which is in the holle vi^s viii^d.

Ex^r. per me David Clayton."

Smeaton.—From *Dr. Burton* we learn that Simon, fon of Algar de Smeaton, with his corpfe gave half an oxgang of land here. This property, together with what the monks had in Scawfby, Campfal, and Afkern, was valued in 1535 at 11s. 5d. per annum.

Snaith.—Edmund de Lacy, conftable of Chefter, granted and confirmed to the monks all that they held in his focage of Snaith, in the year of Grace 1158. *(See Tickhill.)*

Stainford.—The monks had property here in 1231. *Mr. Hunter* gives the following account of the foundation of a chapel at this place:—"On the day of Pentecoft, 1355, an indenture was made between the Abbot and Convent of Roche on the one part, and Thomas de Rillington and fix others, parifhioners of the Church of Hatfield, on the other part, that the faid Abbot of Roche having the Church of Hatfield appropriated, granted and permitted that the faid parifhioners and other the inhabitants of the town of Stainford might, by the Archbifhop's licenfe, maintain at their own coft a chaplain to celebrate divine fervice in the Chapel of Stainford, newly builded, for the fpace of three years daily, excepting on Sundays and other great feftivals, whereon they were to repair to

[a] Mifcellaneous, No. 58.

the Parish Church of Hatfield. This agreement was confirmed by the Archbishop's vicar-general on November 17th, 1355."

The tithes which the Abbot of Roche derived from Stainford were valued at £5 per annum, out of which he had to pay 4s. 2½d. to the Provost of Stainford. The monks held their property here till the dissolution.

Stainredale see **Oneash**.

Stainton.—In 1202 Hugh de Stainton granted 30 acres of land, reckoned by the perch of 18½ feet, in the fields of Stainton, at Rokkehill, to the Abbot of Roche and his successors for a pure and perpetual alms. In such sort that the said Abbot or his successors make no building on the aforesaid 30 acres of land without the consent and will of the aforesaid Hugh or his heirs. And if the same Abbot or his successors lose anything of the same 30 acres of land by default of warranty of the aforesaid Hugh or his heirs, the said Hugh or his heirs shall make exchange of their land which lies on the side next the said 30 acres of land on the east to the extent that they have lost.*

The Abbot of Roche bought land in Stainton of Richard Baret, which was confirmed by John, son of Hugh de Stainton.

William Wasteneys, of Stainton, gave the monks half an oxgang of land here.

The property of the Abbot of Roche in this place is supposed to have exceeded 370 acres of wood and pasture. This calculation of course includes what he had at Lambcote Grange.

Stanhege see **Chatsworth**.

Stansal.—Among the evidences of Godfrey Higgins, Esq., of Skellow Grange, *Mr. Hunter* found a charter dated 1236, by which William Chaworth and William, the son of Eudo, chief lords of Wadworth, declare that they release all claims in lands of Sir Jordan Fitz-Payne, lord of Stansal, Wellingley, and Willsic, which the said Jordan has given to the monks of Roche in pure and perpetual alms, to wit, from that ditch which lies between Magilldhylls across as far as the bounds of Wadworth, and the fee of Wellingley and Stansal, and so runs from the arable land of Wadworth on the west until it comes opposite the town of Stansal on the east, lengthwise, and from the said ditch to another ditch which has been made in Littlemorye, from the south through the whole of that land which is in the western district as far as the arable land of Stansal and the bounds of Wadworth.

* Fines, Ebor. 4 John.

Jordan Fitz-Payne must have made this grant before 1231, as it appears among the names of places confirmed to the monks in that year by Hen. III.

Stirrup.—Gerard de Stirrup gave turbary here before the year 1186. Stirrup is in Nottinghamshire, and is not identical with Tristrop, as *Dr. Burton* has it in his "*Monasticon Eboracense.*" The latter place is now called Streetthorpe, and lies near Doncaster.

In 1276 the Abbot of Roche held twenty acres of meadow and a toft and croft in Stirrup of the fee of Tickhill, the former being the gift of Hamel de Bugthorpe, in the time of Henry III.*

Robert Burton was bailiff of Stirrup at the dissolution, and received from the Abbot 10*s.* per annum.

In 1563 Robert de Hitchcock obtained possession of that messuage in Stirrup in the occupation of Richard More, late belonging to the Monastery of Roche.

Streetthorpe.—At this place, which was formerly called Stirestorp, Tristrop, and Stristerop, the monks had property of which we learn the following from the "*Particulars for Grants*":—

County of York.

Grantee, Richard Stapleton. 6 *Edw. VI.*

All the rents and profits in Streetthorpe, in the County aforesaid, are worth in :—

The rent of one tenement, with all lands, meadows, pastures, and commons to the same belonging, thus demised to Brian Hastings, of Fenwek, by Indenture under the common seal of the late Monastery of Roche, freely resigned, dated 24 Jan., in the 24th year of the reign of King Henry VIII., to have to the said Brian Hastings, Elizabeth his wife, and Franc his son, from the date of the presents to the end and term of their lives, paying thence at the terms of St. Martin and Pentecost equally £2 6*s.* 8*d.* per annum.

Memorandum. That this particler was delyvered to Sir Brian Hastings, knight, the 12th daye of Decembr, 6 Edw. VI., for a purchace.

Ex^{r.} per Willm. Notte, Audit.

Strafford.—The monks paid to the bailiff of the King of the wapentake of Strafford 6*s.* 8*d.* per annum.

Templeborough.—The Roman encampment known by this name, which is situated on the south bank of the Don about half a

---

* Hundred Rolls.

mile from Rotherham, came into the hands of the monks of Roche in the time of Hen. III. *Mr. Hunter* found among the Johnston MSS. a charter by which Ralph, son of Richard de Savile, gave with his body to the Abbot of Roche a carucate of land in Brindsworth, which Peveril held, and Templeborough in the territory of Brindsworth. Witness, Peter de Wadworth.

Twenty years after the dissolution the property which the monks had held here is described in an inquisition of Lionel Reresby, Esq., of Thriberg, as "two mills and twenty acres of pasture called Templebarrow, with appurtenances in Ikkyls, held of the Queen as of her Monastery of Roche lately dissolved, in socage, by fealty and rent of 13s. 4d. for all services and demands."

Thorne.—William gave the monks the tithe of the eels taken at his fishery here, after the full tithe had been taken, which belonged to the monks of Lewis. The tithes here were valued at the dissolution at £7 per annum.

Throapham.—The monks held property here at the dissolution. *(See Laughton.)*

Thurnscoe.—The monks had considerable property in this place before 1186, the gift of William Vavasor.

They also had two carucates of land in Thurnscoe, which belonged to William Paynel, and which he held *in capite* of the lord the King of the barony of Hooton.[a]

In 5 John, 1203, there was a fine between Galfred Luterel and Frethesant his wife, and Isabella, sister of the said Frethesant, plaintiffs; and Osmund Abbot of Roche, tenant of twelve bovates of land with the appurtenances, in Thurnscoe. Verdict for the Abbot and his successors, save foreign service to the said Galfred and Frethesant and Isabella, and the service to the said Frethesant, which the aforesaid land owes to them.[b]

In 20 Hen. III., 1236, there was a fine between William, son of Richard de Barnby, plaintiff; and Robert Luterel, whom Reginald Abbot of Roche called to warranty, and who made warranty to him of ten messuages, one mill, and twenty bovates of land, with the appurtenances in Thurnscoe. Verdict for Robert Luterel.[c]

Andrew Luterel confirmed all that the monks had in Thurnscoe.

In the thirteenth century the monks obtained the two following charters:—

[a] Hundred Rolls.   [b] Fines, Ebor. Augmentation Office.   [c] Ibid. No. 134.

Charter of Ralph de Rainville.

"Know all, &c., that I, Ralph de Rainville, of Thurnscoe, have granted, given, and by this my present charter have confirmed for the welfare of my soul and those of all my ancestors and heirs, to God and Saint Mary and the Monks of Roche, the attachment of the pond of their mill of Thurnscoe upon my fee of Holme, in pure and perpetual alms, free and quit from all service, exaction, and demand. And in accordance with which it shall be lawful for the said monks at their will to raise, strengthen, repair, and amend the said pond, as they shall think expedient, and to take land upon my fee of Holme as often as shall be necessary, without contradiction or impediment of me or my heirs, for raising and repairing the said pond. And I, Ralph, and my heirs will warrant, quit, and defend all the aforesaid to the said monks against all men for ever. Witnesses: Lord Robert de Wykereflay, knight; Peter de Waddeworth, Thomas de Lasci, Hugh de Lascy, Wm. de Tatewyc (Todwick), serving man; Johanna Whiethwait."[a]

Charter of Hugh, son of Hugh Lascy.

"Know all, &c., that I Hugh, son of Hugh Lafcy, of Thurnscoe, have granted and by this my present charter confirmed to God, St. Mary, and the Monks of Roche all the land which my father granted to the same in exchange for ever at Hoxebrigge, and all the meadow which they hold of the gift of my father, as his charter testified. Moreover, I have remised and quitclaimed to the said monks from me and my heirs and assigns for ever all right and claim which I had or might have had in the meadow of the aforesaid monks, as it is bounded by the ditch before the gate of the grange of Thurnscoe after the manner of a farm or common herbage-ground. In such sort, however, that if any cattle of those of my heirs by reason of a defect in the ditch shall enter the said meadow we shall not quarrel about it, and for making greater security to the said monks in all the aforesaid, I have corroborated the present page by placing my seal. Witnesses: Jordan, son of Jordan de l'Isle, Jordan de Mar, Adam Paynel, Robert Lafcy, Adam de Thurnscoe, Payn de Mar, Richard de St. Paul, John Grimbald."[b]

Hugh, son of Reiner de Darfield, gave the monks an oxgang of land here. Richard de Thurnscoe also gave another oxgang of land in this place.

---

[a] Dodsworth's MSS., vol. VIII. fol. 31 B. [b] Dodsworth's MSS., vol. VIII. fol. 32 A.

In 1316 the Abbot of Roche was certified purſuant to writ teſted at Clipſtone 5th March, as lord of the townſhips of Armthorpe and Thurnſcoe, and joint lord of Todwick. The Abbot had a charter of free warren here from Richard II. The property which the monks had at Thurnſcoe at the diſſolution was valued, together with 8*d*. perquiſites of courts, at £12 10*s*. 8*d*. per annum.

From the following "*Particulars for Grants*" we learn the deſtination of the monk's property here at the diſſolution:—

County of York.
Grantees, Doddington and Jackſon.

Thurnſcoe, Blitheſhaw manor, worth in the rent of one parcel of land, demiſed to John Anne, Eſq., by Indenture under the common ſeal of the late Monaſtery of Roche, as it is ſaid, to pay at the term of St. Martin only 5*s*.

Memorandum. The premiſs are no parcell of the aunchient inheritaunce of the crowne, nor of the duchies of Lancaſter or Cornwall, but came to the Kinge's Majeſtie's handes by ſurrender of the ſaid monaſtery.

23rd Dec., 1559. Jno. Gifford.   Per me, Antho. Rous.
At 28 yeres purchas.

County of York.
Grantees, Jno. Wright and Thos. Holmes. 7 Edw. VI.
The Manor of Thurnſcoe is worth in :—

	£	s.	d.
The rent of a grange there, called Thurnſcoe Grange, with the appurtenances, thus demiſed to Triſtram Feſh, by Indenture under the common ſeal of the late Monaſtery of Roche, dated 4 Nov., in the year of the reign of the late King Henry VIII., for the term of 21 years then next following, paying thence at the terms of St. Martin and Pentecoſt equally	2	0	0
The rent of a meſſuage and bovate of land, with the appurtenances there, in the tenure of Wm. Ellys, paying at the terms aforeſaid	0	13	4
The rent of a cottage and two acres of land, with the appurtenances there, in the tenure of Hugh Ellys, paying	0	6	0
Carried over	£2	19	4

	£	s.	d.
Brought forward	2	19	4
The rent of one messuage and one bovate of land, with the appurtenances there, in the tenure of James Ellys, paying	1	6	8
The rent of one messuage and one bovate of land, with the appurtenances there, in the tenure of the said Hugh Ellys, paying	0	13	4
The rent of certain lands there, in the tenure of the heirs of — Meres, paying	0	12	0
The rent of one cottage, with certain lands belonging to the same, in the tenure of the heirs of Wm. Ellys, paying	0	7	0
The woods not valued. Total	£5	18	4

Thurstonland.—Mr. *Morehouse* thinks the manor of Thurstonland was given to the monks at the same time as the advowson of Hatfield by Earl Warren. At the dissolution the annual rents amounted to £8 19s. 7½d.; Thomas Green being steward, and Henry Gillott, bailiff here, and each receiving 20s. per annum. The grange of the monks possessed a right of stray and pasturage for twenty sheep upon the commons and waste lands in the lordship of Shelley, a privilege which no doubt had been granted by one of the early lords of Shelley.[a]

In 1532 John Walker, of Thurstonland, clothier, obtained a lease from the Abbot and Convent of Roche, of lands in Thurstonland, given under the seal of the monastery.[b]

In 1540 the King granted " to John Storthes, of Shyttylyngton, gentleman, all his manor of Thurstonland with all his rights, membres, and appurtenances, &c., late to the Monastrye of Roche, and now dyssolved, belonging, &c., and all other messuages, houses, byldyngs, mylnes, granges, londs, tenements, meadows, pastures, comons, waters, fysshyngs, lyng, and heth, &c., to hold of the said sovereign lord the King, his heirs and successors in cheff, by the suyt of the xx part of a knight's fee, and yelding, therefore, yerely 20s. to the King's Cort of Augmentacon of the Revenues of his Crowne."

Tickhill.—In the "*Monasticon Anglicanum*" we find the following:—

[a] History of Kirkburton.   [b] Ibid.

Charter of Edmund de Lacy.

"Know prefent and future that I, Edmund de Lacy, conftable of Chefter, have granted and by this my prefent charter confirmed to God and the Bleffed Mary and the Abbot and Convent of Roche of the Ciftercian order, all the gifts and fales made to them in my barony of Pontefract, in my conftabulary, in my barony of Tickhill and in my focage of Snaith, which they held at Eafter, 1258, according to the tenure of the charters of the donors and vendors, and this conceffion and confirmation I have made to them for the welfare of my foul and of my father, John de Lacy, and of Margaret my mother, and of Alice my wife, and of all my anceftors and heirs. Witneffes: Adam Abbot of Kirkftal, Sir John de Hoderode, fenefchal of Pontefract; Robert de St. Andrew, John Beke, knights; Sir Ofbertus, rector of Silkfton; Sir Robert de Nottingham, rector of Almonbury; Mr. William de Lichfield, rector of Braiton, and many others."

Tinsley see Winelepe.

Todwick.
—The firft property which the monks had in this place was given them before 1186 by Ralph Tortemayns. This is given upon the authority of the "*Confirmation of Pope Urban III.*" In the Hiftory of the Manor, written by a monk of Roche, and printed in the "*Monafticon Anglicanum,*" it is ftated that Ralph Tortemayns fold to the Houfe of Roche "Little Todwick," and whatfoever appertained to it.

William Tortemayns gave all his wood to the monks with the land on which it grew. He alfo confirmed the grant of pafture for eight fcore fheep in the common pafture in Todwick.

Gregory de Todwick and Alice his wife gave two acres of land in Todwick with their right to the advowfon of the church of the fame place.

Nicholas de St. Paul confirmed the grant of Gregory and his wife, and gave all his meadow lying between his houfe and the road towards the north in Todwick. He alfo confirmed the grant of ten acres of land and pafture for fixty fheep, given by his father (William de St. Paul), and gave all his land between Botyldwellwang and the grange towards the north of the way leading from Afton to Anfton; and on the other fide of the way towards the fouth he gave one acre and a half, with pafture for nine fcore fheep in Todwick, together with common pafture through his land for all the monks' cattle going from Todwick grange.

The monk's account, in the document above referred to, of the gifts of William and Nicholas de St. Paul, is as follows:—"William and Nicholas gave to the House of Roche all their land between Botyldewellwange and the Grange, and all lordship and services pertaining to seven bovates of land, and also all the land, wood, and rent *quæ dirationavit* of Michael de Mawoners."

In 1316, pursuant to writ tested at Clipston, March 5, the Abbot of Roche was certified as joint Lord of Todwick.

All the above gifts were confirmed by Maud de Lovetot.

Charter of Maud de Lovetot.

" To all the sons of the Holy Church present and future, Maud de Lovetot, formerly wife of Gerard de Furnival, greeting. Be it known to your community that I, in my widowhood and in full power over my body, have given and by this my charter confirmed to God and the Blessed Mary and the Monks of Roche, for the welfare of my soul and of my lord, Gerard de Furnival, and of all my ancestors and heirs, all the lands in the territory of Todwick, with their appurtenances, which Ralph Tortemayns and William Tortemayns, and William de St. Paul and Nicholas de St. Paul gave to the said monks, to have and hold, as the charters which they have from them testify. Witnesses: Robert, parson of Misterton, seneschal; Ralph de Ecclesal, Philip Scrope, Walter de Heyr, Roger Whiston, William de Lindrick, Ralph de Bauuent."

In 1309 King Edward II. granted licence to Edmund de Wastenays to give and assign twenty acres of land with the appurtenances in Todwick to the Abbot and Convent of Roche, in exchange for twenty acres of land with the appurtenances in the same place.

All the property which the Abbot had in Todwick was granted October 15th, 37 Hen. VIII., to William Ramsden and Ralph Wyse, and John and Roger Wyse, sons of Ralph. It is thus described in the grant:—" All that grange of ours (the King's) called Todwick Grange, with the appurtenances in Todwick in our said county of York, lately belonging and pertaining to the monastery de Rupe, otherwise called Roche, in the said county of York, now dissolved, and parcel of the possessions lately thereto belonging, and all the houses, edifices, barns, stables, dovecotes, gardens, orchards, lands, meadows, pastures, commons, and hereditaments of ours whatever in Todwick and elsewhere, wheresoever in our said county of York, in any way appertaining or belonging to the said grange, called Todwick Grange, or being with the said grange demised, let,

THE POSSESSIONS.

used, or occupied; and also all that messuage and tenement called the *Abbot's House*,[a] with the appurtenances, now or lately in the tenure of Janet Henfrew and Hugh Henfrew of Throapham, situated in the vill of Todwick, in our said county of York, formerly appertaining and belonging to the said late monastery de Rupe or Roche, and parcel of the possessions thereto lately belonging, &c., and which said grange called Todwick Grange and the rest of the premises in Todwick aforesaid now extend to the clear annual value of £5 10s. 8d. To have and to hold, &c., rendering from the said grange and the rest of the premises aforesaid 11s. 8d.[b]

Torworth.—There was a fine levied at Leicester the first Monday after the feast of St. Andrew, 10 John (1208) between Osmund Abbot of Roche, petent, and Thomas de Sandal and Matilda his wife, summoned to warrant to the said Abbot one bovate of land with the appurtenances in Torworth, whereof the said Abbot and Convent had the charter of the said Matilda in these words:—

Charter of Matilda de Moles.

"Be it known that I, Matilda de Moles, have given and by this my charter confirmed to God and St. Mary of Roche and the monks there serving God, one bovate of land with the appurtenances, in Torworth; viz., that which was Alexander Crassis, and one culture of land of thirty-eight acres in the territory of the said town, and pasture for a hundred sheep everywhere in the common pasture of the said town, and furthermore all the lands which the men of Blythe held of Hugh de Moles, my brother, and afterwards of me in the fields of Serlby and Torworth, and all the rents of those lands, &c."

From the "*Hundred Rolls*" we learn that the Abbot had in 1276 one hundred acres of land of the gift of Hugh and Matilda de Moles in the time of King John.

In 1246 there was a fine levied between "William" Reginald (?) Abbot of Roche, petent, and Adam de Holtal and Donysia, his wife, of six acres of land with the appurtenances in Torworth. Verdict for the Abbot.

In the time of Edw. III. the Abbot was summoned to answer to the lord the King on the plea by what warrant he claimed to

[a] The "Abbot's House" here mentioned still exists, in a ruined condition, in Todwick, and is known by the name of the "Old Hall." It is a good specimen of early English Domestic Architecture, and well deserving of a visit. In the wall of the gable on either side of the chimney is an oval-shaped aperture in the form of a "vesica piscis." At the upper angle of each is carved a beautiful little cross.

[b] I am indebted to W. H. G. Bagshawe, Esq., of Ford Hall, for these particulars.

hold his lands and tenements in Torworth in free and perpetual almoign, free and quiet from all gelds, &c. Verdict, that the Abbot for the prefent go thereof without a day, the right of the King being preferved.

In 1552 the property which the Abbot of Roche had poffeffed in Torworth was granted to two perfons of the names of Green and Hall.

Particulars for Grants (Grantees, Green and Hall.)
Parcel of the poffeffions of the late Monaftery of Roche, in the County of York.
Rents and profits in Torworth, in the County of Nottingham, valued in

	S.	D.
The profits of one field called Grangefield there, in the tenure of Robert Burton, paying thence per annum .	6	8
The profits of certain lands there, in the tenure of John Newcombe, paying thence per annum	0	6
The profits of certain land there in the tenure of Geoffery Bylton, paying thence per annum	0	6
The profits of two acres of land there, in the tenure of Carver, paying thence per annum	0	$3\frac{1}{2}$
The profits of three acres of land there, in the tenure of Geoffery Darell, paying thence per annum	0	9
The profits of three acres of land there, in the tenure of William Ingleby, paying thence per annum . . .	1	0
The profits of eight acres of land there, in three parcels, in the tenure of Robert Burton, paying thence per annum	2	0
The profits of five acres of land there, in the tenure of John Leweftye, paying thence per annum	1	3
The profits of four acres of land there, in the tenure of Hugh Thornell, paying thence per annum	1	0
The profits of certain lands there, in the tenure of John Smith, paying thence per annum	3	4
Clear yearly value	17	$3\frac{1}{2}$

Memorandum. The premyffeys are no parcell of anye of the Kynge's Majeftye's mannors or lordefhypps, neither do theye lye nye anye of his grace's howfes, parkes, foreftes, or chaces; and thefe benne the fyrfte partyculars herof made unto annye perfonne, and there ys no more lande in Taworthe belonginge to the late Monafterye of Roche aforfayde.

Ex^{r.} 26 Januarii, 1552, per me, Willm. Rygges, Audit.

THE POSSESSIONS.

The clere yerelie value of the premifes above
    rememberyd is .. . . xvii$^{s.}$ iiii$^{d.}$ ob.
Which rated at xxv yeres purchafe amoun-
    teth to . . . . xxi$^{li.}$ xii$^{s.}$ iiii$^{d.}$ ob.
    To be paid within xx dayes nexte.

The Kyng to difchardge the purchafer of all encumbrances except leafes and covenants of the fame.

The tenure in focage laft part.

The iffues from the feaft of St. Michel the Arch.

The purchafer to be bounde for the valewe of the woodes.
                                        Thoms. Norwicen.

At the diffolution the Abbot paid the Prior of Blyth one fhilling per annum for land in Torworth.

Wadworth.—Reginald Gurvy de Tickhill quitclaimed all his right in the mill at Wadworth.

Maud, relict of Matthew de Tickhill, gave two acres of land here.

Eudo, fon of Godfrey de Wadworth, gave lands to the monks in Wadworth, and confirmed what Maud, relict of Matthew de Tickhill, had given them.

Peter de Wadworth gave the monks forty-fix acres of his woodland lying on the weft fide of the wood extending from the weft field of Wadworth to the north. He alfo gave three oxgangs of land on the north fide of the north field; thirty-five acres and one rood in the weft field; and thirty-nine and a half acres and half a rood in the eaft field, in confideration of eighteen marks lent to him by the Abbot of Roche in his great neceffity, and alfo of fifty marks which he owed, and which the faid Abbot paid to Aaron the Jew, at York, and his brother. The witneffes to this deed were Ralph de Normanville, knight; Reginald de Kettleburgh, John de Armthorpe, H. de Bilham, Alexander de Stubbs, Peter de Roffington, Peter de Letwell, Ingeram de Stirap, Otho, fon of Mo. de Wilghefich (Wilfick), Adam Leming, and others.

Stillingflete's "Abftract of the Acquittance of the Jews" is as follows:—"The charter of Aaron, fon of Jofey, and of Leo, bifhop, and of Samuel, his fon, Jews of York. Be it known to all the faithful of Chrift, &c., that Peter de Wadworth and his heirs are acquit, &c. Moreover, be it known that we have quitclaimed to the Abbot and Convent of Roche three oxgangs of land and forty-fix acres which they have of the gift of the faid Peter, &c. In witnefs whereof we have put hereto our Hebrew letter and our feals."

The monks did this good act to their old benefactors, the Wadworth family, in the time of Henry III., during whose reign Peter de Wadworth lived.

William, son of John de Vavasour, quitclaimed in 1277 all his right in wards, escheats, &c., in Wadworth.

The monks held what they possessed in this place up to the time of the dissolution.

Walkeringham.—The monks had considerable property in Walkeringham, Lincolnshire, particulars concerning which may be seen in the following:—

Confirmation of King Edward II. of lands in Walkeringham.[*]

"The King to all to whom, &c., greeting.

"The grant, gift, and confirmation which Henry, son of Richard de Walkeringham, by his charter made to the monks of Roche of two tofts, 55¼ acres of land, and 11½ acres of meadow, with the appurtenances in Walkeringham, and of a certain plat of land with the Walcre, and of all the pasture which belongs to that bovate of land of the said Henry, which is called Wlger-oxgang, everywhere in the whole common pertaining to the vill of Walkeringham;

"The grant, also, and gift, and confirmation which the said Henry by another charter which he made to the said monks of one plat of land, with the appurtenances, in the aforesaid vill of Walcre, and two bovates and seven acres of land and meadow, with the appurtenances in the aforesaid vill of Walkeringham;

"The gift, grant, and confirmation which Richard, son of Henry, son of Richard de Walkeringham, by his charter made to the said monks of all that plat of land, with the appurtenances, in the said vill of Walkeringham, and with all things contained within the said plat, which he recovered from the said monks before the justices sitting at Nottingham;

"The grant, also, confirmation, and quitclaim which the said Richard by the same charter made to the said monks of all rents, lands, possessions, meadows, pastures, tenements, homages, services, wards, reliefs, and escheats, with all liberties and easements which they had by the gift and sale of the said Henry his father;

"The grant, moreover, gift, and confirmation which Adam, son of William de Walkeringham, by his charter made with the aforesaid monks of one toft with the appurtenances, in the said vill of Walcre, and with the passage to the said toft pertaining, and of 38

---

[*] Pat. 6 Edw. II. pars. 2. M. 7.

acres and one rood of land and meadow with the appurtenances in the aforesaid vill of Walkeringham;

"The grant, also, gift, and confirmation which Henry, son of Robert Arnewy of Walkeringham, by his charter made to the said monks of 5 roods and one selion* of land, and of all the land which the said Henry had at Frithesend, and of all the pasture which belongs to a half bovate of land, with the appurtenances in the whole common of Walkeringham;

"The grant, gift, and confirmation which Henry, son of Robert, son of Arnewy of Walkeringham, by his charter made to the aforesaid monks of all his land in Upper Walton, and of three selions and two acres of land, with the appurtenances, in the aforesaid vill of Walkeringham, and of all the meadow which the said Henry had in Monkeboye;

"The grant, also, gift, and confirmation which Henry, son of Robert Maumirr of Walkeringham, by his charter made to the aforesaid monks of three acres and a half of meadow and the mediety of one rood of meadow with the appurtenances in the said vill of Walkeringham, and of all the pasture which pertains to the mediety of one bovate of land everywhere in the whole common of the said vill of Walkeringham;

"The grant, moreover, and confirmation which the said Henry by the same his charter made to the aforesaid monks of all that culture in the field of Walkeringham, with all its appurtenances, which the said monks have of the gift of Roger, the chaplain.

"The remission, also, and quitclaim which the said Henry by the same charter made to the said monks of a certain yearly rent of 4*d*., which the said monks used to pay the said Henry for the culture aforesaid;

"The grant, moreover, gift, and confirmation which the said Henry by the same charter made to the aforesaid monks of the homage and whole service of Henry, son of Isabella, and his heirs, which the said Henry, son of Isabella, was wont to render to the aforesaid Henry, son of Robert, for the whole tenement which he held from the same in Walkeringham, and also of 12½ acres of land and seven roods of meadow, with the appurtenances in Walkeringham;

"The grant, moreover, and confirmation which Adam, son of William de Walkeringham, by his charter made to the aforesaid monks of 4 acres of meadow at Drengefflete, which they had of the gift of Roger de Osberton, of the fee of the said Adam;

* A ridge of land lying between two furrows, uncertain in quantity.

"The grant, alfo, gift, and confirmation which the faid Adam by the faid charter made to the faid monks of the whole fervice of Geoffery de Fulham and his heirs, which the faid Geoffery ufed to do to him for a certain particle of land in a place which is called Morfurlung, and alfo of one toft, with the appurtenances, in Schepewykes, and of three acres and a half of land and meadow, with the appurtenances in Walkeringham;

"The grant, gift, and confirmation which Geoffery, fon of Alan de Trent, by his charter made to the aforefaid monks of thirty acres and a half of land and meadow, with the appurtenances, in Walkeringham, with the homage of Walter de Mifterton and his heirs, and all the fervice which he owed to him for two acres of land in Colmanhaghe, and alfo of the whole pafture which belongs to the mediety of one bovate of land everywhere in the whole common of Walkeringham, and all the fervice of Geoffery Fulholm and John, fon of Roger, and their heirs;

"The grant, moreover, gift, and confirmation which the faid Geoffery by another charter made to the aforefaid monks of four acres and one felion of land and three roods of meadow, with the appurtenances, in Walkeringham, and of all his meadow which he had at Helpol and Monkebothe and in the meadows of Walkeringham;

"WE, holding thefe ratified and granted for us and our heirs, as much as in us lies, to our beloved in Chrift the Abbot and Convent of the place aforefaid and their fucceffors, grant and confirm as the aforefaid charters reafonably teftify. In witnefs, &c., witnefs the King at Canterbury, 20th day of May, by fine of ten marks."

The monks had two pieces of meadow in Walkeringham from Robert de Ripers, for which they had to pay William de Walkeringham 6*d.* per annum.

King Henry VIII. by his letters patent, dated 11th November, 1544, granted to Sir Richard Lee, knight, and his heirs, the grange and farm of Walkeringham, with all the lands, meadows, and paftures late belonging to the Monaftery of Roche.

Wallingwells.—*(Nottinghamfhire.)*—The monks had property here at the diffolution. At this place was a Houfe of Benedictine Nuns, founded about the fame time as Roche. Its inmates confifted at the diffolution of a Priorefs and eight profeffed.

Warely.—The name of this place occurs in the "*Confirmation of King Henry III.*," 1231, as one in which the Abbot of Roche had property.

THE POSSESSIONS.

𝔚𝔢𝔩𝔩𝔦𝔫𝔤𝔩𝔢𝔶.—Robert Fitz-Payne gave lands, and Jordan Fitz-Payne pastures, in this place. King Richard I. confirmed to the monks the grange of Wellingley, and from that time up to the dissolution it seems to have continued in their possession.

𝔚𝔦𝔠𝔨𝔢𝔯𝔰𝔩𝔢𝔶.—Richard Fitz-Turgis de Wickerfley, one of the founders of Roche Abbey, gave the monks fifty loads of wood out of his wood in Wickerfley.[a]

𝔚𝔦𝔩𝔰𝔦𝔠𝔨.—Jordan Fitz-Payne gave the monks land in this place.

𝔚𝔦𝔫𝔢𝔩𝔢𝔶.—In Stephens' continuation of the "*Monasticon Anglicanum*" the following charter occurs:—

Charter of Walter Abbot and the Convent of Roche.[b]

"Know, present and future, that Walter Abbot and the Convent of Roche have granted and by the present charter confirmed to Robert, son of Roger de Tinfley, for his homage and service two bovates of land, with the appurtenances, in the vill of Wineley, which he had of the gift of Walter his brother, to have and to hold to him and his heirs of the said Abbot and Convent of Roche freely and quietly, paying thence per annum to the said Abbot and Convent of Roche eight shillings in the grange of Roche, to wit, four shillings at Pentecost and four shillings at the feast of St. Martin in the Winter, for all service save foreign, as far as belongs to two bovates of land of the said fee in the said vill. With such understanding, however, that the said Abbot and Convent are not bound to make warranty of the feoffament of the said land to the said Robert or his heirs. In witness whereof the said Abbot and Convent and the said Robert to the parts of this charter have alternately set their seals. Witnesses: Johann de Stevinton (Swinton?) * * * Robert Bruerton, Peter de Lettewell, Galfrid de Helgheby. 1260."

(Much obliterated, and the Seals lost.)

Owing to the obliterated condition of the original charter when this transcript was made, it is probable that the mistake of writing "Wineley" for "Tinfley" has occurred. This also is the opinion of learned topographer, Samuel Mitchell, Esq., of Sheffield.

𝔚𝔦𝔫𝔱𝔢𝔯𝔱𝔬𝔫.—Winterton, in Lincolnshire, is mentioned in the "*Confirmation of King Henry III.*" as one of the places in which the monks had property. Whatever it consisted of it seems to have remained in their hands up to the time of the dissolution, when it was valued at £1 1s. per annum.

[a] See page 5.   [b] Transcript in the possession of Sir W. Calverlay, Bt.

Winteringham.—Hamelin Bardolph and Katherine his wife, and Robert, son of Eudo, gave the monks land in this place, which Hugh, son of Ralph Bardolph, confirmed. Winteringham is situated in Lincolnshire, about three miles north of Roxby Grange. At the dissolution what the monks had here in pasture was valued at 10s. per annum.

Wyvelsworth.—This place is mentioned in the "*Confirmation of King Henry III.*" as one of the places in which the monks had property.

Woodhouse Mill.—The Abbot of Roche received £1 9s. per annum rent from the mill called "Wodhousemyll."

York.—Agnes, the Prioress of the Convent of St. Clement, at York, granted to the monks a certain piece of land leading from their orchard to the river Ouse, for which they paid £3 sterling.

Oblations, Alms, etc.

The oblations amounted at the dissolution to £1 per annum. This sum was distributed yearly at the Supper of the Lord. The sum of £1 9s. per annum was expended in burning wax daily before the altar of the foundation of Richard Furnival, and 5s. was given yearly at the celebration of the obit for the soul of Thos. de Bella Aqua.

The Architecture,
Monastic Buildings, and their Remains.

THE ARCHITECTVRE — ROCHE ABBEY

HE architectural peculiarities and beauties of Roche Abbey have, until lately, been either misrepresented or neglected altogether. Not long since it was common for historians to devote nearly their whole attention to the possessions and genealogies of persons, and to content themselves with describing any buildings they might meet with, as of the earlier or later Gothic periods. Thanks, however, to the publication of books of sound information on the subject, and to the establishment of Archæological and Architectural Societies, the public have become more conversant with Architecture, and the pleasures of this magnificent art are now widely enjoyed. In proof of the ignorance we have mentioned, let any one take up a book describing the ruins of Roche Abbey Church twenty years ago. He will, almost certainly, find the two east walls of the transepts pointed out as the remains of the nave.

But besides being misrepresented by the pen, the architecture of Roche has received even worse treatment from the pencil. Drawings and engravings of the ruins may be met with, which can only be recognized by exercising the most vivid imagination and by referring to the name inscribed below. Round arches are pointed, and pointed arches are rounded. Windows are turned into doors, and doors into windows. In fact every sort of liberty is taken, including the rounding of the square abacus. But the artist has had to move on, as well as the topographer. Photography has appeared, and put to shame the clumsy daubs of former years. The difficulty of getting an exact representation of a building no longer exists. The most delicate and minute work may now be copied with marvellous exactness and ease. Photography gives us the form of arches, capitals, and mouldings; the position of every stone, beauty, flaw, crack, and stain.

It is left only to the imagination to obtain any idea of what the general appearance of the Abbey muſt have been, before it was "put to the ſpoil." (See p. 91.) We have the evidence, however, of William, Earl of Warren, who in 1345 admiring the magnificence of the ſtone work as well in the buildings of the ſaid Abbot and Convent, as in their Monaſtery, made the monks a conſiderable grant. We have alſo the evidence of Cuthbert Shirebrook, who ſays that the Abbey at the time of its diſſolution "was a very fair builded houſe, all of freeſtone; and every houſe vaulted with freeſtone and covered with lead." And we have ſufficient ſtill ſtanding to prove how extenſive and how beautiful the whole muſt have been: at all events we have every reaſon to be pleaſed with what remains, when we remember, that the only fragment left of Newminſter Abbey, the Mother of Roche, is the north door.

In 1776, Mr. Brown, the landſcape gardener, committed ſuch havoc in the way of pulling down and covering up, that nothing leſs than an extenſive diſinterment can enable us to diſcover how much of the ruins of Roche remain underground. *Mr. Gilpin* gives us an account of theſe operations; "theſe ruins" he ſays, "and the ſcenery around them were in the rougheſt ſtate, when Mr. Brown was employed to adorn them. He is now at work; and has nearly half completed his intention. This is the firſt ſubject of the kind he has attempted. Many a modern place he has adorned and beautified: but a ruin preſented a new idea; which I doubt whether he has ſufficiently conſidered. He has finiſhed one of the vallies which looks towards Laughton ſpire: he has floated it with a lake, and formed it into a very beautiful ſcene. But I fear it is too magnificent and too artificial an appendage, to be in uniſon with the ruins of an Abbey. An Abbey, it is true, may ſtand by the ſide of a lake; and it is poſſible, that *this* lake may, in ſome future time, become its ſituation; when the marks of the ſpade and the pickaxe are removed—when its oſiers flouriſh; and its naked banks become fringed and covered with wood. In a word, when the lake itſelf is improved by time, it may ſuit the ruin, which ſtands upon its banks. At preſent the lake and ruin, are totally at variance. Mr. Brown is now at work in the centre part of the three vallies, near the ruin itſelf. He has already removed all the heaps of rubbiſh, which lay around; ſome of which were very *ornamental*; and very *uſeful* alſo in uniting the two parts of the ruin. They give ſomething too of more conſequence to the *whole*, by diſcovering the veſtiges of what once exiſted. Many of theſe ſcattered appendages alſo, through length of time, having been covered with earth, and adorned with

wild brushwood had risen up to the windows, and united the *ruin to the soil* on which it stood. All this is removed: a level is taken, and the ruin stands now on a neat bowling green, like a house just built, and without any kind of *connection* with the ground it stands on. There is certainly little judgment shewn in this mode of improvement. The *character* of the scene is mistaken. If Mr. Brown should proceed a step further—pull down the ruin and build an elegant mansion: everything would then be right, and in its proper place. But in a *ruin* the reigning ideas are *solitude, neglect*, and *desolation*."[a] As Mr. Gilpin predicted, time has done a great deal, towards rendering Mr. Brown's work more in keeping with the ruin. All true lovers of Architecture will, nevertheless, always deplore the pulling down of detached fragments, and the heartless covering up of the ground plan, which we know still exists in great perfection. And for the present, we must content ourselves by hoping that the noble owner will, ere long, enhance a hundred-fold, the interest of the lovely spot he has the privilege to possess, by lifting the dark veil of earth which has for a century hidden from all eyes innumerable objects of interest and beauty.

Whatever may be the truth of the legend which attributes to Durandus a superstitious motive, in choosing the site for his Abbey, we have abundant proof, that there were not wanting many substantial reasons to confirm him in his selection. Among these may be mentioned, not only the beauty of the situation, for beautiful it must ever have been, from its natural combination of rock, wood, water, and meadow, even before it had received the attentions of Mr. "Capability" Brown; but also its complete seclusion from the outer world. Thus rendering it peculiarly suited to the requirements of the stern and rigid rule of the order of its occupants, one of whose special principles it was, in the selection of sites for their houses, that "they should never be constructed except in places separated from all converse and neighbourhood of men."[b] In both these respects it bears a striking resemblance to the parent Abbey of Fountains, as it does also with regard to another essential circumstance to an establishment of this kind, namely, an abundant supply of clear and excellent water. A further inducement to the monks to settle in this choice spot must have been the existence here of a splendid building stone, beautiful in colour, easily worked, and yet very durable, as is sufficiently testified by the admirable state of preservation in which the remains of the Abbey Church continue to

---

[a] Picturesque Beauty, vol. i. page 21.
[b] Cistercian Rule quoted by Mackenzie E. C. Walcott, in his "Church and Conventual Arrangement," from Harl. MS. 3708, f. 18.

this day, notwithstanding their exposure to the weather for so many centuries. The reputation, indeed of the Roche Abbey quarry, has long been widely spread, and so highly is it now esteemed, that when the new houses of parliament were about to be built, and search was made throughout the country, for the best materials for that purpose, the stone from this quarry was one of those ordered to be examined and reported upon.

It is evident, therefore, that these early Cistercians exercised no ordinary degree of judgment, no less than of taste, in selecting this place as the site of their future Abbey. And here, no doubt, they commenced as soon as their circumstances would permit, the erection of their conventual buildings. These, in all probability, may have been at first of a temporary character, until increasing wealth and prosperity enabled them, in that respect, to rival their parent and kindred houses of Fountains and Kirkstall, as seems to have been the case when Roche was brought to its full maturity and perfection.

As, it has been observed, the monastic remains of Roche Abbey are, at least as to what is visible above ground, of so limited an extent, it must be left very much to conjecture to determine what the buildings were when entire. Yet fortunately, our conjectures here need not be of a vague and wholly uncertain character. For, it is a well ascertained fact, that the arrangement of institutions of this kind, very much followed an established plan. And it is upon record as regards these Cistercian monasteries that they were, as far as circumstances permitted, built according to a fixed rule. We constantly read in the accounts which are preserved in the "*Monasticon Anglicanum*" respecting the establishment and the erection of the buildings of the monasteries, which were derived from the great Abbey of Fountains, that this was done "*de more*"—according to established custom, or "*secundum formam ordinis,*"—according to the form of their order. Now, though the remains here are certainly scanty, and those of the immediately parent Abbey of Newminster are reduced to the smallest fragment, yet in the kindred monasteries of Fountains and Kirkstall they are very ample. And from these we may, with considerable confidence, form an opinion as to what the general arrangement must have been at Roche.

From those examples then, as well as from others, we learn that the main offices of the Abbey were erected round a cloistered court, of which the nave of the church formed the northern side. That on the eastern side of the quadrangle were found, beyond the south transept of the church, first an apartment, which appears to have been a vestry, communicating with the church by a doorway, which

THE ARCHITECTURE, &c.

yet remains at Roche. Beyond this veſtry, was the chapter-houſe, which in the early times of the erection of theſe abbeys, *i. e.*, in the 12th century, is always found in the parallelogram form: and of this building again, veſtiges have been diſinterred here ſufficient to verify this ſtatement. On the ſame ſide of the court at Kirkſtall are two vaulted apartments, the uſe of which is not very obvious, they are dark and dreary, and perhaps may have been places of confinement for refractory monks, or poſſibly merely ſtorehouſes. It ſeems not improbable that ſomething of the kind exiſted alſo at Roche, as the length of this ſide, as indicated by a corner maſs of maſonry ſtill remaining, muſt have afforded confiderable ſpace beyond the chapter-houſe. At the ſouth-eaſt, no doubt, there would be alſo a paſſage. On the ſouth ſide of the court would, almoſt certainly, be found the Refectory, with its accompanying offices, as buttery, kitchen, &c. The weſt ſide of this court would, no doubt, be occupied by a large apartment, extending its whole length, and perhaps even beyond it, to the ſouth, as is the caſe at Fountains, where it is ſtill pretty perfect, and was alſo the caſe at Kirkſtall, as is plainly ſhown by the veſtiges which remain there. This noble apartment would reſt upon an undercroft, as in the examples juſt referred to, having a groined roof ſupported in the centre by a row of pillars. At Fountains the length of this erection, built at two different periods, is not leſs than 300 feet; of that at Kirkſtall about 175 feet. The upper chamber formed *one* of the dormitories in theſe Abbeys; for from the early account we have of Kirkſtall, preſerved in the "*Monaſticon Anglicanum,*" it is evident there were two dormitories erected from the firſt foundation of the monaſtery, "*utrumque dormitorium, monachorum ſcilicet et converſorum,*" *i.e.*, one for the monks and the other for the lay-brethren. And the ſame was probably the caſe alſo at Fountains and at Roche. On the weſt ſide of the cloiſter court, we may conclude, was the dormitory of the lay-brethren, a portion of which, ſeparated from the reſt, may have formed the ſleeping apartment of other dependents of the monaſtery, who no doubt were numerous, as the Ciſtercians were great agriculturiſts;* and alſo occaſionally, at

---

* It is remarked reſpecting the Benedictines, of whom the Ciſtercians were a reformed and ſtricter branch, in Stephenſon's Introduction to "Chronicon Monaſterii de Abingdon," publiſhed under direction of the Maſter of the Rolls, that "Benedict thought it good that men ſhould be daily reminded that in the ſweat of their face they ſhould eat bread, and day by day they toiled in the field, as well as prayed in the church. After having been preſent at the ſervice of Prime, the Monks aſſembled in the chapter-houſe, each individual received his allotted ſhare of work, a brief prayer was offered up, tools were ſerved out, and the brethren marched two and two, and in ſilence, to their taſk in the field. From Eaſter until the beginning of October they were thus occupied from ſix o'clock in the morning until ten, or ſometimes till noon. Beſides the monks, lay-brethren and ſervants were engaged, who received payment in coin. And as by degrees more land was brought into tillage than the monaſtery needed, the ſurplus was leaſed out to lay occupiers. Thus each monaſtery became a centre of civilization, and while the rude chieftain, intent on war or the chaſe, cared little for the comfort either of himſelf or his retainers, the monks became the ſource, not only of intellectual and ſpiritual light, but of phyſical warmth and comfort, and houſehold bleſſings."

leaſt, of ſtrangers. To this latter concluſion we ſeem led by the fact that at Fountains, where this part of the Abbey is found in a more perfect ſtate than it exiſts elſewhere, one acceſs is gained to this dormitory by a flight of ſteps placed on the *outſide* of the cloiſter court. The dormitory of the monks, there ſeems little doubt, was an apartment which ranged over the chapter-houſe and other buildings on the eaſtern ſide of the court, and from this apartment acceſs was gained to the choir of the church by a doorway opening upon a flight of ſteps within the ſouth tranſept. Theſe ſteps ſtill remain at Fountains and Kirkſtall, or at leaſt the inclined plane on which they ſtood. And we may conclude that a ſimilar arrangement exiſted at Roche, as we may obſerve that here a doorway, already referred to, leading from the ſouth tranſept into the veſtry, is not placed in the centre of this wall, but, as is alſo the caſe at Fountains and Kirkſtall, conſiderably to the eaſt ſide, in order, no doubt, to give room for the ſtaircaſe.

Judging from the fragments of maſonry which ſtill remain and which appear to have formed the boundaries of the cloiſter court, its dimenſions were about 180 feet on the eaſt and weſt ſides, and 125 feet on the north and ſouth.

Beyond the court on the ſouth-eaſt it is evident that extenſive buildings exiſted. A conſiderable block of maſonry ſtill remains at the diſtance of about 90 feet to the ſouth of that, which we may ſuppoſe formed the ſouth-eaſt corner of the court, and which has been already alluded to. This maſonry, it is probable, marks the boundary of the buildings in that direction. Here very likely may have been the Locutorium or monk's parlour, and to the eaſt of this, the reſidence of the Abbot. This appears to have been the arrangement at Kirkſtall: and there the foundation of a rather large building has been recently laid bare, to the north of what we may ſuppoſe to have been the Abbot's lodge. The plan of this building has been very much that of the nave of a church with a middle alley ſeparated from aiſles by an arcade of four arches on each ſide. It ſtood eaſt and weſt, and had two entrances on each ſide of the latter end: it alſo ſhows veſtiges of three, if not four, fire places. It ſeems probable that this was the Infirmary of the Abbey, as ſuch was the uſual arrangement of this monaſtic appendage. It is not unlikely that at Roche alſo the infirmary may be looked for in this direction, it being the uſual one, although at Fountains it has been thought to have ſtood over the river immediately to the weſt of the great dormitory.

There is another conſiderable block of maſonry remaining here,

THE ARCHITECTURE, &c. 169

which ſtands to the ſouth-eaſt of the ſites juſt referred to. This is ſaid to be a fragment of the Abbey mill, and near it, beſide the foot bridge, down in the bed of the ſtream, may be obſerved a beautiful Early Engliſh light cluſtered column. Again, to the ſouth-weſt of the cloiſter court, there appear to have been other conſiderable buildings, the foundations of which it is ſtated, in dry ſeaſons may be obſerved extending beyond the ſtream. It is probable that the Hoſpitium or gueſt houſe of the Abbey may have ſtood here.

The Abbey Gatehouſe, of which there are conſiderable remains of great intereſt, will be deſcribed more at large hereafter, ſtands at ſome diſtance to the north-weſt of the church.

Such appears to have been the general arrangement of the monaſtic buildings at Roche. But their relative poſition and the plan of the whole Abbey precincts, together with its boundary wall, of which traces ſtill remain, will be better underſtood by reference to Plate I.

The principal, indeed as already intimated, almoſt the only remains of this once extenſive Abbey, are thoſe of the church and the gatehouſe, both of which are of great intereſt and excellence. Theſe we will endeavour now to deſcribe and to point out their architectural features.

The Church.

The church, when entire, muſt undoubtedly have been a very beautiful and noble ſtructure, extending in length more than 200 feet, and having a breadth at the tranſepts of about 100 feet. Perhaps we may form the beſt idea of what it muſt have preſented to the eye, by viſiting the church of Kirkſtall, which it certainly much reſembled in its general plan and architectural character, though apparently a few years later in date. Kirkſtall Abbey church, with the exception of a breach made on the north ſide by the fall of a portion of its tower, and the loſs of ſome of its roofs, happily remains entire and unaltered, *with very ſlight exceptions*, as it came from the hands of its original builders. And a more noble and impreſſive ſtructure it is ſcarcely poſſible to enter. It is true that it exceeds the church of Roche by about 20 feet in length, and in breadth of tranſept by about 18 feet. Still there having been the ſame number of arches on each ſide of the nave, the ſame bold lofty tower arches, arcades, and groined aiſles, the general effect muſt have been very ſimilar in both examples.

The ground plan of both theſe churches is that of a croſs, with a tower at the intersection. The naves were spacious and lofty, the transepts without aisles, but having chapels on their eastern sides, here two in each transept, while at Kirkstall there were three; with short eastern limbs or structural choirs. (See Plate II.) The naves had each an arcade of eight arches with aisles, which no doubt here, as at Kirkstall, were groined. This also may have been the case with the nave itself, although it was not so at Kirkstall; and in that example neither the tower area nor the transepts appear to have been vaulted over, while at Roche such vaulting evidently existed, as may be seen from the shafts and springers which still remain. In both cases the choirs were groined over.

Of the noble church of Roche, as already intimated, only the eastern sides of the transepts, with a portion of their chapels and of the choir still remain. But these are sufficient to give us a knowledge of what the general architecture of the building must have been, and to enable us to fix its date with tolerable precision.

As regards what remains of the transepts, we have on each side two beautifully proportioned pointed arches of three orders, they rest upon bold clustered piers, with a vaulting shaft between them of the pointed boutell form, as are also the shafts which support the soffits of the arches, while the intermediate ones are either square or of the torus form. The form of the arches is that termed by *Rickman* the "drop arch,"[*] the centres being found within the width of the arch. They are also slightly stilted, their mouldings are formed of the pointed and round boutell used in alternation; and the abaci of the capitals are square, with a rather deep-cut moulding. Above the points of the arches is a bold stringcourse, passing round the vaulting shafts, and also round the pier of the central tower. Upon this stringcourse is an arcade of blank pointed arches, two over each principal arch; these are perfectly plain and devoid of ornament or shafts, having only the jambs slightly chamfered. Above these again is another stringcourse upon which, in each compartment, stands a round-headed window, also perfectly plain but having a dripstone. Above this string are the springers of the groined roof, which was evidently of very bold and good character: the diagonal ribs resting upon corbels which terminate in a conical form, and having capitals slightly enriched with foliage.

The arches of the transepts, as already intimated, opened into chapels, of these, those on the southern side are still entire, while those on the north are mostly in ruins. They seem to have been

[*] Ascertained by actual measurement, but only in a slight degree, and from the fact of the arches being stilted, a lofty character is given.

divided by a wall, raised only a few feet from the floor, and not as at Kirkstall, reaching to the roof. The most southern of the chapels has a round-headed window on its south side, beneath which is a piscina also with a circular head. And there can be no doubt that similar windows were originally found on the eastern sides of both these chapels, as well as of those in the north transept. Here, however, it is evident, that these original windows were superseded by insertions of larger dimensions, of the 14th century. A sufficient portion of the tracery of that next the choir still remains to afford pretty certain evidence of what the window was when entire. This will be found represented in Plate VII. fig 12. It seems very probable that one of these chapels was dedicated to the Virgin, and that in it was interred Matilda of York, Countess of Cambridge, who died A.D. 1440, having in her will directed that her "body be buried in the monastery of Roche, in the chapel of the blessed Mary, before her image, situated in the *southern* part of the church of the said monastery." She also directs that "there lie over her grave a stone of alabaster, raised aloft after the manner of a tomb, with an effigy."[a] It seems, very probable, that the figure of the noble lady may have rested on the wall, which divides the chapels: no other site being apparently available, for a tomb of such character, in areas of such limited dimensions as these chapels are. In support of this conjecture too, it is observable that the stone adjoining the central pier is cut away as if to receive the head of a figure.

The northern chapels seem altogether to have resembled those on the south side: in the one next the choir is a piscina like that in the south chapel, and round its arch and in the neighbourhood of it, are lines marked in a light red colour, with further plain indications that the stone work was also marked out in black lines. These are drawn upon a very thin coating of plaster, or rather of whitewash, which may be found also in other parts of the building.[b] These chapels were all groined over, and had bosses at the intersections of their ribs, some of which still remain.

The eastern limb or structural choir of the church, as already stated, is of short dimensions, extending in length only about 37 feet. It is without aisles or communication with the chapels. In these respects it agrees with the nearly coeval choirs of Kirkstall and Louth Park, and also with the original one at Fountains, which, however, was rebuilt, on a very enlarged plan, about a century after its first

---

[a] See p. 58.

[b] It was not uncommon, in early times, to whitewash the walls of churches, thus we are informed that in 1214, Robert de Lindsey, Abbot of Peterborough, "dealbavit" (whitewashed) the choir of that church.

erection. In all these cases the chorus cantorum, or choir for divine service, extended under the central tower, and probably a compartment or two beyond it. That such was the case at Fountains may be seen from the foundations of the stalls which yet remain there.

The eastern limb at Roche has had triple sedilia on the south side, which appear to have been surmounted by lofty canopies. These have entirely vanished: they appear not to have been original, but to have superseded sedilia under a single circular arch, as at Kirkstall, indications of such arch being here still discernable. To the east of these a plain niche of parallogram form contains a piscina, and probably also a lockyer. On the north side opposite the sedilia, are the remains of very rich canopied work of lofty dimensions. It is of the Decorated period, and may have been an Easter sepulchre, or perhaps a tomb of some benefactor.* To the west of this is also a shallow niche, also canopied, but of lower dimensions. This choir was lighted by round headed windows to the north and south, in the part which extends beyond the chapels, in three stages: in the western part, in the clerestory only. Beneath these, standing on a bold string, are two blank arches on each side, at the triforium stage, similar to those in the transepts, but somewhat richer, having shafts at their angles and moulded edges.

There is no means of determining what the arrangement of the east end was, as it has been entirely demolished. The choir was groined in two compartments, with quadripartite vaulting, the transverse rib in the middle resting on pointed shafts, which descend below the triforium stringcourse and terminate in conical shaped corbels, whose capitals are enriched with foliage. The diagonal ribs are supported by similar corbels.

Of the nave of this fine church, as already stated, very little now remains visible: though, doubtless, the whole of its basement lies buried beneath the soil, having been thus concealed by the levelling system of Mr. "Capability" Brown. The west end has, however, of late years been uncovered, and this, together with the fragments of three of the piers, enables us to determine its extent and the character of its architecture. (See Plate II.) Its length was 126 feet 6 inches, and, as we before said, it had an arcade of eight arches on each side, with side aisles. Its breadth was 30 feet 1 inch, that of its aisles, 14 feet 6 inches. The piers consisted of groups of eight

---

* Idonea de Vipont grand-daughter and heiress of Richard de Busli, the co-founder of Roche Abbey, gave *with her body*, to this house, the Manor of Sandbeck, and thus became a great benefactress. (See p. 140.) It is probable, therefore, that she would be buried in a place of special honour, near the high altar. May not this have been her tomb? She died A.D. 1241. Though certainly the canopy work appears of somewhat later date.

pointed boutells: whereof four were principal ones, and the remainder, placed in the angles, of smaller dimensions. The diameter of the piers was five feet. Their form will, probably, be more easily understood from the accompanying plan of their horizontal section, than from the more elaborate figure contained in Plate V. fig. 1.

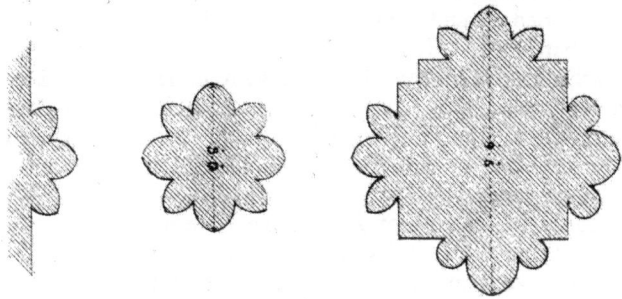

There can be little doubt, judging from the remains of the transepts, that the piers and arches of the nave were very lofty and graceful in their proportions, and must have formed a very noble structure. The aisles were, most probably, vaulted, but as regards the nave itself, it may, perhaps, be questioned whether such was the case. We have no means of determining, with certainty, what was the arrangement of the upper stories. Very likely, however, the same general plan was followed as is found in the transepts and choir, namely, that of blank-arched triforium arcades, with single clerestory windows above.

From the excavations made at the west end, it is evident that the church was entered here by three portals: in this respect differing from the examples of Fountains and Kirkstall, which have each only one west doorway. The central and principal portal at Roche was of three orders, with nookshafts, the bases of which have small foot ornaments. The side doors seem to have been plainer.

The walls of the west end were about six feet in thickness.

As regards the style of the architecture and the date of this fine church, it has been already stated that it is of the character which is denominated Transitional Norman, which prevailed during the latter half of the 12th century. Of this style, however, there are several phases: shewing a gradual advancement from the pure Norman, till we arrive at the perfect Early English. A finer example of the earlier work of this period cannot perhaps be anywhere found than that which has already been so frequently alluded to, the church at Kirkstall. There we have, with the exception of the pointed arches of the principal arcades, a perfect Norman building, showing in its mouldings, capitals and other features, scarcely a vestige of the following style. In that case we know from the records, which have been preserved to us, that the church was begun soon after the settlement of the monks there in 1152, and that the work was carried on and completed at the sole expense of the great patron of that house—Henry de Lacy. It was therefore, doubtless, erected earlier in the history of the convent, more continuously, and in a shorter period than that in which such large structures are usually brought to a conclusion: while for the most part such extensive operations lag, or are for a time altogether suspended from insufficiency of funds.

As regards this church of Roche, we have no reason to suppose that the brethren were so favourably circumstanced: for although their patrons gave them lands, and granted them permission to erect their monastery on which side of the water they pleased, we hear nothing of their having borne the expenses of the buildings. It must, therefore, have been a considerable number of years before they were able to undertake the erection of so noble a church, having, doubtless, had to content themselves, like the parent house of Fountains, for some time, with a much more humble oratory.* And this view of the case before us, is found exactly to accord with the architectural features of the remains of the church, no part of which, it is believed, can be assigned to a date earlier than about the last ten years of the 12th century. It seems most probable, that it was erected during the Abbacy of Osmund, under whose long, able, and active rule the house seems especially to have prospered and increased in wealth and possessions, and who obtained for it both from Pope Urban III and from Richard I, as well as from the Countess of Eu, the great superior lady of the Tickhill fee, under which the land was held, confirmations of all its possessions and privileges. This Abbot presided over the convent from A.D. 1184 to A.D. 1223.

The church, there is little doubt, was, according to the usual custom, commenced at the east end: and here, accordingly, we find marks of the earliest character, such, for instance, as a mixture of

---

* We read also with respect to the monks who were sent out from Fountains to establish a monastery at Barnoldswic, (afterwards removed to Kirkstall,) that the Abbot of the parent house, erected for them there, in the first instance, "*humble* offices, according to the form of their order.". " Et missis fratribus officinas humiles erexit secundum forman ordinis." *Monasticon Anglicanum,* vol. v. p. 531.

Again, as relates to Kirkstall itself, it is recorded. "Abbas itaque—basilican erigit in honore matris Dei semper virginis. Et dispositis exordine humilibus officinis monasterium suum mutato nomine Kirkestall nominavit. An. Dom. MCLII. *Ibid.*

the round and pointed shafts in the piers, with square edges at the angles: while the mixture entirely disappears when we get to the west of the crossing, where all the shafts of the pillars have assumed the pointed form. But even with regard to the earliest part, the tall and graceful proportions of the piers and arches, the lofty form of the latter, the pointed panelling of the triforium story, and the length and narrowness of the round windows, together with the character of the vaulting ribs and shafts, forbid our placing it early in the transitional period, which makes the simplicity and severity of its details the more remarkable, though strictly in accordance with the Cistercian rule.

The Gatehouse.

The only other considerable remain of the Abbey buildings, is a portion of the Gatehouse. This is situated at some distance to the north-west of the church. The lower story of this structure alone is preserved, which bears a considerable resemblance to the Gatehouse at Workfop Priory, and does not appear to differ much from it in date, both being of the Decorated period: and may be assigned to the early part of the 14th century. In one point the gateway of Roche does not resemble that of Workfop, inasmuch as it has a stone groined roof, while in the latter example, there is a beautiful original one of wood. This gateway is divided into two principal compartments of equal magnitude, being separated by the arch in which the gate hung, which had a smaller portal on the north side of it. Each of these compartments had others, into which they opened at their sides, all these varying in dimensions and the whole remaining perfect, with the exception of the one at the south-east angle, of which the greater part has perished. The compartments which remain are all groined over, having very bold diagonal and transverse ribs, the edges of which are merely chamfered. The ribs are supported by conical shaped corbels, and in the principal intersections have carved bosses. In the north-west corner of the inner compartment is a stone newell staircase, which led to the upper story. At the south-west angle of the gatehouse externally, there appears to have been a considerable mass of masonry, which possibly may have supported a staircase communicating with the outside, like the one at Workfop. The archways to the east and west are similar, each being about 15 feet in width, having obtusely pointed arches of three orders, the edges of which are merely chamfered, and are supported by shafts, which have plain capitals and bases. The eastern view of this building is given in Plate XIII; its ground plan Plate XIV; and the details of its architectural features in Plate XV. There can be little doubt that this gatehouse, when perfect, was a very fine building, exhibiting a noble simplicity and massiveness of structure, as may be inferred from what still remains, especially from the groined roof which is of a most marked character, and well worthy of observation.

The stables and farm buildings of the abbey, were probably to the north of the gatehouse, on the site where offices of the same character still remain.

An ancient key of copper, and various fragments of ornamental stonework have been from time to time disinterred, and doubtless an ample crop of similar objects still lie buried beneath the soil. Representations of some of these will be found in Plates XI and XII. Especially a fragment (Plate XI. fig. 1.) which contains a capital of a shaft of the great west door-way. Attention must also be called to the dedication cross, which is incised on the wall on the left side of the west door-way within, a representation of which forms the tailpiece to this section.

There is a large octagonal basin lying near the bridge which leads to the site of the mill. It has a hole through the centre of its bottom, and probably may have been for a fountain in the middle of the cloister court.

There are wells of beautiful water on the premises, especially "the Ladies' Well," or rather, most probably, "the Well of our Lady," which is situated a short distance from the site of the abbey court, though across the stream.

A great variety of mason's marks may be found in different parts of the buildings. Such as have been observed are given in Plate IX. as they may probably be of use, to those who are desirous of investigating that interesting subject.

Such are the only visible remains of the once noble and extensive Abbey of Roche. It must doubtless, when in its entire state, have presented a most striking and impressive effect to the spectator, when entering into its precincts, through the gatehouse, extending as it did quite across the valley, and being flanked on the northern side by its fine and lofty church. So extensive were its buildings that it seems evident even in the days of John, Earl of Warren, in the early part of the 14th century, it had out-grown the requirements of its inhabitants.* Or rather, perhaps, we should say, that the number of its monks had dwindled down considerably

* See p p 51, 112

THE ARCHITECTURE, &c.

from what they had been in earlier times. For it is truly surprising to contemplate the rapid increase of this order of Cistercians, on their first establishment, during the former half of the 12th century. This will be more clearly seen by representing the matter in the tabular form of a pedigree, with the dates of the several oundations of Fountains and its offshoots, thus :—

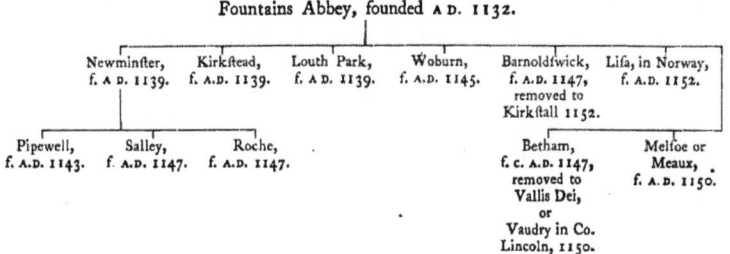

Such was the extraordinary rapidity with which the fame of the piety of the early Cistercian brethren attracted numbers to their society, who flocked to their houses "as doves to the windows." And not only did their numbers thus marvellously increase, but their worldly possessions multiplied in like manner: and the great addition to their earthly wealth, no doubt, was attended with much of its usual consequences, a departure from the primitive simplicity and rigid piety of their order, and the introduction of an amount of laxity and luxury which the early Cistercians so earnestly eschewed. This increasing worldliness would naturally produce its usual effect, the fervour of men's love towards the order, began shortly to abate, and instead of the wonderful increase in the number of members and of houses, which attended their first introduction into the country, after the three earlier quarters of the 12th century, the foundation of an additional monastery was of very rare occurrence. Instead of "the good seed," as the early chroniclers of the order boasted, "taking root and bringing forth an abundant harvest" throughout the land, it would seem, that ere long, the blade began to wither away, till, at the time of the great catastrophe, the number of the monks of these vast establishments had dwindled to a comparatively scanty body, no more than eighteen brethren having been found here at the dissolution, and only about twice that number in the far larger parent Abbey of Fountains. At the kindred Abbey of Louth Park, Lincolnshire, another offshoot from Fountains, we are informed by *Tanner*, that in the reign of King Henry III there were no fewer than sixty-six monks and one hundred and fifty conversi or lay-brethren, while at the time of the dissolution there were not above twelve religious in that house. Truly these establishments had out-lived their day: and in their case was strikingly verified the dictum which comes to us from the highest authority, "Now that which decayeth and waxeth old, is ready to vanish away."[a]

Before taking leave of these interesting ruins and their beautiful environs, it would be ungrateful not to offer a tribute of thanks to the noble family within whose domains they are situated, for the kind privilege which has long been so freely granted to the public to visit them. It is indeed a rich treat, not only to the Archæologian and Architectural student, but to every person who can at all take an interest in what is beautiful in rural scenery, to spend a few hours in this choice retreat. And it is probable that there are few persons residing within many a mile of this spot, or who have ever visited the neighbourhood, who have not, at one time or other, enjoyed the calm and tranquil pleasure of a brief sojourn here: and who will not esteem the day as one to be marked with the whitest stone, which has been spent, it may be in the society of friends who have now passed away, in a summer's ramble among the rocks, and "the high woodlands, which crown this happy valley," or in the enjoyment of a quiet, or, it may, be a festive hour, on the soft green sward, amidst fair Roche's

"White walls and silver springs."

[a] Heb. viii. v. 13.

Addenda.

ADDENDA.

A Flora of Roche Abbey.

THE situation of Roche Abbey is on the magnesian limestone, in a beautiful valley, bounded on the north by a range of perpendicular rocks, and on the south by the "King's Wood." Its fine carboniferous soil, its lake and waterfalls, its old stone quarries and rich banks, unite such a variety of favourable conditions that a Local Flora, worthy of notice, may reasonably be expected.

RANUNCULACEÆ.

R. ficaria. Little celandine, or pilewort.
R. acris. Upright crowfoot.
R. repens. Creeping crowfoot.
R. bulbosus. Bulbous crowfoot.
R. arvensis. Corn crowfoot.
Thalictrum minus. Meadow rue.
Helleborus viridis. Green hellebore.
Aquilegia vulgaris. Columbine.

BERBERIDACEÆ.

Berberis vulgaris. Barberry, in Kingswood and Hedges towards Tickhill, abundant.*

* Barberry used to grow commonly in hedges on the Abbey side of Tickhill; in the same neighbourhood mildew and blight on the cereals were usually mischievous, and the farmer naturally thought that barberry was the cause. A high botanical authority ridiculed the idea, on the ground that the blight on barberry (æcidium) was so different a vegetable to the (ustilago) on barley, or (tilletia) on wheat, that barberry could not be the cause. But facts prove that the spores of fungi, mixed up with the dust of the atmosphere, do mischief both to plants and animals, and we know the spores of one fungus stimulate the growth of the spores of another; we also see daily one fungus parasitic on that of another, and often a third upon that. It is therefore probable that the spores of the fungus on barberry, blown immediately on the wheat when in a moist condition, with rain or dew, would poison the juices of the plant, and so by weakening it, would render it an easy prey to the unwelcome parasites of mildew and blight.

CRUCIFERÆ.

Arabis hirsuta. Rock cress.
Thlaspi arvense. Penny cress.
Capsella bursa-pastoris. Shepherd's purse.

CISTACEÆ.

Helianthemum vulgare. Rock rose.

VIOLACEÆ.

Viola odorata. Sweet violet.
V. canina. Dog violet.

CARYOPHYLLACEÆ.

Lychnis flos-cuculi. Ragged robin.
L. githago. Corn cockle.
Stellaria nemorum. Wood stitchwort.

LINACEA.

Linum catharticum. Purging flax.

MALVACEÆ.

Malva sylvestris. Wild mallow.

TILIACEÆ.

Tilia europæa. Lime-tree.

HYPERICACEÆ.

Hypericum perforatum. St. John's wort.
H. montanum. Mountain St. John's wort.
H. pulchrum. Lesser St. John's wort.

GERANIACEÆ.
Geranium pratense. Crane's bill.
G. columbinum. Purple Crane's bill.

CELASTRACEÆ.
Euonymus europæus. Spindle-tree.

RHAMNACEÆ.
Rhamnus catharticus. Buckthorn.

LEGUMINOSÆ.
Ononis arvensis. Rest harrow.
O. campestris.
Trifolium repens. White clover.
T. pratense. Purple clover.
Medicago sativa. Lucerne.
M. maculata. Spotted trefoil.
Ulex europæus. Furze, whin, gorse.
Sarothamnus scoparius. Broom.
Onobrychis sativa. Saintfoin.
Vicia sylvatica. Climbing vetch.

ROSACEÆ.
Prunus communis. Blackthorn.
P. padus. Bird cherry.
Spiræa ulmaria. Meadow sweet.
Alchemilla vulgaris. Ladies' mantle.
A. arvensis. Parsley piert.
Agrimonia eupatoria. Agrimony.
Geum urbanum. Avens.
G. rivale. Water avens.
Rubus idæus. Raspberry.
Fragaria vesca. Wood strawberry.
Poterium sanquisorba. Burnet.
Potentilla fragariastrum. Cinquefoil.
P. Tormentilla. Tormentil.
Rosa canina. Dog rose.
R. inodora. Slightly-scented sweetbriar.
Pyrus aucuparia. Mountain ash.
P. malus. Crab tree.
Cratægus oxyacantha. Hawthorn.

ONAGRACEÆ.
Epilobium angustifolium. Willow herb.
Circæa lutetiana. Enchanter's nightshade.
Hippuris vulgaris. Mare's tail.

CUCURBITACEÆ.
Bryonia dioica. Red briony.

ARALIACEÆ.
Hedera helix. Ivy.

CORNACEÆ.
Cornus sanguinea. Cornel or dogwood.

UMBELLIFERÆ.
Sanicula europæa. Sanicle.
Angelica sylvestris. Angelica.
Heracleum sphondylium. Hog weed.
Daucus carota. Wild carrot.
Conium maculatum. Hemlock.
Bunium flexuosum. Earth nut.
Æthusa cynapium. Fool's parsley.

SAXIFRAGACEÆ.
Chrysosplenium alternifolium. Golden saxifrage.

CAPRIFOLIACEÆ.
Sambucus nigra. Elder.
Viburnum lantana. Wayfaring tree.
Lonicera xylosteum. The fly honeysuckle

RUBIACEÆ.
Galium aparine. Goose grass or bedstraw.
G. erectum. Upright bed-straw.
Asperula odorata. Sweet woodruff.

VALERIANACEÆ.
Valeriana officinalis. Valerian.
V. dioica. Small marsh Valerian.

COMPOSITÆ
Chichorium intybus. Endive succory.
Apargia hispida. Hawkbit.
Tragapogon pratensis. Goat's beard.
Carduus arvensis. Thistle.
C. pratensis. Meadow thistle.
Arctium lappa. Burdock
Gnaphalium sylvaticum. Cudweed.
Erigeron acris. Fleabane.
Pyrethrum parthenium. Feverfew.
Artemisia vulgaris. Mug wort.
Anthemis arvensis. Chamomile.
Achillea ptarmica. Yarrow.
Chrysanthemum leucanthemum. Ox-eye daisy.
C. segetum. Corn marigold.

ILICACEÆ.
Ilex aquifolium. Holly.

JASMINACEÆ.
Ligustrum vulgare. Privet.
Fraxinus excelsior. Ash.

APOCYNACEÆ.
Vinca minor. Periwinkle.

A FLORA.

GENTIANACEÆ.
Chlora perfoliata. Yellow wort.
Erythræa centaurium. Centaury.

CONVOLVULACEÆ.
Cuscuta europæa. Dodder.
Convolvulus arvensis. Bindweed.

SOLANACEÆ.
Solanum dulcamara. Bitter sweet.
Atropa belladonna, used to grow abundantly about Firbeck churchyard and *Hyoscyamus niger* at Stone, both have disappeared from the locality.

SCROPHULARIACEÆ.
Euphrasia officinalis. Eyebright.
Scrophularia nodosa. Figwort.
Verbascum thapsus. Mullein.

OROBANCHACEÆ.
Lathræa squamaria. Tooth wort.

LABIATÆ.
Mentha sylvestris. Horse mint.
M. arvensis. Mint.
Thymus serpyllum. Wild thyme.
Origanum vulgare. Marjoram.
Ballota nigra. Stinking horehound.
Lamium amplexicaule. Dead nettle.
Nepeta glechoma. Ground ivy.
Symphytum officinale. Comfrey.
Cynoglossum officinale. Hound's tongue.

PRIMULACEÆ.
Anagallis arvensis. Pimpernel.
Primula vulgaris. Primrose.
P. veris. Cowslip.
P. elatior. Oxlip.

PLANTAGINACEÆ.
Plantago media. Plantain.
P. lanceolata. Ribbed plantain.

POLYGONACEÆ.
Rumex pratensis. Meadow dock.
R. acetosella. Sorrel.
Polygonum bistorta. Bistort.
P. persicaria. Spotted persicaria.

THYMELACEÆ.
Daphne laureola. Wood laurel.

EUPHORBIACEÆ.
Euphorbia exigua. Spurge.
Mercurialis perennis. Dog mercury.

URTICACEÆ.
Humulus lupulus. Hop.
Urtica urens. Nettle.
U. dioica. Great nettle.

ULMCAEÆ.
Ulmus montana. Witch elm.
U. suberosa. Common elm.

AMENTIFERÆ.
Alnus glutinosa. Alder.
Betula alba. Birch.
Carpinus betulus. Hornbeam.
Quercus robur. Oak.
Fagus sylvatica. Beech.
Corylus avellana. Hazel.
Populus nigra. Black poplar.
P. tremula. Aspen.

CONIFERÆ.
Pinus sylvestris. Fir.
Taxus baccata. Yew.

TAMACEÆ.
Tamus communis. Black bryony.

HYDROCHARIDACEÆ.
Anacharis alsinastrum. Water thyme. This plant first appeared in the waters at Roche, about 1865; we noticed it in several places growing with great freedom, about half-a-century ago, and then it disappeared as mysteriously as it came.

TRILLIACEÆ.
Paris quadrifolia. Herb paris.

ORCHIDACEÆ.
Orchis pyramidalis. Tall orchis.
O. maculata. Spotted orchis.
Spiranthes autumnalis. Lady's tresses, on the old quarry spoil banks, opposite the farm house, from the high road down to the Abbey.
Neottia nidus-avis. Bird's-nest orchis.
Listera ovata. Twayblade.
Ophrys apifera. Bee orchis.
O. muscifera. Fly orchis.

AMARYLLIDACEÆ.
Narcissus pseudo-narcissus. Daffodil.

LILIACEÆ.
Convallaria majalis. Lily of the valley.

MELANTHACEÆ.
Colchicum autumnale Colchicum.

ARACEÆ
Arum maculatum Wake robin.

JUNCACEÆ.
Juncus conglomeratus Rush.
J lamprocarpus. Rush
Luzula pilosa. Wood rush

CYPERACEÆ.
Carex digitata Sedge.
C fulva Tawny sedge.
C distans. Distant spiked sedge.
C riparia Great common sedge

GRAMINACEÆ.
Phalaris arundinacea. Tall canary grass.
Anthoxanthum odoratum. Sweet vernal grass.
Phleum pratense. Catstail grass
Alopecurus pratensis Foxtail grass
A agrestis. Slender foxtail grass
Agrostis canina. Bent grass
A vulgaris. Common bent grass.
A. alba Fine bent grass.
Holcus lanatus. Soft grass.
H mollis Yorkshire fog.
Aira cæspitosa Turfy hair grass.
A flexuosa. Wavy hair grass.
A præcox. Early hair grass.
Trisetum flavescens. Yellow oat grass
Avena fatua. Wild oat.
A. pratensis Meadow oat.
Poa annua. Annual meadow grass
P nemoralis. Smooth meadow grass
P trivialis. Rough meadow grass
P pratensis Meadow grass
Briza media. Quaking grass.
Cynosurus cristatus Dogstail grass
Dactylis glomerata. Cocksfoot grass
Festuca ovina. Sheep's fescue grass.
F. sylvatica. Wood fescue grass
F. gigantea. Tall fescue grass.
F pratensis Meadow fescue grass
Bromus erectus. Upright brome grass
B asper. Rough brome grass
B. sterilis Barren brome grass
Brachypodium sylvaticum Wood brachypodium.
B pinnatum. Upright brachypodium.
Triticum caninum. Dog wheat.
T repens Creeping dog wheat
Hordeum sylvaticum. Wood barley.
H pratense Meadow barley.
Lolium perenne. Rye grass
L italicum. Italian rye grass.

EQUISETACEÆ.
Equisetum arvense. Horse tail

FILICES (FERNS).
Ophioglossum vulgatum Adder's tongue
Polypodium vulgare. Polypody
Polystichum lobatum. Shield fern.
Lastræa filix-mas. Male fern.
Anthyrium filix fœmina Lady fern.
Scolopendrium vulgare. Hart's tongue.
  A few years back, in an old quarry, on the East side of King's Wood, this sportive fern altered from the common form of two heart-shaped lobes at the bottom of the frond, to one long lobe, full two inches, at a right angle from the mid-rib, the following year it returned to its normal form
Asplenium trichomanes Spleen wort.
A. adiantum-nigrum Black spleen wort.
A. ruta-muraria. Wall rue.
Pteris aquilina. Brake.

MUSCI (MOSSES).
Anœctangium ciliatum Hoary-branched beardless moss.
Bryum ligulatum Thyme thread moss.
B. argenteum. Silver thread moss.
B. palustre. Marsh thread moss.
Dicranum bryoides Lesser fork moss.
D squarrosum. Drooping leaved fork moss.
D scoparium Broom fork moss
Didymodon purpureus. Purple twin-toothed moss.
Encalypta vulgaris. Common extinguisher moss.
Diphyscium foliosum. Leafy double-bladder moss
Funaria hygrometrica Hygrometric cord moss
Fontinalis antipyretica. The greater water moss.
Grimmia pulvinata. Grey cushioned grimmia.
Gymnostomum ovatum. Hairy-leaved beardless moss.

A FLORA.

Gymnostomum microstomum. Small mouthed beardless moss.
Hypnum alopecurum. Foxtail feather moss.
H. commutatum. Curled fern feather moss.
H. cupressiforme. Cypress-leaved feather moss.
H. loreum. Rambling mountain feather moss.
H. molluscum. Plumy-crested feather moss.
H. polyanthus. Many-fruited feather moss.
H. purum. Neat meadow feather moss.
H. rutabulum. Rough-stalked feather moss.
H. schreberi. Schreberian feather moss.
H. sericeum. Silky feather moss.
H. tenellum. Tender awl-leaved feather moss.
H. triquetrum. Triangular-leaved feather moss.
H. velutinum. Velvet feather moss.
Orthotrichum affine. Pale straight leaved bristle moss.
Polytrichum aloides. Aloe leaved hair moss.
P. commune. Common hair moss.
Tortula ruralis. Great hairy screw moss.
T. muralis. Wall screw moss.
T. subulata. Awl-shaped screw moss.
T. rigida. Rigid (aloe-like) screw moss.
Weissia calcarea. Calcareous Weissia.

MARCHANTIACEÆ.

Marchantia polymorpha. Common liver wort.

JUNGERMANNIACEÆ.

Jungermannia asplenioides. Spleenwort scale moss.
Alicularia scalaris. Ladder scale moss.
Scapania nemorosa. Wood scale moss.
Madotheca platyphylla. Flat-leaved scale moss.

LICHENES.

Borrera tenella.
Callema nigrum.
Chroolepsus aureum.
Lepraria flava.
L. alba.
Lepraria viridis.
Lecidea parasemia.
L. rupestris.
L. ulmacola.
L. quernea.
L. ferrugineæ.
Lecanora albella.
L. vitellina.
Opegrapha atra.
O. scripta.
O. vulgata.
O. rufescens.
O. elegans.
Parmelia omphalodes.
P. pulverulenta.
P. olivacea.
P. parietina.
Peltidea canine.
Ramalina fraxinia.
R. fastigiata.
Scyphophorus pyxidatus.
Spiloma nigrum.
Thelotrema lepadinum.
Verrucaria epidermis.
V. cinerea.
V. gemmata.
V. nigrescens.
Variolaria faginea.
V. discoidea.

FUNGI.

Agaricus ceciliæ.
A. excelsus.
A. rachodes.
A. vaginatus.
A. melleus.
A. imbricatus.
A. nudus.
A. infundibuliformis.
A. fusipes.
A. personatus.
A. dryophilus.
A. stipitarius.
A. radicatus.
A. galopus.
A. iris.
A. mitis.
A. vulgaris stylobates.
A. speciosus.
A. mutabilis
A. fastigiatus.
A. trechisporus.
A. crustuliniformis.
A. longicaudus.

Agaricus semiorbicularis.
A. Rubi.
A. melinoides.
A. campestris.
A. arvensis.
A. cretaceus.
A. fascicularis.
A. velutinus.
A. fimiputris.
Æcidium berberidis.
Æ. compositarum.
Æ. crassum.
Æ. violæ.
Aregma bulbosum.
Bolbitius tener.
Boletus parasiticus.
B. edulis.
Bulgaria sarcoides.
Bovista nigrescens.
B. plumbea.
Clavaria amethystina.
C. rugosa.
C. umbrina.
Coprinus atramentarius.
Cortinarius callochrous.
Dothidea betulina.
D. ulmi.
Ergot. Common on the cock's foot grass.
Hirneola auricula-Judæ.
Hygrophorus distans.
H. eburneus.
Lactarius insulsus.
L. piperatus.
L. serifluus.
Lycoperdon cælatum.
L. giganteum.
Lycoperdon pyriforme.
Marasmius urens.
M. peronatus.
M. oreades.
M. insititius.
M. rotula.
M. graminum.
Morchella esculenta.
Nyctalis parasitica.
Paxillus involutus.
Peziza aurantia.
P. coccinea.
Phallus impudicus.
Polyporus lentus.
P. spumeus.
P. ulmarius.
P. vulgaris.
P. betulinus.
P. squamosus.
P. velutinus.
P. versicolor.
Rhytisma acerinum.
R. punctatum.
Russula heterophylla.
R. virescens.
R. nitida.
R. alutacea.
Sphæria berberidis.
S. bombarda.
S. confluens.
S. innumera.
S. ceuthosporoides.
S. mamæformis.
Thelephora terrestris.
T. versicolor.
Xylaria hypoxylon.

ADDENDA.

In addition to the Notices of Grants of the Monastic property of Roche given in the text, the following appear in the *"Inventories of Particulars for Grants preserved among the Records of the late Augmentation Office,"* in Appendices to 9th and 10th Reports of the Deputy Keeper of the Public Records.

"Bellow, John, and John Broxholme, 10th June, 38 Henry VIII, Sec. 4, Request to purchase,"—*Inter alia,*

"Farm at Staynton (York), late of the Monastery of Roche (York), Memorandum and Woods."—*Rep.* 9, *p.* 170.

"Brokylesye, Robert, and John Dyon, 28th May, 36 Henry VIII. No request." —*Inter alia,*

"Valuation of Farms in Wynterton (Lincoln), late of the Monastery of Rupe *alias* Roche (York). Memorandum, summary, and particulars of sale of this"— *Ibid. p.* 177.

"Broxholme, John, and John Bellow, 30th September, 37 Henry VIII. Request to purchase,"—*Inter alia multa,*

"Farm in the city of Lincoln, late of the Monastery of Roche (York)."—*Ibid. p.* 182.

"Butler, William, and others (No date), Henry VIII. No request."—*Inter alia,*

"Woods pertaining to the Manor of Roxbye (Lincoln), late of the Monastery of Roche."

"Woods pertaining to Bramclyffe Graunge (York), late of the Monastery of Roche." *Ibid. p.* 183.

"Girlyington, Nicholas, 12th March, 35 Henry VIII. No request."

"Farms in Roxby (Lincoln), late of the Monastery of Roche *alias* Rupe (York), and Woods."—*Ibid. p.* 213.

"Ramsden, William, of York, 20th February, 37 Henry VIII. Sec. 2. Requests to purchase,"—*Inter alia,*

"Farm in South Annifton (York), late of the Monastery of Roche (York). Memorandum."—*Rep.* 10, *p.* 258.

"Sutton, Charles and John, 12th and 24th February, 36 Henry VIII.—*Inter alia,*

"Woods belonging to a Farm called Scotney, in Roxbye (Lincoln), late of the Monastery of Roche (York)."—*Ibid. p.* 281.

"Welbore, Michael, 13th December: Clyfford, George, 12th February, 36 Henry VIII. Requests to purchase"—*Inter alia,*

"Farms in Scawsby, Smeton, and Camsall (York), late of the Monastery of Roche (York). [The pen has been drawn through the Smeton entry.]"—*Ibid. p.* 296.

Page 159.　　　　　**Charter of Abbot Walter.**

This charter is strangely included among those of Kirkstall Abbey, with which it has no connexion, in the *Monasticon Anglicanum,* Edit. Caley, Ellis, and Bandinel.

May not the Wineley there mentioned be a contracted form of Wellingley? The Fitz-Paynes, lords of this latter place, were certainly closely allied to the family of Tinsley. They appear also under the name of De Hotens, from Hoton Roberts, where they held half a knight's fee of the crown: Henry de Tenneflowe holding the other moiety.—*See Kirby's Inquest.*

Sir Henry de Tinfley, married Lucy, daughter of Sir Robert de Hoton Roberts.—*Hunter's South Yorkshire, p.* 399.

Page 169, 8th line from top.

It has been suggested that the hospitium, or guesthouse of the Abbey, was contained in this gatehouse, which seems to have been the case at Workfop, and in some other examples, but this opinion is open to considerable doubt here, for, in the first place in these Ciftercian Abbeys, the hospitium generally formed a separate building of considerable magnitude, as at Fountains and Kirkftall, in the former of which there seem to have been two; and secondly, the arrangement here, on the ground floor at leaft, differs from the case of Workfop, inafmuch as the fide compartments are not separated from the gateway, as they are in that inftance where they form diftinct apartments or offices, as would be required for a guesthouse. Here all is open, as if made for the shelter of a confiderable concourse of people while waiting for some purpose; this would be likely to be the case with those who were expecting the diftribution of the monaftic alms. We may therefore, perhaps, with more probability, conjecture that the gatehouse at Roche formed the almonry, as well as the porter's lodge, of the Abbey.

That the gate was the usual place for the diftribution of alms, both in monaftic and private eftablifhments is shewn by the following passage from a curious old poem much quoted in "*Parker's* Domeftic Architecture of England," speaking of the *aumonere* or *elemosinarius*, it is said:—

> "All the broken mete he kepys y wate.
> To dole to pore men at ye gate."
>
> MS. Sloane, No. 1986 f. 43.

Page 172, 11th line from top, after the word "lockyer," add

Or it may be a credence, from "Credenza," *(Ital.)* a cupboard or shelf, on which the elements and facred veffels were placed, before confecration. This, if not a separate table, was frequently formed of a shelf in the niche or fereftella, over the pifcina. The arrangement found here is very unufual, though the same thing exifts at Kirkftall under a round-headed arch.

Page 173, 5th line from bottom.

"About the laft quarter of the 12th century:" thus the passage was originally written, but was altered as it ftands in the text, in deference to the opinion of a very experienced and judicious Antiquarian.

ERRATA.

Page xvii, 14th line from top "Anflem" should be "Anfelm."
Page 4, 3rd line from bottom "Aorman" should be "Norman."
Page 22, last line of note "Pantage" should be "Pontage."
Page 114, 16th line from bottom "1355" should be "1535."
Page 156, 9th line from top "Lincolnshire" should be "Nottinghamshire."
Page 159, 7th line from bottom insert "the" before learned.
Page 174, 4th line from bottom "forman" should be "formam."

Index.

INDEX.

A

Aaron the Jew at York	155
Abbey of Sancta Maria de Rupe	xx
A B C, by William Thorpe	67
Abdy	99, 108
Aberdeen	42
Abingdon	55 (*n*)
Abbots of Roche, list of	2
Abbot's House	153
Abbot and Convent of Roche	155
———Robert, of Whitby	7
———of Newminster, Letter from	60, 62
———of Fountains Abbey	6
———of Peterborough	171 (*n*)
———Alexander, of Kirkstall	9
———of Kirkstead	81, 151
———of Newminster	60
———of Roche, Afton John de	55
"Abbreviatio Rotulorum Originalium"	110 (*n*)
Abstract of the Acquittance of the Jews	155
Act for the Dissolution of Smaller Monasteries	74
Acton in Suffolk, legend at	26
Acworth, Thomas	85
Acuto, Adam de Monte	141
Adam de Gigglefwick	50
Adam, son of Ralph de Armthorpe	100
Addenda	181
Advowson	126
Aggecroft	15, 17, 99
Agnes, daughter of Robert de Brunnington	100
Agreement between Abbot and Convent of Roche, Thomas Rillington, and others	114
Alan, the parson of Malthy	120
———, Abbot of Roche	34
Albus, William	108
Alexander the IV., Pope, Bull of	31, 110
Almonbury	151
Algret	106
Alice, Countess of Eu	17
Alteration in Custody of Seals of Religious Orders	45
Alverley	99, 120, 142
Alz, William de	10
Amabill de Brampton	109
Andrew, Saint	83
Anes	15, 21
Anne, John	149
Anne, William de	48
Annifton, South	187
Anfton	21, 120, 141
Anfelm	xvii
Antonie, John	71
Archbishop of York	24, 25, 36, 37, 40, 43, 49, 54, 55, 58, 60, 62, 64, 66, 79, 114

Architecture, The	xvii, 163
Arcy, Henry de	111
Armthorpe, Henry de	100
———, John de	155
———, Ralph de	100
———, Thomas de	15, 100
———	16, 21, 28, 34, 35, 89, 100, 101, 125
Arnaldus	4 (*n*)
Arncliffe	101
Arnethorpe	100
———, Thomas de	100
Arneldthorpe	100
Arnewy, Henry	157
Ashenbeech	101
Ashton, Arthur	134
Ashover	15, 16, 21, 101
Aske, Robert, at insurrections	78-80
——— executed at York	81
Askern	21, 101, 144
———, Maurice de	101
Atheling, Edgar	xvii
Afton	100
Aexoure	21, 101
Avenell, William	15
Avenal, William, Lord of Haddon	123
Averpenning	22 (*n*)
Augmentations, Court of	134
Augi, Countess of	xx
———Henry, Earl of	xxii

B

Bacon, William	121
Bagshawe, W. H. G.	153
Balne	101
Banke	131
Bankewell, Simon de	54
Banks, James	89
Bauuent, Ralph de	152
Barbot, William	10
———, Richard	5
Bardolf, Hamelin	15
Bardolph, Hamelin	160
———, Katherine	160
———, Hugh	160
———, Ralph	160
Baret, Richard	10, 145
Bargo, Hugh de	23
Barker, Bobert	122
Barlings, Abbot of	81
Barnby	15, 16, 21, 32, 89, (*n*) 101, 102, 104
———, Benedict, Rector of	101
———, Richard de, William, son of	147
Barneby, Gervase de	5, 15, 32, 101, 104
———, Richard de	32, 102

Barneby, Hugh de	32
———, Alexander de	32
———, Thomas de	32
Barnoldfwick	103
Barnoldfwic	174 (n)
Bartlett, Cromwell's fervant	70
Barton, Great	27
Barry, Richard	55, 126
Barvile, William de	103
Baffett, William	123
Battle of Bannockburn	48
——— Boroughbridge	48
Bawtry	12, 21, 103
———, Richard de	106
Bayonne	37
Becket, Thomas à	9, 83
Beggam in Suffex	68
Beke, John	151
Bella Aqua, Thos. de	160
Bell, Adam	93
Bellewe, John	123
Bellew, Thomas de	122
Bellftring Lands	104
Bellow, John	187
Benedict, Saint	37
Benedictines	167 (n)
Benedictine Nuns	158
Beatrix, fifter of Roger de Bufli	xx
Bently, Lord of	xxiii
Bereus, Robert of	12
Beresford, Edward	122
Bergh, Roger de	122
Bernard, Saint	xviii
Bernehill	21
Berwick-on-Tweed	47
Bere, John	121
Betham	177
Bigod, Sir Francis	80
Bilham	103, 121, 126
———, Hugh de	126, 155
Bildewas, Abbot of	133
Bircheworth	117
Bifham Abbey	91 (n)
"Black Book" of the Monafteries	74
Blackftondelf	134
Bladefworth, William de	104
Blakehills	26
Blithefhaw	103, 149
Blodwith	22 (n)
Bloxolme, John	122
Blund, Richard le	144
Blythe, 11, 12, 21, 87, (n) 103, 118, 141, 144, 153, xx	
Blythe, Caftle of	xx
——— Priory, Regifter of	103
———, Prior of	103
Bodleian Library	87 (n)
Bohler, Mr. J.	vi
Bolgate	11
Boniface VIII, Pope	40, 133
Booth, Laurence	63
Botildewellewang	104, 151, 152
Bowes, Sir Robert	80
Boxley Abbey	83
Boyvill, Sir R. de	140
Braithwell	21, 104
———, Artrop de	104
Braiton	151
Bramclyffe	187
Bramley	16, 21, 104, 115
Brampton, Robert de	109
———, Michael de	109
Bramwith	15, 16, 21, 102, 104, 105
———, Nicholas de	32

Brancliffe	15, 16, 28, 34, 35, 100, 105, 125
Brathmere, Fifhery of	114
———, fee Hatfield	106
Brettvile, Robert de	108
Bridlington	105
———, Prior of	81
Brindfworth	147
Brinton, Robert	122
Britifh Mufeum	82
Brochard, Girard	23
Brokylefye, Robert	187
Brookhouse	105
Broom Riddings	105
Brother Thomas	102 (n)
Brown, Mr.	164, 165, 172
———, Ralph	139
Broxholme, John	187
Bruce, Robert	46, 47, 48, 49
Bruerton, Robert	159
Brumpton, William de	137
Brunington, Robert de	100
Bruntat, John (?)	109
———, Eudo de	109
Bug, Thomas de	140
Bugthorpe	106
Bugthorpe, Hamel de	146
———, Nicholas de	106
Building of Roche Abbey	6
Bull of Pope Urban IV.	30
———, Alexander IV.	31
Burgh, Thomas Lord	139
Burgundy, Duke of	xviii
Burnet, Bifhop	72, 79, (n) 81, (n) 84
Burnell Family	126
———, William	130
Burton, Dr. v, 15, (n) 36, 50, 56, 61, 110, 111, 144, 146	
———, Richard	120
———, Robert	146, 154
———, William	65
Burton's "Anatomy of Melancholy"	82 (n)
Bury, Sir Thomas de	140
——— St. Edmunds	27, 40
Bufli, Ernaldus	xx, xxii
———, Idonea de	140
———, John de	xxii, 11, 12, 125
———, Jordan de	xxii
———, Richard de xxi, xxii, 4, 5, 6, 9, 11, 15, 94, 110, 119, 120, 125, 126, 172 (n)	
———, Robert de	10
———, Roger de	xx, xxi, xxii
Buteiler, William le	5
Butler, William	105, 187
Byland Abbey	45
Bylton, Geoffery	154
Bynd, of Eels defined	114 (n)

C.

Callinglow	106
Calverlay, Sir W.	159 (n)
Cambridge, Countefs of	58, 83, 127, 171
Cambridge, Earl of	xxiii
Campfall, Mr. W. H.	vi
Campfall	106, 126, 144
Canby, Mr.	94
Canterbury	47, 107, 158
Carlifle	44, 46
Carlton	106, 107
Carucages	21
Carr	107
Carter, William	86, 88
Carver	154

INDEX. 193

Carzon, Robert . . . 32
Caſtage 22
Caſtello, Gena de . . 109
Caſtleſhaw . . . 107
Catwick . . . 107
Cawood 54
Cauz, Alfred le . . 23
Cellarer of Fountains Abbey . 14
Chalons, Biſhop of . . xviii
Chalons-ſur-Saone . . xvii
Chaucer 50
Chaucomb, Warine de . 136
Chaucumbe, John de . . 139
Chapel, Alan Fitz . . 34
———, Henry de . . 23
Chapter Houſe . . 86, 89 (*n*)
Charter Houſe . . 90 (*n*)
——— of Richard de Buſli . 4
——— of Richard Fitz Turgis . 5
——— of William, Earl of Warren . 28, 108
——— of John de Warren, Earl of Surrey 51
——— of William de Roſſington . 108
——— of Amabill de Brampton . 109
——— of William de Chaworth . 111
——— of Henry de Shelley . 117
——— of John Levet . . 126
——— of Walter, Abbot of Roche 122
——— of Adam Fitz Burnell . 125
——— of Warinus de Scargill . 131
——— of Philip Paynel . 138
——— of Idonea de Vipont . 140
——— of Abbot Richard and Robert de Ripers 142
——— of Ralph de Rainville . 148
——— of Hugh, son of Hugh Laſcy . 148
——— of Edmund de Lacy . 151
——— of Maud de Lovetot . 152
——— of Matilda de Moles . 153
——— of Walter Abbot, and the Convent of Roche . . . 159
Chaworth, Henry de . . 111
————, John de . . 111
————, William de . 111, 145
Chatſworth . . . 107, 145
Cheſter . . . 144, 151
Chetham, Chriſtopher and Ralph 134
Chriſt's Church College, Oxford 68
Church, The . . 169
——— of St. George, Doncaſter . 109
Ciſteaux . . xvii, xviii, 47, 49
Ciſtercian Devotions . . xix
Civita Vecchia . . 31
Clayton, David . . 131, 141, 144
Clifford, Henry, Earl of . 83
————, Robert de . . xxii
————, Lord Roger . . xxii
————, Lord Thomas . xxiii, 59, 83
————, Inquiſitions . . 126
Clifton, Alan de . . 142
Clinton, Lord . . 122
————, Lord Admiral . 117
Clipſtone . . 103, 149, 152
Clyfford, George . . 187
Cobcroft, Sir Robert . . 91
Coc, Reginald . . 108
Cokewald, Henry de . . 139
Cole MS. . . . 93
Coleton, William de . . 139
Collys, Nicholas . . 86, 88
Colmanhaghe . . 158
Common Seals . . 46, 118
Compendium of Diſcoveries at Roche, by Drs. Legh and Layton . 82
Coningsbrough, King of . 109
Coninsborough . xxiii, 15, 21, 34, 58, 104, 107
————, Lord of . . xx
———— Caſtle . . xx
Conference between Royal Army and Rebels at Ferribridge . . 79
Confirmation of Counteſs of Eu . 17
——— of King Henry III. . 20
——— of King Richard I. . 16
——— of Pope Urban III. . 14, 151
——— of King Edward II., of lands in Walkeringham . . 156
Corngilds . . . 21
Cornwall, Duchy of . . 149
Cotes, Allandel . . 114
———, John . . . 114
Council at St. Paul's, London . 45
Counhal, William de . . 34
Counties . . . 21
Courcy, Richard de . . 135
Couſen, Joane . . . 122
Coventry . . . 48, 82
Craſſis, Alexander . . 153
Cramcumb, Godfrey de . 23
Craven, Hiſtory of . . 7
Creſſi, William de . . 18
Cromwell, Thomas 70, 71, 74, 78, 79, 80, 91, 92 (*n*)
Croxton, Sir John de . . 140
Croyland Abbey . . 6
Croyton, John de . . 140
Crumbewell, John de . xxi, xxii
Cudworth . . . 108
Cumberland, Earl of . 82, 83, 127, 129, 130
Cumberworth . . 108
Cundal, Henry, Abbot of Roche 67, 72, 84, 86, 87
. . . . 88, 94
Cundall, Thomas . . 86

D

Dadeſley . . . xx
Danegilds . . . 21
Darcy, Lord . . . 79
Darell, Geoffery . . 154
Darley, Henry de . . 144
Deepcar . . . 108
De la Roche . . . 125
De Rupe . . . 125
De Hotens . . . 187
Denſhaw . . . 108
Derby . . . 84, 99, 123
Deſcription of a Monaſtery . 69
——— Monk . . 69
Dionyſius, Abbot of Roche . 9, 10
Diſcontent in the Roman Catholic Church in the time of Henry III. . 24
Diſſolution, The . . 67
Docelin, Maſter, the Chancellor . 23
Doddeſworth, John . 82, 86, 87, 88
Doddington, Grantee . . 149
Dodſworth 103, 104, 111 (*n*), 125 (*n*), 138 (*n*), 148 (*n*)
Domeſday Book . . 12
———— Survey . . xx, xxii
Doncaſter xx, xxiii, 21, 79, 80, 81, 83, 108, 109, 146
————, Deanery of . . 94 (*n*)
Doncaſtre, John de . . 132
Dover . . . 47
——— burnt by the French . 39
Draft of an Act of Parliament after the Suppreſſion . . . 95
Drax, Richard . . 86
——, Prior of . . 135, 136, 139
——, Priory of . . 136
Drengeſflete . . . 157

25

Drigwrt, Hugh de	15, 119
Dr. Layton's Letter to Thomas Cromwell	70
Drs. Legh and Layton and the Act of Suppreſſion	77
Dromore, Biſhop of	61, 64, 65
Dugdale	xxi
Duningeton, William de	10
Dunſcroft	31, 110
Durandus	3, 4, 6, 8, 9, 37, 165
Durham	60
Dyon, John	187

E

Eaſtwood, Rev. J.	vi, 91 (n)
Eccleſfield	91 (n), 108
Eccleſhall, Ralph de	108
Eccleſal, Ralph de	152
Edinſor, Adam de	107
Edmund, brother of King Edward	38, 41, 43
———, Earl of Cornwall	43
———, Saint	82
Edward I. King of England	38, 39, 40, 41, 42, 100, 106, 125
——— II. „	46, 48, 100, 118, 152
——— III.. „ Royal Charter of	112
——— III. „	xxiii, 127, 152
——— VI. „	146, 149
———, Prince	32, 33
Edwin, Earl	xx
Eſſarts	22
Eglifton Abbey	45
Eilrichethorpe	4, 5, 9, 10, 110
Ellercar, Sir Ralph	80
Ellis, Sir Henry	91 (n), 92 (n)
Ellys, William	149, 159
———, Hugh	149, 150
———, James	150
Elmiſhall	125
Elizabeth, Queen of England	xxii
Elſi	xxi, 5
Elmfall	126
Ennuſe	110
Engleis, Hugh le	12
Erdeſale, Nicholas, ſon of Jeffery de	144
Errata	188
Eſpeke, Walter	xviii
Eſton, John de	121
Eu, Counteſs of	xx, xxii, 17, 99, 120, 125, 174
Eudo, Robert, Fitz	15
———, William, ſon of	145
———, Robert, ſon of	160
Everſham	33
Ewes or Ehus	110
———, John, ſon of Gilbert de	141
Exeter, Thomas, Duke of	59 (n)
Execution of the Abbot of Barlings, at Lincoln	81
———————————————Fountains, at Tyburn	81
"Excerpta é Rot. Fin."	xxii (n)

F

Fac-ſimiles of the ſignatures of the monks of Roche at the diſſolution	86
Fairwath	16, 21
Farworth	110, 112
Fenwick	146
Ferribridge	79
Ferrars, Earl of	123
Feſh, Triſtram	149
Feyrford, Matilda de	112
"Fines, Ebor."	145 (n), 147 (n)
Firbeck	104, 111
Fiſhlake	28, 111

Fitzwilliam, John, Lord	127
————, Thomas	121
Fitz-Payne, Robert	159
————, Sir Jordan	145, 146, 159
Fitz-John, Richard	xxii
Fitz-Turgis, Richard	xxiii
Flanders	47
Fleming, William the	119
Flemenfrith	22
Flixburgh	111, 135, 139
Flomenwith	22
Flora of Roche	181
Florence	26
Foſſard's	12
Foljambe, George Savile	46
Fogſwell	5
Ford Hall	153
Forſtal	22
Foſſard, Nigel de	xxii
Fountains Abbey	6, 7, 14, 50, 92 (n), 166, 167, 168, 171, 172, 174 (n), 177
————, Abbot of	81, 88 (n)
Foundation Charter of Richard de Buſli	4, 9
————of Richard Fitz-Turgis	5
————of John de Buſli	11
Franc-pledge	22
France	50
Freeman, John	91 (n)
Fretwell, Roger	104
Froude, quoted	78, 79
Frankland	131
Frithefend	157
Friar Mere	132
Fulham, Geoffery de	158
Fuller, Hugh	130
Furnival, Richard	160
————, Gerard de	19, 23, 152
Furneys, Richard de	107
Fyſhburn, Richard	86, 88

G

Gamul	4
Gamel, Filius Beſingi	5
Garth, William	127
Gaſcony	47
Gatehouſe, The	175
Gaunt, Robert de	135
Gaveſton Piers	46
Gebod, Robert, ſon of	111
Gerard, William Fitz	15, 142
Gerbode, William, ſon of	104
George, ſon of Lord Lumley	80
Gerwedon, Abbey	45
Gifford, John	149
Gigglefwick, Adam de	50
————, its well	50
Gilbert, the Chaplain	117
Gildingwells	111
Gilds	21
Gillott, Henry	150
Gilpin, Mr.	164, 165
Girlyington, Nicholas	187
Glaſ, Robert, ſon of	107
Glouceſter, the Earl of	26
Goderic-Riding	111
Goſeker	105
Grafton	74
Grandimont Order, Peter of the	xviii (n)
Grangefield	154
Grant, Royal	134
Gray John, Abbot of Roche	60
Greasborough	121

INDEX.

Green, Grantee	154
——, John	102
——, Thomas	89, 150
Grendon, Henry de	127
Grimbald, John	148
Guienne, Duke of	38
——, war in	39
Gunhale	100
Gunnora	xxiii
Guvry, Reginald	120
Gwarine, Abbot of Pontiniac	9

H

Haddon	123
Haimfoken	22
Haket, Ralph	122
Haloghby, Henry de	127
Hall, Grantee	154
Halyhton, Adam of	105
Hampol	125
Harleian MS.	165 (n)
Hartington, H.	123
Harold, Earl	xx, xxiii
Harworth	110, 112
——, Gamellus de	112
Haftings, Brian	146
Hatfield	xxiii, 101, 110, 112, 150
——Park and Woods	114
Haugh	108, 115, 117
Haytfeld, Church of	113, 114, 144, 145
Heathcote	123
Heden, Gerard de	144
——, Simon de	144
Helgheby, Galfrid de	159
Helias, Abbot of Kirkftall	18
Hellaby	115
Henfrew, Hugh	153
——, Janet	153
Hengwith	22
Henry I., King of England	xvii
—— II.	120
—— III., King of England	xxii (n), 100, 101, 105, 106, 110, 125, 139, 146, 147, 156, 158, 159, 160, 177
——Summons of	32
—— V.	xxiii
—— VI.	120
—— VIII.	70, 101, 102, 105, 110 (n), 122, 123, 128, 130, 131, 134, 146, 149, 152, 158
——, Abbot of Newminfter	18
——, Prior of Roche	7
Helpol	158
Herthwic, Robert de	105
Herfy, Baldwin de	108
——, Malveifin de	108
Heflington, John, Abbot of Roche	67
Hefley	115
Heftwell	116
Hewett	131
Hewet, Robert	119
——, Agnes	119
Heyden, Richard de	34
Heyr, Walter de	152
Hidage	21
Higgins, Godfrey	145
Hillbrigthorpe	116, 125, 132, 133, 134
"Hiftory of the Manor of Todwick"	94
Hitchcock, Robert de	146
Hoderode, Sir John de	151
Holme	116, 148
Holmes, Thomas, Grantee	149
—— Carr Wood	116

Holtheng	110
Holy Trinity, Prior of	136
Hooton	xxii, 116, 127
——, Slade	116, 144
——, Levet	116, 126, 127, 144
——, Jordan	116
——, Roger	116
——, Allen de	105
——, Barony of	147
—— Roberts	116, 118, 144, 187
——, Sir Robert de	188
Hope	116
Horbiry, Richard de	140
——, Ralph de	122
Hofpital of St. John of Jerufalem	113
Holtal, Adam de and Donyfia his Wife	153
Hoxebrigge	148
Hugh, the Clerk of Rotherham	10
"Hundred Rolls"	106, 120, 146 (n), 147 (n), 153
Hundefdon, Lord	104
Hunt	131
Hunter, Mr.	xxiii (n), 104, 110 (v), 144, 145, 147
	188

I

Ichells	117
Ickles	117, 118
Idle, River	134
Idonea, Widow of Robert de Vipont	xxi
Ikkyls	147
Images burnt at Smithfield	83
Image of the Crucifix on a Rock at Roche	82
Index	191
Infangthef	22
Ingbirchworth	117
Ingleby, William	154
Injunctions given by the Commiffioners on leaving Monafteries	73
Innesby	117
Infpections	22
Infula, William de	105
——, Jordan de	116
Introduction	xvii
Inventory of Roche Abbey	88
Ifabel	xxi

J

Jackfon, Mr. Charles	vi
——, Charles	104, 120
——, Grantee	149
Jeffcock, Rev. J. T., F.S.A.	vi
Jeffry and Watt	93
Jeremiah, parfon of Roffington	100, 126
Jervaulx, Abbot of	81
Jeroval Abbey	45
Jews at York	13, 155
John, King of England	101, 105, 106, 135, 136, 147, 153
——, the Forefter	34
——, Abbot of Roche	42, 43
——, fon of Phillip	23
Johnfton MSS.	147
Jordan, fon of Phillip de Marr	121

K

Karleol, W.	23
Keeper, John	89
Ker, John	117
Ketelbergh, Reginald de	109, 155
Kilnhurft	118
——, Roger de	118

Kilnhurſt, Thomas de	118
Kimberworth	xxi
"Kirby's Inqueſt"	100, 121, 187
Kirkburton, Hiſtory of	108 (n), 117 (n), 150 (n)
Kirkſtall	18, 19, 103, 166, 167, 168, 169, 170, 171, 172, 174 (n), 177, 187, 188
Kirkſtead	xxi, 177
Kiveton	103, 118
Knight's fee, defined	100
Knot Hill	132
Knott, legend of	26
Kyrkeby, John de	137
Kyveton, John de	103, 118

L

Laci, Henry de, Lord of Pontefract	9
Lacy, Roger	18
——, Robert	148
——, Edmund de	144, 151
——, Henry de	116, 174
——, John de	151
——, Margaret de	151
——, Alice de	151
Lambcote	15, 16, 119, 145
Lambcroft	15, 119
Lancaſter	99
————, Thomas, Earl of	48
————, Duchy of	149
Landſdown MSS.	82
Langdon Abbey	70
Langley, Edmund de	xxiii, 52
Langthwaite, Hugh de	5, 109, 126
————, Richard de	121
Laſci, Thomas de	148
Laſcy, Hugh	148
Laughton	18, 43, 48, 105, 111, 120, 147
————, Lord of	xx
Layton, Dr.	70, 71, 72, 80, 81, 82, 83, 91 (n)
Lee, Sir Richard	158
Leek, John	106
Legend of Acton	26
———— Roche	25
Legh, Dr.	70, 71, 72, 77, 80, 81, 82, 83
Leiceſter	153
Leirwith	22
Leming, Adam	155
Leon	109
Letter from the Abbot of Newminſter	60, 62
———— on the ſuppreſſion of Roche Abbey	89
Letewell, Peter de	155, 159
Levet	xxii
——, John	55, 126
——, Richard	116
——, William de	xxiii, 126, 127
——, Hammond de	116
——, Conſtantia	126
Lewes	28, 32, 52, 92 (n), 112
——, Monks of	147
Leweſtye, John	154
Leybun, Roger de	xxii
Librate	107
Lichfield	123
————, Biſhopric of	82
————, Mr. William de	151
Ligulf	16
Lincolnſhire	xxi, 91 (n), 111, 134, 135, 159, 160
————, Biſhop of	136
————	43, 44, 84, 99, 120
Lindric	15, 17, 21, 120
Lindrick, William de	152
————, near Tickhill	120
———— Brook	120

Lindrick Common	120
———— Dale	120
Lindſey, Robert de	171 (n)
Liſt of Abbots	2
———— Subſcribers	viii
L'Iſle, Jordan de, Jordan ſon of	148
Liſa	177
Littel, Thomas de	117
Littlemorye	145
London	33, 40, 41, 42, 46, 102
Longſword, William	12
London, Dr.	90, 92
Louth Park	77, 171, 177
Louweder, Richard de	144
Loverſal	99, 120, 142
Lovetot, Maud de	152
Lowthwaite	4
Lucius, Pope	14
Ludham, Euſtachius de	106
Lumby	100, 120
Lumley, Lord, eldeſt ſon of	80
Luterel, Andrew	137, 147
————, Galfred, and Fretheſant Wife of	147
————, Robert	147
Lyvet, James de	122
————, Richard	122

M

Magilldhylls	145
Maidſtone	83
Malcolm III.	xvii
Maltby	xxi, xxii, 4, 7, 11, 21, 120
———— Mill	116
————, Lord of	xxiii
Malgerio, Maſter	23
"Mancheſter Guardian"	134
Mandate from King Edward II.	48
Manſelyn of Doncaſter	116
———— of Brodſworth	116
Manvers, Leo de	15, 100, 105
Mapes, Walter	54
Maſter of the Rolls	167 (n)
Matilda of York	58, 59
Margens, Thomas	114
Mariſco, Henry de	100
Mar	21, 121
——, Roger de	15
——, Jordan de	148
——, Payn de	121, 148
Marr, Roger de	122
————, The Grange of	121
Marſh, Henry de	109
Mary, Queen of England	82
Maſon, William	104
Maude, daughter of Thomas, Lord Clifford	xxiii
Mauger, ſon of Roger de Stokes	115
Maumirr, Henry	157
Mawoners, Michael de	152
Medyltun, Thomas	86, 88
Meleton, William de	127
Melroſe, Chronicle of	18 (n)
Melſoe or Meux	177
Melton, William de	47, 49
Memers, Richard de	108
Merlay, Ranulph de	6
Merſſh, Robert de	127
Meteham, Thomas de	127
Michael, ſon of Leo de Manvers	100
Micklebring	121
————, Eugenia	121
Middleton	123
Mileri, William de	5

INDEX.

Misterton, Robert de 144
———, Walter de 158
———, Robert, parson of 152
Mitchell, Mr 46, 159
Moles, Matilda de 141, 153
———, Hugh de 141, 142, 144, 153
———, William de 15, 142
Molesme, Robert de xviii
"Monasticon Anglicanum" 110, 122, 150, 151, 159, 166, 167, 174 (n), 187
"——— Eboracense" v, 36, 146
Monastery, description of 69
——— de Rupe 152, 153
Monkeboye 157
Monkebothe 158
Monk Bretton 121
———, description of 69
Monks Bridge 105
——— of Pipewell 7
——— of Salley 7
——— of the Rock 4, 7, 18, 125
Monby, Sir J de 140
Monteby, John de 140
Montfort, Simon de 32, 33
Montforth, John 118
Monyash 121
Morton, Robert, Earl of xx, xxii
Mores, Edward Rowe, Esq 110
More, Richard 146
Morfurlung 158
Morley 121, 122
Mortimer 33
Mortmain Act 35
Morpeth, John, Abbot of Roche 66
——— 7
Morehouse 108 (n), 117 (n), 150
Moslay, Richard 86, 88
Mowbray, John de 48
Moyle, Mr 130
Multhorpe, John 127
Munkegate, Peter de 29

N

Newhum 16
Newhall 21, 122
Newland 122
Newerth 115
Newminster Abbey 7, 18, 66, 164, 177
———, John, Abbot of 60
———, Robert, Abbot of 7
Newmarch, Adam de 5, 6, 15, 122
Newmarches xxiii
Newcombe, John 154
Newsome 15, 122
New Visitation of Religious Houses ordered 81
Neuflet 114
Nevil, Geo Reg 59 (n)
Nicholas, clerk of Laughton 120
———, parson of Tickhill 12
Norfolk, Duke of 79, 80, 81
Northumbland, Duke of 101
Northampton 46
North, Edward 130
Normandy, Robert, Duke of xvii
Norwich, Galfrid de 29
Normanville, Ralph de 122, 155
Norwicen, Thomas 155
Nostel, the Prior of 121
"Notes and Queries" 27 (n)
Notte, William 146
"Nottinghamshire, History of" xxii
——— xx, 106, 123, 146, 158

Nottingham xx, 41, 84, 103, 115, 122, 141, 156
———, County of 154
———, Sir Robert de 151

O

Oblations, Alms, &c 160
Odenell, son of Nicholas D'Aubeney 105
Odo, Filius Johannis 5
Oldcotes 16, 21, 123
———, Philip de 122
Oneash or Anes 15, 21, 99, 106, 121, 123, 145
Ormesby, William de 41
Orm 16
Osbertus, Sir 151
Osberton, Roger de 157
Osmund, Abbot of Roche 13, 14, 16, 17, 18, 19, 20, 25, 101, 105, 120, 147, 153, 174
Outfangthef 22
Oxford 68
———, Earl of 79
Oxgang 99, 107

P

Painell, William 135
———, Hugh 137
———, Jordan 5
Parcel of the Possessions of the Monastery of Roche 128
Paris, Matthew 12, 25, 26 (n)
Parker's Domestic Architecture of England 188
Parks, John Del 114
Pannage or Pawnage 22
Particulars for Grants 101, 102, 104, 106, 117, 120, 122, 128, 130, 141, 144, 146, 149, 154, 156, 187
Passage 22
Patent Rolls 138, 139
Paul's Cross 83
Paul, Nicholas de Saint 99, 151, 152
———, St Richard de 148
———, St Robert de 29
Payne, Robert Fitz 12, 15
———, Geffery Fitz 115
Payn, Robert, son of 111
Paynell, Ralph 135
———, John 137
———, Phillip 138
Paynel, Adam 148
———, William 147
Pension to the Abbot of Roche 87
Penrice 83
Percy, William 28
Peter, John Fitz 114
Petre, Doctor William 87
Peterborough, Abbot of 171 (n)
Philis's Hole 27
Philippa, Queen of England 52, 53, 113, 114
Philip, Abbot of Roche 34, 35, 136
———, King of France 38, 41
Piers Ploughman's "Vision and Creed" 55
"Pilgrimage of Grace" 78
Pipewell 7, 177
"Placitorum Abbreviatio" 31
Plantagenet, Richard 59
Pleas 21
———, Roll of 135
Plesley, Simon de 15, 101
Podensac, Governor of 39
Pocklington 106
Pollington 100
"Polyolbion" of Drayton 50

Pontefract	79, 117, 151
Pontiniac	9
Pontage	22
Pope, the	20, 24, 25, 33, 50, 73
———, Nicholas	123
Portman, John	92 (*n*)
Portsmouth	39
Possessions, the	99
Premonstranses Order	45
Prior of Blythe	141
——— of Drax, the	25
——— of York, the	25
——— of Workson	43
Profits of Rectory of Hatfield	115
Prophetic Parable	56
Pryme, Mr De la	94

Q

Queen Philippa's gift to Roche	53
Questions asked by the Commissioners on Visiting Monasteries	72
Quick	132

R

Radcliffe on-Trent	103, 118
Rainville, Ralph de	148
Ralph the Priest	10
———, Bishop of Chichester	23
———, son of Nicholas	23
———, son of Robert Fitz-Payne	12
Ramsden, William	128, 131, 152, 187
Rastal, Mr	xviii
Rawmarsh	108, 115, 118
Raveni, Willielmus Filius	5
Reference to Plates	xii
Reginald, Abbot of Roche	19, 20, 25, 105, 147, 153
——— the Bailiff	109
——— the Presbyter de Doncaster	126
——— the Tailor	109
Reine, Robert	82
Reresby, Lionel Esq	147
Reprisals	115
Rhodes, Peter de	121
———, William de	141
Richard I, King of England	12, 16, 20, 23, 100, 141, 159, 174
——— II,	149
———, Abbot of Roche	28, 29, 34
———, son of Hugh	23
——— the Granger	34
Richmund, Roger	23
Rice, Ap Dr	70, 71
Rickman	170
Rievaulx, Abbot of	81
Rillington, Thomas	114, 144
Riparius, Robert de	99, 120
Ripers, Robert de	142, 158
Risby	17, 21
Robert, Abbot of Roche	43, 44, 46, 47, 48, 56, 57
———, son of Glai	15
———, Saint	7
——— the Cellarer	29
Robin Hood	93
Robynsone, John	82, 86, 88
Roche, Adam de la	116
———, William de	122
Rochester, Bishop of	83
Rochdale	101, 108, 116, 131
Rodmerchewyet, Hugh de	106
Roger, son of Hugh Fitz Walter	100
Rokkehill	145
Roll's House	81, 96 (*n*), 106 (*n*), 125 (*n*)
Rome	24
Romburgh	68
"Rood of Grace"	83
Rossington	100, 115
———, Jeremiah de	109
———, Peter de	109, 116, 155
Rothwell, Robert de	139
Rothell, parson of	117
Rotherham	29, 89, 99, 103, 117, 147
———, S de	43
Rot Fin	xxi (*n*)
Rous, Antho	149
Roxby	13, 15, 21, 89, 134, 135, 136, 137, 138, 139, 160, 187
Royal Charter	106, 118, 137
Rufford Abbey	45
Rupe, Monastery of	134
———, William de	29
Rupibus, William de	23, 29
Rumsey	xvii
Ryevall, Abbot of	133
Rygges, William	154
Rypun, Nicholas de	32
Ryvall	xviii

S

Saddleworth	134
Sake	22
Salley	177
Sally, Abbot of	7 (*n*)
Sandal, Thomas de	32, 126
———, Madilda	153
Sandall	21, 139
Sandbeck	xxi, 11, 33, 89, 140, 141, 172 (*n*)
Sandebi, William de	10
Sanderson, John	110
Saunderson, Robert	141
———, Sir Nicholas	xxii
Sarah, relict of Richard de Bawtry	106
Savile, Richard de, Ralph son of	147
Sbyson, Thomas	29
Scalzebi, Robert de	5, 6, 15, 122
———, Knight of	10
Scarborough	80
———, Earl of	vi, xxii, xxiii
Scausby, Hugh	12
Scawsby	21, 141, 144, 187
———, Adam de	109
Scelhall, Hugh de	140
Schepewykes	158
Schofelde, Lord Thomas de	132
Scoreby of Marr	16
Scoteni, Walter de	15, 135, 136
Scotage	21
Scotney	187
Scotland	47, 48, 49
Scroby	44, 60
Scrope, Philip	152
Scutage	21
Seals of the Abbey	45 46, 118
Seal of the Cell of Roche	110
Secretum of the Abbey	45, 46
Selesai, Henry of	108
Serlby	103, 141, 153
Sezacres	15, 142
Shaw, G Esq	132 (*n*)
Sheffield	87 (*n*)
Shelley	142, 150
———, Henry de	117
Sheldon, Thomas	123

INDEX.

Shepwick	142
Shepley, Mathew de	18, 108
Shires	21
Shirebrook, Cuthbert	89, 164
Shyttylyngton	150
Shrewsbury, Earl of	79
Sibylla	xvii
———, de Sancta Maria	29
Silkstone	151
Simon de Montfort	33
——— de Baukewell	54
———, Fitz Simon	117
———, Precentor of York	29
Skellow	126
———, Grange	145
———, John de	126
Slade Hooton	5, 99, 107, 120, 142, 143
Sloane, MS.	188
Smeaton	144, 187
———, Alan	117
———, Simon son of Algar de	144
Smetheton, Alan de	32, 34
Smithfield	83
Smith, Mr. Theophilus	vi
———, John	154
Smythe, Thomas	86
Snaith	144, 151
Soke	22
Sonke	21
Southerfell	26
"South Yorkshire"	xxiii (n), 110 (n), 188
Spalding Abbey	45
Spencer	104
Sprotbrough	121
Sprotburgh, Lord of	102
Stacye, Rev. J.	vi
Stainton	16, 21, 119, 145
———, Hugh de	5, 145
———, Hugh, John son of	145
———, John de	140
———, William de	140
Stainforth	21
Stainford	144, 145
———, John Fitz Peter de	114
———, Provost of	145
Stainredale	145
Stallage	22
Stanhop	49
Stanhope, Sir Edward	xxii
Stansal	21, 145
Stanhege	107, 145
Stapelton, Lord Robert de	131, 132
Stapleton, Robert de	117
———, Richard	146
Statute relating to Seals of Monasteries	45
Stather, North and South	111, 137
Staynton	187
———, John de	122
Stelle, Robert	89
Stephen, Abbot of Roche	37, 40, 41, 138
———, King of England	xix, 4
———, Cardinal	18, 25, 120
Stephenson, Thomas	120
Sterndale	123
Stevinton, Johann de	159
Stillingflete	155
Stirap, Ingeram de	155
———, Gerard de	16, 146
Stirrup	16, 21, 146
Stokes, Thomas	127
Stone Edge	132
Storthes, John	150
Stowe	53
Strafford	146
Strie, William	109
Stristerop	146
Streetthorpe	146
St. Paul, Robert de	29
— Agatha Abbey	45
— Clement at York, Agnes, Prioress of	160
— Mary of Roche	153
— Andrew, Robert de	151
— Roche	125
— Mary's, York	68
— Paul's London	45
— John's Church, Laughton	120
— Omer, Sir William de	136
— Leonard, Hospital of, at York	141
Stubbs, Alexander de	32, 155
Styrrup, Ralph de, Robert son of	112
———, Robert de	112
Suffolk	26
Summons to Stephen, Abbot of Roche	38, 39
——— to Parliament	32, 38, 39, 43, 44, 47
Suppression of Monasteries	94 (n)
——— of Roche Abbey letter on	89
Surrey, John, Earl of	51, 52, 112
Surrender Deed of Roche Abbey	84
Surdeval, Richard de	xxii
Surtees Society	28, 59 (n)
Sutton, Charles	187
———, John	187
Swain, Fitz Swain	7
Swaincroft	134
Swayn, Adam Fitz	16
Swift, Mr. W.	vi
Swinton	122, 159
———, Raynder de	122
———, William de	122
Sykes, Dr.	vi, 109 (n)
Symon, son of Symon	15
Sywardthorp, Hugh Marshal de	141

T

Takewith	16
Tange	21
Tanner	101, 177
Tatewyc, William de	148
Taxation of Pope Nicholas	137
Templeborough	117, 146, 147
Tenneflowe, Henry de	187
"Testamenta Vetusta"	59 (n)
"——— Eboracensia"	59 (n)
Testification of Richard de Boyvill	140
Theam	22
Themantale	21
Theodare, a Monk	19
Thethingpenning	22
Thomas, Abbot of Roche	36
———, the Granger	32
———, son of Artrop de Braithwell	104
Thomas, William Fitz	101
Thoc, Thomas	32
Thornsham, Robert, Steward of Anjou	23
Thorne	28, 147
Thornhill, Robert	110
Thornell, Hugh	154
Thornabye, Robert	139
Thoroton, Dr.	v, xxii
Thorpe	37
———, William	67
Thoresby's MSS.	18, 53
Thriberg	147
Throapham	120, 147, 153
Thundercliffe Grange	xxi

Thurftonland	89 (*n*), 142, 150
Thurne, Thomas, Abbot of Roche	64
Thurnfcoe	15, 16, 21, 103, 116, 126, 147, 148, 149
——, Adam de	148
Tickhill	xx, 11, 12, 17, 18, 21, 48, 103, 106, 112, 143, 144, 146, 150, 151, 174
—— Caftle	xx, xx, 48, 121
——, Roger de, Abbot of Roche	11, 12
——, Reginald Guvy de	155
——, Mathew de, Maud, relict of	155
Tikill, William, Abbot of Roche	62, 63
Tilli, Ote de	104
Tinfley	151, 187
——, Sir Henry de	188
——, Robert de	159
"Tin Trumpet" quoted	69
Todwick	15, 21, 94, 104, 148, 149, 151, 152, 153
—— Grange	151
——, "Old Hall" at	153 (*n*)
——, "Hiftory of the Manor" of	151
——, "Little"	151
——, Gregory de	151
Toffred, Abbot of Croyland	6
Toft defined	100
Toll	22
Torr	110
Tortemayns, Ralph	15, 151, 152
——, William	151, 152
Torworth	16, 21, 103, 118, 141, 153, 154, 155
Tower Hill	81
Trent, River	49, 52, 111, 134
——, Alan de	158
Triftrop	146
Trithings	21
Turbary	21
Turgis, Richard Fitz	4, 5, 6, 94, 125, 126, 127
Turke, Richard	102, 105, 141
Turlavefton, Ralph de	10
Turmifton, Jeffery de	144
Twell, Thomas	86, 87, 88
Twing, Robert	25
Tyrrell, Henry	128, 130, 131

U

Ulecotes, Philip de	18
Ullay, Robert de	141
Upland, Jacke	23
Urban, Pope III	14, 16, 30, 116, 117, 119, 123, 125, 135, 142
—————— IV	107
Urnethorp, Hugh de	117

V

Vallambrofa	26
Vallis Dei or Vaudry	177
"Valor Ecclefiafticus"	101, 105
Vavafour, William	15, 99, 147
——, John de	156
Verona	16
Verum, Richard de	123
——, William de	123
Vefci, Lords of Rotherham	xxiii
Vickers, Mr G Naylor	vi
Vipont, Robert de	140, 141
——, Idonea de	xxii, 140, 172 (*n*)
Viteri Ponte or Vipont, Robert de	xxii
Vivian, Archdeacon of Derby	23

W

Wadworth 15, 21, 111, 120, 142, 143, 145, 155, 156

Wadworth, Peter de	13, 109, 140, 143, 147 148, 155, 156
——, Eudo de	111, 155
——, Godfrey de	15, 111
——, Ralph, Prieft of	111
——, Hugh de, Abbot of Rocke	13, 16, 135
Wakefield	133
——, John, Abbot of Roche	58, 59, 60
Walcott, Mackenzie E C	165
Walcre	156
Wales	47, 84
Walent, Henry	117
Wallbran, Mr	92 (*n*)
Wallingwells	158
Wall, Robert	81
Walker, John	150
Walkerfall	118
Walkeringham	110, 120, 142, 156, 157, 158
——, Richard de	156
——, Roger, Chaplain of	157
——, William de	143, 156, 158
——, Adam de	157
——, Henry de	156
Wakling, John de	108
Walfingham	83
Walter, fon of Leon	109
——, Abbot of Roche	30, 137
Walton, Upper	157
Warmfworth, William de	109, 110
Warpening	22
Warren, the Goldfmith	88 (*n*)
——, William, Earl of	18, 28, 34, 41, 108, 111, 112, 114, 164
——, John, Earl of	50, 51, 52, 92, 112
——, William de	xx, xxiii
Warely	21, 158
Warwick	92 (*n*)
Wafteneys, William	145
Waftenays, Edmunde de	152
Waftenayes, Lord Edmund de	132
Watt	93
Waverley	xviii
Weighton Common	79
Welbeck Abbey	45
Welbore, Michael	187
Wells, Thomas	86, 88
Well, the "Ladies"	176
Wellingley	15, 16, 21, 111, 143, 145, 159, 187
Wentworth	117
——, W de	43
——, Thomas	117
Weftminfter	38, 39, 44, 46, 78, 119, 138
Weftrafen	138
Weftnis	100
Wetelay	117
Wheland, John	82
Whalley, Abbot of	133
Whiethwait, Johanna	148
Whitehall	83
Whitehead, Henry	133
Whitaker, Dr	7
"White Monks"	xviii
Whitwell	15, 107
Whifton Roger	152
Wickerfley	5, 21, 159
——, Richard de	9, 116, 126
——, Robert de	116, 140, 148
——, Richard Fitz Turgis de	159
Wilfick	145, 155, 159
Wilfon, Henry	82, 86, 88
——, W	104
William, Abbot of Roche	49
——, Chaplain of the Caftle of Tickhill	12

INDEX.

William, son of Richard de Barnby	102
———, son of Gilbert de Catwick	107
———, son of Henry de Marisco	100
———, son of Edward III.	52
———, son of Richard de Busli	10
———, Sir William Fitz	100 (n)
——— the Fleming	16
——— the Conqueror	xxii
Williams, Sir John	122
Will of Matilda of York, Countess of Cambridge	58
Wilkynson, John	119
Wilghesich, Mo. de Otho, son of	155
Winchester	23
———, Bishop of	xix, 22
Windsor	47
Wineley	151, 159, 187
Winterington	15, 17, 21
Winterton	159
Winteringham	160
Wlger-Oxgang	156
Wlrington, Robert de	144
———, Herbert de	144
———, Thomas de	144
Wlvethwait, John de	140
Woburn	177
Wolfpit	5
Wolvethwait, John de	110, 111
Wolsey, Cardinal	68, 70
Woodhall	121
Woodhouse Mill	160
Worksop	xx, 94 (n), 175, 188
———, Prior of	19, 43
Worcester	33
Wortley	xxi
Worthley, Henry de	103
Wrigley, John	134
Wright, Jno.	149
Wulsagh	108
Wyk, Hugh de le	139
Wynkyn de Worde	12 (n)
Wynterton	187
Wyn, Miles	100 (n)
Wyse, Ralph	152
———, John	152
———, Roger	152
Wyvelsworth	21, 160

Y

Yorkshire	xxii. 84, 99, 120
——— Churches, notes on, by a Monk of Roche	94
York	xx, 60, 79, 80, 81, 82, 112, 135, 160
——— Fabric Rolls	28, 29
——— Cathedral Church	29
——— Castle	82
———, St Mary's Abbey	7
———, Matilda of	171

ROBERT WHITE, PRINTER, PARK-STREET, WORKSOP.

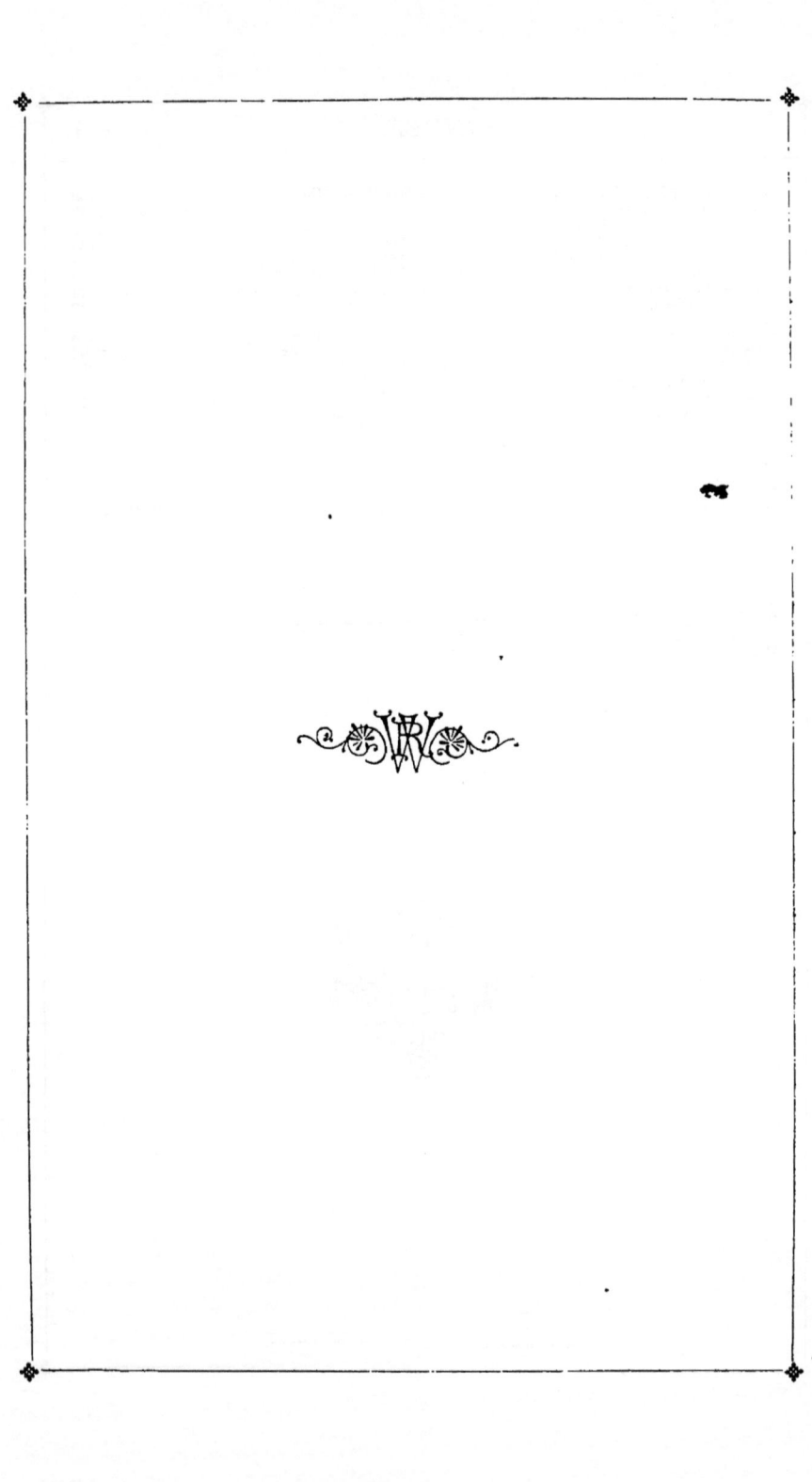

Lightning Source UK Ltd.
Milton Keynes UK
UKHW020654120520
363107UK00010B/3025